BURGLARY AND THEFT

BURGLARY AND THEFT

By

JOHN M. MACDONALD, M.D., F.R.C.P.(E).
Professor of Psychiatry
University of Colorado School of Medicine
Director of Forensic Psychiatry
University of Colorado Medical Center
Denver, Colorado

With Contributions by

Captain C. Donald Brannan
Commander, Crimes Against Property Bureau
Denver Police Department
Denver, Colorado

and

Lieutenant Robert E. Nicoletti
Director, Bureau of Laboratories
Denver Police Department
Denver, Colorado

CHARLES C THOMAS · PUBLISHER
Springfield · Illinois · U.S.A.

Published and Distributed Throughout the World by

CHARLES C THOMAS • PUBLISHER

Bannerstone House

301-327 East Lawrence Avenue, Springfield, Illinois, U.S.A.

© *1980, by* CHARLES C THOMAS • PUBLISHER

ISBN 0-398-03962-3

Library of Congress Catalog Card Number: 79-19351

With THOMAS BOOKS *careful attention is given to all details of
manufacturing and design. It is the Publisher's desire to present books
that are satisfactory as to their physical qualities and artistic possibilities
and appropriate for their particular use.* THOMAS BOOKS *will be true
to those laws of quality that assure a good name and good will.*

Library of Congress Cataloging in Publication Data

Macdonald, John Marshall, 1920-
    Burglary and theft.

    Includes bibliographies and index.
    1. Burglary—United States. 2. Larceny—United
States. 3. Burglary investigation—United States.
I. Brannan, C. Donald, joint author. II. Nicoletti,
Robert E., joint author. III. Title.
HV6658.M26   364.1′62   79-19351
ISBN 0-398-03962-3

Printed in the United States of America

C-1

to my wife

PREFACE

Each year in the United States burglary, larceny-theft and motor-vehicle theft account for over 90 percent of the Crime Index offenses recorded in the *Uniform Crime Reports* of the FBI. These are the crimes that are reviewed in this book, and these are the crimes that occupy so much of a police officer's time. They are important crimes which have not received the attention they deserve.

Many citizens no longer feel safe in their own homes. Victims of burglary are outraged by the violation of their privacy and go in fear of the burglar's return. The problem of theft affects everyone directly or indirectly through higher prices for goods and higher insurance rates.

This study is based upon psychiatric evaluation of over one hundred burglars for the courts and interviews with a fence and with many other burglars, sometimes in their own homes. Victims have also had their say. The experience of riding in a police car with burglary detectives on night duty provided insights not otherwise readily available. The aim has been to provide a broad review of these crimes and the persons who commit them. A glance at the table of contents will show the range of inquiry.

The two police officers who have contributed to the chapters on criminal and scientific investigation speak from many years of practical experience. It is hoped that the book will be of value to law enforcement officers as well as to others with an interest in these crimes, the offenders and their victims.

J.M.M.

ACKNOWLEDGMENTS

I AM PARTICULARLY grateful to Police Chief Arthur G. Dill of the Denver Police Department for his generous cooperation and assistance over a period of many years. Division Chief Paul A. Montoya, Captains C. Donald Brannan, Donald L. McKelvy, and Donald B. Mulnix, Lieutenants Lester Beaulieu, David J. Gross, and Robert E. Nicoletti were most helpful.

It is not possible to name all the burglary detectives who contributed to this study, but I would mention Detectives Gordon Reed and Robert B. Turner who took me on weekends to the scenes of many burglaries and other assorted crimes during their long hours on night duty, also Detectives Raymond B. Henry and Thomas A. Orecchio whom I accompanied on a vehicle theft ring investigation. Many officers from other police departments within and beyond Colorado also provided assistance.

My thanks are due to authors and publishers who have permitted reproduction of material. Mrs. Berniece Hindmarsh has been helpful in obtaining books and articles from libraries throughout the United States.

Dr. Stuart Boyd of St. John's College, Santa Fe, New Mexico, made many valuable suggestions, and his editorial advice was very welcome. Mr. Leonard Chesler who practices, lectures, and writes in the field of criminal law provided advice on legal definitions.

Mrs. Carolyn Zwibecker was especially helpful in typing the many drafts of this book. Her efficiency and remarkable patience are appreciated.

CONTENTS

BURGLARY AND THEFT

CHAPTER 1

BURGLARY: THE BILLION DOLLAR CRIME

The contagion of crime is like that of the plague.
—Napoleon Bonaparte, *Sayings of Napoleon*

EACH YEAR IN THE United States the number of burglaries is more than three times the total number of aggravated assaults, robberies, forcible rapes and criminal homicides. There are over 3 million burglaries each year in this country, and the annual cost to victims exceeds 1½ billion dollars, ten times the financial loss from robberies.

It is impossible to estimate the full costs of this crime. Citizens have to buy better locks for their homes and pay higher premiums for burglary insurance. Indirectly, citizens pay more for goods and services because businesses and public utility companies pass on the costs of their security systems, merchant guards and losses from burglaries.

Taxpayers meet the costs of an inefficient criminal justice system that has not been notably successful in catching, prosecuting and rehabilitating burglars. For some years, less than 20 percent of burglaries have been cleared by arrest, and almost 30 percent of those arrested have not been prosecuted. Of the adults prosecuted, about 60 percent have been found guilty as charged (*Uniform Crime Reports*).

Citizens pay not only for the prosecution of burglars, but also for their defense in the law courts. Public defenders, paid by the state, are playing an increasingly important role in the defense of persons charged with serious crimes. Rehabilitation of the offender, as well as his punishment, is at the expense of the taxpayer and may cost more than educating one's son or daughter at Harvard University.

Many citizens go in fear of the burglar, not only because they fear the loss of possessions of great sentimental or financial value, but also because they fear that an unexpected encounter with an intruder may lead to physical injury or even death. Women also face the risk of rape or other sexual assault by a home invader.

This study is based in part upon the psychiatric evaluation for the district courts of Colorado of over 100 burglars and upon interviews with many burglars in jails, penitentiaries, the security ward of a city general hospital and in their own homes. Information obtained directly from these men and from police officers, both within and beyond Colorado, contributes to the clinical examples provided throughout this book.

The opportunity to accompany police officers in their search of a dark warehouse or home, to follow the chase of an intruder who has been flushed from his hiding place, over fences, through backyards and down alleys, and to observe victims in their state of shock following an unexpected encounter with a burglar provided a much more intimate grasp of burglary than the official police reports and statistics on this crime.

BURGLARY DEFINED

Burglary is defined in English common law as *the breaking and entering of the dwelling house of another in the nighttime with intent to commit a felony.* This common law definition has been greatly modified by state statutes so that generally burglary can occur in the daytime and without forcible entry into other structures, including tents, commercial buildings and even telephone booths. The meanings of the words in the original definition have been broadened.

BREAKING. Actual breaking is unnecessary; the essence of the term is unauthorized entry, and it is sufficient if a door or window is pushed open even though it is unlocked. Although some courts have held otherwise, the mere unauthorized act of opening wider a door or window already partly open but insufficient for the entry is generally held to be a breaking (10). *Constructive breaking* refers to entry by some trick or fraud, for example, by impersonating a telephone company employee. If an employee opens a door for an accomplice, both commit burglary.

ENTERING. The slightest entry is sufficient, such as one finger inside a window while pushing out a pane of glass.

NIGHTTIME. Most modern statutes do not restrict burglary to the period from sunset to sunrise.

FELONIOUS INTENT. No breaking and entering amounts to burglary at common law unless there is an intent to commit a felony such as theft, rape, robbery, kidnapping or murder. Thus a man who breaks into a home on a freezing winter night to keep warm commits a trespass, which is not a felony, and he has not committed a burglary at common law, no matter how forcible his breaking and entry. Burglars sometimes give such an explanation of their forcible entry, but their burglarious intent can be shown by their possession of burglary tools, their ransacking of the premises and their piling of valuable items inside the place of entry.

Some courts have taken the very commonsense position that an unexplained intrusion into the dwelling of another at night will support a jury's finding of an intent to steal, and as Perkins also notes, a prima facie presumption of burglarious intent arising from such unexplained conduct has sometimes been provided by statute. These presumptions are generally disfavored because they call upon the accused to disprove the presumption and therefore conflict with a "presumption of innocence."

DEGREES OF BURGLARY. Some state statutes describe first, second and sometimes third degree burglaries. First degree burglary, which provides for more severe punishment, may cover burglary of an occupied building, burglary at night, the possession of a deadly weapon by the burglar or the commission of an assault during the burglary.

STATE STATUTES. There are variations among the states in the definitions of burglary and other crimes. In the *Uniform Crime Reports* of the Federal Bureau of Investigation, offenses are classified according to *UCR* definitions, which may differ from some state or local codes.

ROBBERY. The term *robbery* is often used incorrectly to describe acts of burglary. Robbery is a crime that takes place in the presence of the victim to obtain property or a thing of value from a person by use of force or threats of force. The criminal who breaks into an unoccupied office, opens the safe and takes or attempts to take the contents commits a burglary. If an employee walks into the office during the burglary and is forced to open the safe by the criminal, the crime becomes a robbery as well as a burglary, but the offender is usually charged only with the more serious crime of robbery.

BURGLARY RATES

In recent years in the United States, the annual burglary rate has been over 1,400 offenses per 100,000 population. The crime is most frequent in densely populated metropolitan areas, less frequent in the suburbs and much less frequent in rural areas. Metropolitan areas had over 1,600 burglaries, cities outside metropolitan areas over 1,000 and rural areas over 700 burglaries per 100,000 population (*UCR*).

The incidence is much higher than that recorded in official statistics, as many burglaries are not reported to the police. The President's Commission on Law Enforcement and Administration of Justice initiated the first national survey of criminal victimization. The National Opinion Research Center of the University of Chicago made a random survey of 10,000 households. An adult in each household was interviewed to see whether any member of the household had been a victim of crime during the preceding year, whether the crime had been reported, and if not, the reason for not reporting.

It was found that the burglary rate was three times the rate reported in the *Uniform Crime Reports*. The survey technique, as applied to criminal victimization, has been described as beset with a number of methodological problems, and it is possible that some of the unreported crimes would not be substantiated by thorough police investigation. Nevertheless the survey does provide a guide to the extent of unreported burglaries. The most frequent reason given for not notifying the police was lack of confidence in the effectiveness of the police.

The burglary rate tends to be higher in the summer months, when people are more likely to be away from their homes, but some studies have failed to show any significant difference in the number of burglaries from season to season. Nonresidential burglaries occur more often at night and on weekends when commercial and industrial buildings are less likely to be occupied. Residential burglaries are more likely to occur during the day on weekdays. Scarr found that almost half of all residential burglaries occurred between 10 AM and 4 PM (14).

Ferdinand, in his study of the criminal patterns of Boston between 1849 and 1951, found that severe economic depressions have consistently been accompanied by a high rate of burglary. Unlike robberies, however, burglaries have not increased during wartime; indeed, the burglary rate in Boston has declined during all three major wars in the last century (3).

THE BURGLAR AND HIS SKILLS

There is great variety in the ranks of burglars, from the crude window smasher who shows little finesse in his chosen occupation to the highly skilled cat burglar who has mastered the art of circumventing burglar alarms. Some operators confine themselves to burglary, while for many, this crime is just a sideline, sandwiched between other nefarious activities.

In their youth, many burglars serve an informal apprenticeship, learning their trade from more experienced associates. Other criminals in their twenties or thirties turn from armed robbery to burglary after learning from painful personal experience the much longer penitentiary sentences for stickups.

Postgraduate courses in burglary are available at reformatories and penitentiaries. Among the skillful burglars are a small number of men who turn to crime for the first time in their late twenties or thirties and who take advantage of their training as security guards, police officers, locksmiths or electronic experts.

Walsh gives the following example of a skilled professional burglar (15):

> Greg is a jewelry and fur specialist who has taken a gemology course in order to evaluate and learn about the property he steals. He has jewelers' tools and removes stones from their settings to weigh and safely secure them. His main targets are the homes of wealthy persons who, he takes the pains to discover, have such property in their homes, rather than in a bank vault. Greg spends

considerable time, before contemplating a theft, researching possible victims in order to build a profile of them. He searches the social register, the social and financial pages of the newspapers, the city directory and the directories of corporate officials. He visits the neighborhoods of the wealthy at different times and days to get a feel for their living patterns. When satisfied that an individual not only is likely to possess property in which he might be interested, but also maintains a life-style which includes substantial periods away from home, Greg will add him to a list of possible targets. This list includes the name, address and phone number of that individual as well as a notation about any item that he may have heard about or seen worn by one of the occupants (in a news photo, for example) that particularly interests him.

When he is ready to pull a job, he has a group of three or four other burglars with whom he works. They begin by calling individuals on Greg's list until they find a home with no one answering. Next they proceed toward the target, stopping at a phone booth to try the residence again. If still no one answers, the drama begins.

They are equipped with two police radios and a walkie-talkie. One of them is designated as the driver and he lets the others out of the car somewhere near the preferred approach to the house. The driver then proceeds to a phone booth and giving his cohorts approximately ten minutes he calls the home once more. If no one or someone unfamiliar answers, he proceeds immediately to a pre-determined pick-up point. If his friends answer, he gives them his number and begins waiting at the booth monitoring police calls and phoning them intermittently to be advised of their progress.

In the house the thieves again divide the labors. One of them waits for the phone call and mans the walkie-talkie if it becomes necessary for them to be separated on different floors of the house. The first step is to find the luggage owned by the occupants, for they will be using this to transport the property from the house. This done, they proceed to steal what they will, opening a safe if that is necessary or merely lifting what is around of value. Their ease of operation will depend on what they have calculated to be the maximum time they will have to operate inside. Thus, if they know the occupants to be at a social function, they will use the luxury of several hours to do a thorough job. If, however, they have determined that their victims are out dining, they may allow themselves less time to complete the job and execute their exit.

When they have finished, they notify their driver with whom they have been in intermittent contact, and proceed to the arranged pick-up point, leaving as they came, through a side door or a back window with suitcases in hand. Anything that they decide is of little value, costume jewelry for example picked up by mistake, is put back in the suitcases and bag and baggage is taken to another predetermined safe place and disposed of. (Their preference was for a desolated wharf area from which they would drop the merchandise they didn't want into a swift-flowing channel.) *

Selection of Partners

Burglars have the same problem as businessmen in finding dependable, honest assistants. The man who is unpunctual, given to strong liquor or to the abuse of drugs cannot be relied upon to fulfill his duties. The negligent behavior of an intoxicated employee can cost a company thousands of dollars, but an intoxicated accomplice in a burglary can cost his partner not only money but also time behind bars.

It is readily understandable why a master craftsman is reluctant to imperil his future by working alongside someone who may open his mouth too wide, telling his friends about exploits that should be kept hidden or bartering this information to the police to save his own skin. The accomplice with no sense of loyalty who talks to the police may gain his freedom but lose his life from a knife between his ribs or a bullet in the night. "You don't want a drunk, if he does show up he will be high; you don't want a lover, he'll tell every broad in town what he does; you don't want a flasher, he'll be overdressed, cracking $100 bills when he goes in a joint; you don't want a junkie, I can spot them, their oily complexion, always kind of run down. I pick people who've got a bit of nerve. If anything happens he won't fall apart."

In this profession one needs a cool head, sufficient mechanical dexterity to work quickly and efficiently on locks and alarms, and great patience. In a crisis, a burglar confronted by a suspicious householder or warehouse employee will need all the poise and quick thinking of an experienced confidence game swindler to talk his way out of a sticky situation. A friendly wave to a security guard and a self-assured comment may be necessary to avoid arousing suspicion. "I was carrying a TV

---

* Pages 164 to 166 taken from *The Fence: A New Look at the World of Property Theft* by Marilyn E. Walsh and used with the permission of the publisher, Greenwood Press, Inc., Westport, Connecticut.

set out of the house and a neighbor came running up. Oh, hell! I asked her what she wanted. 'Do you fix TVs?' 'Certainly do.' We fixed hers too."

An assistant lacking in self-confidence and of dull intelligence may run when he should walk, or through some other ill-considered act, draw unwelcome attention at an inopportune moment. It is not surprising that many burglars prefer to work alone except when they need a lookout to warn of danger or an assistant to help remove large items to a nearby vehicle. There are, of course, burglars who need company to bolster their courage so that they can complete their crimes rather than flee at the first hint of danger.

Equipment

Many burglars carry no more than a large screwdriver or pry bar and perhaps a piece of plastic for use on door locks. One cautious burglar always purchased a new screwdriver and pry bar before every burglary so that if he were arrested in possession of these tools, scientific investigation of tool marks on prior burglaries would not match the tools he was carrying.

One professional burglar told police, "I never carried any tools except a three-bladed pocket knife and a small flashlight. That's all you need. My knife had one heavy blade which made a fair pry; a medium sized blade for cutting screens and a small blade for working locks." Channel locks, vice grips or a pipe wrench to twist off doorknobs, bolt cutters, pliers and masking tape for use on windows to prevent the glass from shattering loudly when broken are other useful aids, but the less the burglar has to carry with him the better.

The burglar may have a radio scanner in his car to monitor the police band, but he will seldom carry it with him. If he does so, he will use a compact scanner with an earplug receiver so that no one else can hear the transmission. In major burglaries, walkie-talkies may be used to enable the lookout to warn of danger. Equipment used in safecracking will be reviewed later.

No special clothing is required except by the impersonator who wears the uniform or work clothes appropriate to his assumed role as a telephone company or public service employee.

Dark clothing and perhaps a mask are worn by some night burglars. ("I use a little girl's leotards, size 6, as a mask. I've been stopped half a dozen times by the police, they didn't pay any attention to the leotards on the back seat.") Shoes with rubber soles are an advantage by day or night. Cotton gloves, surgical gloves or sox are used to avoid leaving fingerprints.

Weapons

When questioned by police, burglars will usually deny carrying guns during their crimes. It would not be to their advantage to admit such behavior, and it is difficult to estimate the percentage of burglars who go armed. An experienced offender reported: "Yes, I think that the majority of people who commit burglaries are dangerous people—I'd say two-thirds of them carry weapons. I carried a weapon, I never had set plans, but I thought if he (the householder) would shoot then I would shoot too. It would be either him or me if he would shoot." One burglar carried a sawed-off shotgun. "Just the sight of it would put a lot of people in shock."

RESIDENTIAL BURGLARIES

There are almost 2 million residential burglaries each year in the United States, almost two-thirds of all burglaries, with losses totalling almost $1 billion. These burglaries are more frequent in the summer months of July and August, when people are away from their homes. There is another peak in December, when the burglars are filling their Christmas stockings.

It is difficult to obtain accurate records on the times of burglaries because so often no one is present when the burglar breaks in, but *UCR* figures suggest that just over 50 percent of residential burglaries occur between 6 AM and 6 PM. Scarr's study showed that almost 50 percent of all residential burglaries for which the time of occurrence could be estimated happened between 10 AM and 4 PM. A five-year study in Washington, D.C., showed that 75 percent of residential burglaries were committed during the day (11).

At night, burglars are most active between 7 PM and 10 PM,

the hours when householders are most likely to be attending some social activity, and the burglar's presence on the streets is less likely to attract attention than in the early hours of the morning.

HOME BURGLARIES

Selection of Targets

Juvenile burglars without transport tend to operate in their own home neighborhood or in neighborhoods between school and home. A juvenile will often have knowledge of those homes near his own that are unoccupied during the daytime. Many adult burglars travel far from their homes to well-to-do neighborhoods, preferably those that are infrequently patrolled by the police. Some burglars prefer average income residential areas because in these homes there is often more cash lying around than in very expensive homes. "I don't fool with Jewish people, their money is in the bank, valuables in a safety deposit box or stashed in the house so well, you couldn't find it in three days. They have valuable furniture, but you can't carry a sofa out."

Various factors influence the criminal's choice of a particular home for burglary. Houses on street corners are favored by many burglars because they are able to get a good look at the two sides of the house that face adjoining streets, they do not have to worry about neighbors on either side seeing or hearing them and they do not feel hemmed in on two sides. Shrubbery that obstructs the neighbors' views of the front or back doors of the target house appeals to the burglar because he can make a forcible entry without being seen.

Valuable items such as antique rifles readily visible through a front living room window arouse temptation. The presence of an antiburglary iron grill in front of windows suggests something of value within. "I pick houses with burglar proof bars held in place with nails, you can pull them right off. I know because I've installed them." One burglar judged a home by its garage. "If the garage is real neat, the people have got a little class, they've got to have something. Most people who've got nice things keep everything neat, in order. These people have got something, nine times out of ten."

Anyone at Home?

Various methods are used to determine whether a house is occupied. Much is made of the fact that burglars select houses that have an accumulation of newspapers on the porch and overflowing mailboxes. Certainly it is unwise for householders to advertise their absence, but burglars would very soon be out of pocket if they pillaged only these homes. The presence of a single newspaper in the front yard suggests that no one is at home, especially if there are clues such as an open garage door but no car either inside the garage or in front of the house.

Burglars cruising a target area may see a housewife driving off to do her shopping or the whole family leaving the driveway in the early evening to dine out. Some offenders can sense whether or not a house is occupied. "I don't know if it's an instinct or not, but you can tell if people are there. It's like a job, it gets to be a habit, you have a feeling if nobody's there." An old trick is to telephone the home of the intended victim; if the phone is still ringing when the burglar arrives, he assumes that no one is at home.

There are those housebreakers who watch the society columns of the newspapers to find who will be vacationing in the Bahamas or on the ski slopes at Vail. These burglars also check newspaper wedding announcements and then visit the bride's or groom's home during the wedding ceremony. One burglar studied the night duty roster of young resident physicians at a large general hospital. Then there are the warped individuals who read the obituary notices and find the home addresses of recently deceased persons so that they can pay a visit at the time of the funeral.

A carefully cultivated friendship with a maid or chauffeur in a rich person's home may provide useful information on the owner's activities or even duplicate keys to the home. Women seen purchasing or wearing expensive jewelry are followed to their homes, which are placed under surveillance and later broken into. A nationwide group of burglars would note expensive cars with out-of-state license plates and then telephone their colleagues in that state. By checking the license numbers, they could obtain the addresses of the vacationing car owners.

The burglar who works by night watches in the early evening hours for homes with drapes open and no lights on or just the the porch light on. He knows that many persons leave lights, TV, or radio on when they go out in the evening, but even so, he may not take the risk of finding someone at home and may not even check for occupancy by ringing the doorbell. "If there are lights on at night or the sound of radio or TV, I'll pass it by. I'll think to myself, 'Is somebody *really* there or are they fronting it out?', but there's no way I'll take the chance" (1).

The night provides protective cover; in residential areas fewer people are on the streets, and drawn blinds reduce the likelihood of a burglar being seen by a householder in an adjoining home. But as one burglar said, "Most of the time people use a gun is at nighttime, that's why I don't pull any nighttime burglaries."

A burglar may be deterred by the presence of a barking dog or a burglar alarm system. Some burglars, however, pride themselves on their ability to handle burglar alarms and dogs. "I just stare at them, pick up something, or close the door on them." Small dogs, which bark incessantly, may be more of a problem than a large friendly watchdog.

Once a house is chosen for breaking and entering, the burglar will walk up to the front door. There may be a note attached to the door that shows that no one is at home. "What made it so sweet was that somebody had left a jar of jelly that was homemade and it had a little note on it that said, 'We came by and left this for you, happy birthday, see you later, Tom.' So I knew right then that these people were gone because the jelly is sitting right in the door."

Usually the burglar will ring the doorbell as a final check to see whether there is anyone inside. If someone answers the door, request can be made to speak to Miss Jones or some other imagined person. This approach shows little subtlety and may arouse the suspicion of anyone who has read police leaflets on burglars and their methods of operation.

Many persons today are also suspicious of callers making marketing surveys and of door-to-door salesmen who offer merchandise or services at outrageous prices unlikely to result in a sale. An enterprising offender obtained a stack of handouts used by Jehovah's Witnesses; he would hand one of these to anyone who answered the door.

Place of Entry

If no one answers the door, the burglar may make a quick check to see if the door is locked and, if so, whether a door key is hidden under the doormat, in a flower pot or taped under the mailbox. Usually entry is made by forcing open the front, rear or sliding glass patio door. (One study showed that a door was the place of entry in 61.4%, a window in 33.7%, the roof in 0.2% and other sites in 4.7% of residential burglaries. *UCR*, 1961).

Channel locks and vice grips can be used to force the door lock open, or a screwdriver or pry bar can be used to open the door. Some doors are so poorly constructed that they can be opened simply by applying pressure to the doorjamb so that the lock bolt slips out of its slot.

A very cautious burglar will leave the house when there is no response to the doorbell, return later, force the door open, leave once again, return to loot the house, place the stolen items under a bush or in the alley, and once again leave the area before returning to pick up the loot. Thus the burglary involves four trips to the house, with a careful check for police response after each trip.

One man would force open the back door, walk through the house, unlock the front door, leave the area, then return later, and enter through the front door, as if someone had opened it for him. One youth was observed by a surveillance team sitting on the lawn of a home for twenty minutes. During this time he rang the doorbell twice before he walked around the back of the home and forced open the door.

In a study of 219 Boston residential burglaries with entry through a door, Reppetto found that the burglar entered through an open door in 10 percent of the cases (13). The most frequent technique of door entry was direct impact (39.3%), followed by pry door (19.2%), attack lock (15.0%), open door (10.0%), passkey (5.9%), loid door (5.5%) and pick lock (5.0%). Loiding refers to the use of a credit card, plastic strip or other thin flexible material which is slipped between door and jamb to move the bolt.

In another study of 383 Boston residential burglaries with entry through a window, Reppetto found that the burglar entered through an open or unlocked window in 28 percent of the cases (13). The most frequent technique of window entry was break glass (38%), followed by pry catch (33%), open or unlocked window (28%) and cut glass (1%).

Other points of entry include milk chutes, the holes cut in rear doors to let household pets in and out (for small juvenile burglars), occasionally through the roof and, very rarely, down the chimney. A fire department had to remove bricks from the lower part of a chimney to rescue a thirteen-year-old burglar who became stuck in the chimney. "We decided to go break into this house and they decided that I was the smallest so I would have to go down the chimney and that was when I got stuck. They tried to pull me out with a garden hose and then Joe called the fire department and Paul said that as soon as the fire department got me out, he told me to run and said if I didn't do it he would beat me up."

Inside the Home

Once inside, the burglar may take immediate action, either to prevent someone else entering the home by propping a chair against the door or to provide for quick escape from all rooms by opening windows and unlocking doors. Many burglars do not bother with these protective measures but proceed immediately about their business. Victims of a burglary finding their home in disarray are quick to conclude that the burglar has made a thorough search. This is seldom the case, as the able burglar usually wants to be on his way with the least possible delay. "I think a good burglar knows within two minutes if he's into something good or it's just a waste. We've been in and out in five minutes, get everything we wanted." He knows what he is after, and from experience he knows where he is most likely to find what he is looking for. Providing he completes his search within ten minutes, he has a good chance of avoiding capture by police responding to a telephone call from a neighbor who has noticed something suspicious.

> Mostly I get in and out as fast as I can, usually in eight or nine minutes. If somebody sees you in the yard, then sees you disappear, they're going to wait two or three minutes then call the police. It takes them three minutes to get the police on the telephone and three or four minutes for the police to put the dispatch out. It's ten or fifteen minutes before the police get there unless they're real close. I don't go in vicinities that are well patrolled and I stay away from hot areas that are burglarized real heavy.
>
> I just look as quickly as I can at the most likely places. It's not an intensive search, I don't tear the house up searching. Most people keep money in the game room or the bedroom. I guess they feel since that's their favorite room, that's the safest. Bedrooms mostly, I look through the drawers first. I start at the top drawer, then close the drawer and work down. I don't make messes of houses, I don't throw things around. I look some under boxes, under drawers, in containers, between papers, between mattresses, under carpets, in books. I just feel pockets.
>
> Usually I don't bother to look in shoes. Only in one house of all the houses I've been in, I found money in shoes. I go through all the rooms quickly. Now and then I take electric combs from bathrooms. I've found shotguns in bathrooms. I'm after jewelry, guns and money. I put all the stuff together, what I can carry, wrap it in a blanket, walk out to the alley, act like it's a bunch of trash, leave it by the trash can. Then I get the car and pick it up. . . .
>
> There's seldom anything in the living room. If there's something expensive in the front room, it's right where people will see it. Bedrooms, that's where generally people leave money and valuables; closets, shoes, shoe boxes, under rugs and under mattresses. Women hide money in lingerie or roll it up in their panty hose. Another place is in the shades, once I pulled the shades down and four or five hundred dollars came tumbling out. I wanted to close the shades so nobody would see in. Sometimes they put money under a dictionary.

Another burglar emphasizes the importance of the bedroom as a hiding place for valuables, and he notes that search of a kitchen is seldom rewarding: "First the master bedroom, then the other bedrooms, the dining room area if there's a buffet in it, the living room last, maybe the kitchen room briefly. It's usually in the master bedroom, the top dresser drawer, the bottom of the closet right on the floor. I pull the bottom dresser drawer all the way out and look under it for jewelry. I found $4,300 in cash there one time. I seldom find anything under the mattress."

Burglary of Occupied Homes

Most burglars take steps to avoid breaking into an occupied home, but there is always the risk that someone is asleep inside, even in the daytime, who does not hear the ring of the doorbell or the sounds of surreptitious entry. "I walked into a bedroom and to my horror discovered a couple asleep there. I could feel myself turning white and sweating all over. I just ran downstairs as quickly as I could, out the back and away. I'd hate to hurt anybody, I really would, but obviously if it came to the crunch . . ." (1).

Victims are often so surprised by the appearance of a burglar that they take no effective action, and many burglars count on this reaction. "They're so surprised they don't know what to do. Before they come to their senses you get out." "The reason I got away with so much, fifteen houses a day, was because I didn't care what happened to me. People would walk in on me, they're so shocked they don't know what to do anyway." One burglar had a ready answer when surprised by someone in a home asking, "What are you doing here?" He would reply, "Your nephew's downstairs, he invited us in. Go ask him." As he told me, "Everybody over thirty or thirty-five has got to have a nephew." Another burglar, when surprised by his victim, would say, "I'm from Hartford Insurance Company. I must have got the wrong house" then hurry out "with a pillowcase of goodies."

The greatest fear of the burglar is the person who lies in wait with a revolver or shotgun and does not respond to the doorbell. "One guy pulled a gun on me, he was waiting for us. He didn't answer the door. He started firing first, then said, 'Stop you S.O.B.,' but he was too excited. I pushed my friend out the door then went out. I was expecting a bullet, but by luck he didn't hit me. Most time people use a gun is at night-time, that's why I don't pull nighttime burglaries."

Burglars sometimes gain entry through imposture, as fire inspectors checking for fire hazards or as public service company employees overhauling equipment. For example, one such imposter checking the thermostat on the first floor asked an elderly female homeowner to get some tape from his partner who was "working" on the furnace in the basement. Shortly afterwards both imposters left the house, and the homeowner discovered that cash and credit cards were missing from her purse.

There are those burglars who deliberately break into occupied homes, usually at night. Some of them like the greater challenge and greater risk. Sometimes entry is made while the family is seated for dinner or huddled around a television set in the living room. "The best time is when people are still up and about, with the radio on, talking, having a drink, making noises. As long as the night's full of noises, you're pretty safe if you happen to knock something over. The worst time is when everybody's gone to bed and there are no noises. That's when you can't afford to make a sound" (5).

Another nighttime burglar of occupied homes described his operations to police officers.

> Once inside, and if the weather was cool, I would turn up the thermostat. The popping and cracking of the furnace would cover up my noise and was normal and unnoticed by the residents. I was always careful to turn it back to its original setting just before I left. If it was a warm night, and the windows were open, I might detect snoring. I didn't worry about people who were steady snorers. Generally, I operated only the living area, and not the sleeping area of a house; but I believe I could have moved the bedroom furniture out of some of those places and never wakened the people.

Francis Hohimer, a cat burglar for the Mafia, claimed to have made millions of dollars from the burglary of homes of socially prominent persons in Grosse Point, Michigan; Shaker Heights, Ohio; Denver, Colorado; Scottsdale, Arizona; Beverly Hills, California and other cities across the United States. The victims were often home at the time of the burglary, and Hohimer would not hesitate to wake them.

Hohimer was indicated by his brother and by a Mafia fence named Leo Rugendorf as the killer of Valery Percy, the twenty-one-year-old daughter of U.S. Senator Charles H. Percy. The girl was stabbed to death in 1966 during the burglary of Senator Percy's home in Kenilworth, a suburb of Chicago. Hohimer denies having committed this crime, and he has not been charged with either the murder or the burglary.

In his book, *The Home Invaders,* Hohimer describes his instruction in the craft of burglary at the Illinois State penitentiary by "Oklahoma" Smith, an accomplished burglar, who apparently was never arrested for this crime but received a life sentence for the murder of his wife. Much of Smith's advice is routine and straightforward, suitable for any novice embarking on a career of crime, but some of his recommendations are intriguing.

> Don't even bother checking children, they will sleep through anything, noise will hardly wake them up. Check the refrigerator the very first thing. If there is a small baby in the house, ninety-nine times out of a hundred there will be a formula in the refrigerator. Heat it up, find the baby and put the bottle in his mouth, and then change the diaper. If that baby wakes up, a mother's instinct is to wake up the second that baby cries hungry or wet. . . .
>
> When you get back to the car, change clothes as soon and as fast as possible, throw shoes and all out along the highway. If some crime lab wishes to check them out for soil or material they're all theirs, they don't belong to you. . . .
>
> Never wear deodorant or shaving lotion, the strange scent might wake someone up. The more people there are in a house, the safer you are. If someone hears you moving around, they will think it's someone else.
>
> If they call, answer in a muffled sleepy voice. They can't see well in the dark, your eyes are accustomed to it.
>
> Never turn on any lights, use a small pen light.
>
> Listen to their breathing. If they are awake they are controlling their breathing, asleep it's normal.
>
> Never be afraid of dogs, they can sense fear. Most dogs are friendly, snap your fingers they come right to you. Call them lightly right out of the house, roll them a ball, throw a stick, they will go get it.

Never, never hook up with the outfit or Mafia. They are the dirtiest son of a bitch's on earth.

Never carry any ID, you may lose it, or anything in your pockets that will jingle (6).

Rugendorf selected homes for burglary and provided Hohimer with pictures, lists of valuable items for removal and sometimes door keys. Hohimer chose his associates and paid them from the money he received from Rugendorf. His life-style was expensive, and he travelled across the country either by first class jet or in Cadillacs and other expensive cars, often in the company of a girl friend.

Hohimer and his accomplice would check into a motel near the home of the intended victim. They would register under assumed names and give fictitious home addresses, usually in Chicago or some other Illinois city. They would correctly describe their car on motel registration cards but would mix the numbers of the license plate. If not accompanied by women, they would check out of the motel before the burglary. If accompanied by women, they would return to the motel after the burglary, wake their female companions and leave the city.

Entry into the home was usually between 2 AM and 5 AM, the victims were awakened at gunpoint, and their hands and feet were tied with surgical tape. They would usually take jewelry, furs and money. Sometimes the victims would be asked for the location of a wall safe. The telephone cords or the telephone lines leading out of the home were cut, and the burglars would leave in the victim's car, which was left near the scene or near their motel. They carried automatic pistols and revolvers, as well as the following equipment in a small black attaché case or dark blue gym bag: two black ski masks, one with red trim and one with blue trim around eye and mouth openings, a pair of brown cloth work gloves, three pen flashlights, a propane fuel tank with torch head, a pry bar seventeen inches long, a screwdriver twelve inches long, a pair of channel lock pliers, a pair of wirecutters, a glasscutter and six rolls of surgical tape.

Selection of Items

Burglars seldom strip a home of all objects of value. They would need a large moving van to remove all the loot, and a large moving van is likely to attract attention, especially at night, and is also relatively easy to trace. When there is a wide sweep of a house, including even the owner's shirts, then revenge rather than economic gain is probably the motive. In one such case, the burglar had been cheated by a drug dealer and was exacting revenge.

What is surprising is that so often items of value are left undisturbed by the burglar even though he could easily remove them without significant additional risk or inconvenience to himself. Burglars are creatures of habit, and they tend to take the same range of items in all their burglaries. Thus, some burglars take only jewelry and cash, others concentrate on television and stereo sets. Indeed the burglar may have a shopping list, and like the housewife bound for the super-market, he knows exactly what he, or rather his fence, wants. Like the prudent housewife, he avoids temptation and passes by attractive items that catch his attention but may not prove to be wise "purchases."

A pair of antique duelling pistols worth over $1000 may fetch only a few dollars, but if the fence has a customer who wants these pistols, he will be willing to pay a good price for them. It is important to know what the fence wants.

The fence is as sensitive to fluctuations in the marketplace as any buyer for a department store. A change in fashion, the appearance of a new fad and oversupply can all affect the value of some item. At the height of demand for CB radios, the theft rate was very high because fences were eager to buy this item, but when prices fell and the demand decreased, fences quickly lost interest. An enterprising burglar worked at an auction house where he had no difficulty disposing of his loot. "Flea markets" where persons sell secondhand goods also provide an opportunity for the burglar to sell his wares.

A burglar has described jewelry as "the easiest to pawn and the hardest to identify." Unless jewelry is unique in appearance it is hard to trace and identify, but fences take advantage of burglars who do not realize the true value of stolen items. Inexperienced thieves cannot distinguish between expensive and cheap jewelry, but the expert is very selective and does not bother to take imitation or cheap jewelry. Class rings sometimes find a ready sale to collectors. Trinkets may be taken as gifts for girl friends, which is an unwise move that may lead to the burglar's arrest, for example, when the girl friend wears earrings of usual design that are noticed by the victim or one of her friends. Silverware may have a distinctive pattern that can be identified, but once it is melted down it can no longer be traced.

Valuable antiques are often passed over, for example, a $10,500 antique coffeepot, in favor of cheap items, because the burglar is no connoisseur. One offender ransacked a house and took only three *Playboy* magazines. Sex offenders look for women's underwear and may masturbate into panties or slash underwear with a knife.

Stolen credit cards can be used to purchase goods from department stores, airline tickets, stereo equipment and so on, but there is the risk of arrest. Many burglars sell credit cards or enlist accomplices to make use of them. One quick-thinking burglar, when told by a store clerk that a check with the credit card company showed that the card had been stolen, responded that he had reported it stolen but later found it and forgot to notify the credit card office.

Burglars who break into the home of a known narcotics dealer will often go to great lengths in their search for drugs, tearing apart furniture, cutting up sofas and mattresses, as well as removing baseboard heater grates and air conditioning vents. The burglar, acting on a tip from an informant, goes straight to a wall safe hidden behind a picture to obtain a large amount of money. But before he leaves, he tips over mattresses, scatters items from drawers and leaves a TV set near the rear door to make it look as though someone searching the home happened to find the wall safe.

Deliberate vandalism is rare and usually points to juvenile burglars or an act of revenge. Ketchup is splattered on the furniture, honey is streaked on the carpet, dishes are smashed, paintings are slashed and obscene words are scrawled on the walls. One youthful burglar, on seeing family pictures including the children, would often respond by breaking articles in the house. His companion commented, "I guess [he did it] because his mom and dad had such an unhappy marriage. He liked his mom and dad and [was angry when] they were separated."

Envy of others in better financial circumstances may also lead to resentment and destruction of their property. The burglar may believe that he has knocked over an expensive lamp through carelessness and may not be aware of the psychological factors underlying his destructive behavior. One burglar would take things of sentimental value, mementoes and other items that could not easily be replaced, in the hope of sharing the owner's pleasure in their possession. But when his magical expectations were not fulfilled, he would throw these items away.

APARTMENT HOUSES

Burglars tend to avoid those luxury apartment houses with guards on duty at all times at the entrance and closed-circuit TV, but they seldom have difficulty gaining entrance to other apartment houses either through the front door or the underground garage door. The burglar will push the intercommunication buttons alongside each tenant's name on the wall of the lobby. A tenant will unlock the entrance door by remote control either without making any inquiry or in response to some ambiguous message.

Back doors to apartment houses are often propped open because a tenant is moving his belongings in or out or in the summer because of a failure in the air conditioning system. The lock on the garage door may be less secure than the entrance door lock; if it is difficult to overcome, then the burglar can slip through the door after a tenant drives in or out. Once inside, all the burglar needs to slip the lock on many apartment doors is a plastic card. Even when there are dead bolt locks, many tenants neglect to use them. "I like nicer apartments. Homes you got neighbors, they notice you. You're a lot less looked at when you approach an apartment house. The front door is easily pried with a screwdriver. If there's a double bolt action on the apartment door I don't mess around with them, but you'd be surprised that people don't use their double bolts."

The burglar may break into twenty or more apartments; if he lives in the apartment complex, he can quickly hide the stolen items. If he seeks only cash or jewelry, he can conceal the loot on his person. Larger items can be taken to the underground garage or stored in a maintenance closet for later removal. Most apartment house burglars operate in the daytime, but some work at night, especially those who rappel down the side of the building or climb from one balcony to another. The climbing skills of these burglars compel admiration even as we murmur our disapproval.

> An apartment tenant heard a noise about 3:50 AM and when he went to check he saw a man with long hair standing alongside his television set. The burglar jumped through a sliding glass door, shattering the glass, and he climbed over the balcony and scaled down the side of the building going from one balcony to the next. Meantime the owner's wife surprised another burglar in the bathroom and he also ran out to the balcony and started down the side of the building. By this time several tenants had been aroused by the commotion, and they watched the burglars jump from a third floor balcony to the ground and escape.

The recreation centers in large apartment houses provide many attractive items for the burglar, including expensive furniture. "If you've got enough nerve, you can get away with anything, pick up furniture from the foyer of an apartment house, boldly walk out on the street with it, and no one will pay any attention. In an underground parking garage if you are surprised by the apartment house manager while taking the door off the hinge, just say the owner of the building told you to take the door off and he will say 'OK' and go back inside."

NONRESIDENTIAL BURGLARIES

There are over one million nonresidential burglaries each year in the United States, over one-third of all burglaries, with losses totalling almost half a billion dollars. These burglaries occur more often at night and on weekends, when commercial and industrial buildings are likely to be unoccupied. A recent *UCR* analysis of over 730,000 nonresidential burglaries in which the time of the offense was known showed that 79.4 percent occurred at night (6PM to 6AM) compared with 47.2 percent of over 1,379,000 residential burglaries.

Selection of Targets

An early study of nonresidential burglaries showed that retail stores (37.7%) were the most frequent targets, followed by business or professional offices (14.8%), gas stations and garages (13.8%), public buildings—schools, libraries, etc. (11.6%), warehouses and plants (11.1%) and banks (0.2%). Boxcars, private clubs and other miscellaneous structures (10.7%) accounted for the remaining targets (*UCR*, 1961).

Some burglars specialize in, and for the most part confine themselves to, one type of target, for example, warehouses or taverns, and they tend to use the same mode of entry from one burglary to another. A target may be chosen on the advice of a fence or simply on an impulse. "We were sitting in the Jack-in-The-Box eating. Howard looked across the street and said, 'There's an antique shop, do you want to hit it?' and we did."

Targets may be chosen because they present a greater challenge to the burglar or because they meet some other psychological need. A youth arrested for breaking into a church said that he found a note pinned on one of the doors inside the church. It stated, "No cash left in the building, so if you break in you are wasting your time." The youth said he broke in and stole a cross "to prove that I didn't waste my time and effort." Thirty-one times a burglar broke into a police car pound situated directly opposite a police station and removed car parts. He told a friend "Let's lay it to the pigs." Some of the targets will be further considered.

Hotels

For statistical purposes, hotel burglaries are classified in the *Uniform Crime Reports* as nonresidential. A considerable number of these offenses are committed with the aid of room keys, which can be obtained by posing as a hotel guest, by retaining master keys after termination of employment at the hotel, by failing to return a room key or by making a duplicate key. A prostitute obtained keys from many hotels in the course of her work and returned later to commit burglaries.

Hotel employees have excellent opportunities to enter rooms because often they know when a guest is absent. Those hotels that require guests to register their room numbers on entering the swimming pool provide useful information for employee burglars. If the employee has a legitimate reason to be in the room from which he steals, he commits *theft* rather than *burglary*. As the removal of a television set from a hotel room will often set off an alarm, the set is usually quickly hidden in a laundry cart, maintenance closet or stairwell and not removed from the hotel until several hours later.

Churches

Churches are often left open without any protection against thieves, but even when they are locked, churches are often entered because there are so many inviting items within, such as collection boxes, calculators, tape recorders, electric type-writers, amplifying equipment, pianos, organs and sometimes, especially in the older European churches, priceless stained glass windows and church vessels set with jewels.

> Burglars in Murcia, Spain used a blowtorch to cut through iron bars and chains to steal from the local cathedral crowns from the life-sized images of the Virgin Mary and the Baby Jesus. Together the two crowns contained some 600 precious stones and the total loss was estimated at over $4 million. Burglars in Cologne, Germany entered the city's thirteenth century cathedral by way of scaffolding for repairmen on the outside of the building, evaded electronic alarms and used nylon mountain climber's ropes to make their way through air ducts to a locked treasury. Their loot, which included several gold monstrances, jewelled crosses and bishop's rings, was valued at over $1 million.

Persons involved in devil worship have broken into churches to obtain brass crosses, chalices, cyboriums, altar cloths and other items they use to celebrate a Black Mass. In one such case, the items were placed in a vacant home, and dead cats with knife wounds were found on the altar. One half of an expensive brass cross had been destroyed to make it suitable for satanic purposes.

Vandalism, usually by juvenile burglars, includes tearing pages out of the Bible, writing obscene comments on the walls, urinating on religious objects and setting fires. In some instances youths select churches for acts of destruction to demonstrate their rejection of any symbol of authority.

Mentally disturbed burglars may show bizarre behavior inside the church. One man, who cut his arms and hands in several places breaking into the church, told officers, "The devil broke in here and cut me." Occasionally persons will break into churches for the purpose of suicide in that setting. One man did not lose consciousness after shooting himself in the chest; after three hours, he decided that he wanted to live. He was able to attract the attention of the police by throwing items from the altar through a church window.

Art Galleries and Museums

The demand for works of art and antiques in recent years has resulted in a remarkable increase in their cost. In 1970 the Metropolitan Museum of Art paid a record $5,544,000 for a Velázquez. Prices of fashionable items have multiplied ten to forty times in less than twenty years, and works of art are now being purchased for their investment, rather than only aesthetic values. Art and antiques may well provide a better hedge against inflation than stocks and bonds.

Burglars have not been slow to respond, and two lists of "most wanted" art circulated by Interpol (International Criminal Police Organization) comprise twenty-four works, many of which have a value of at least one million dollars. These works are only a selection from an aggregate of more than 1,000 works stolen within the past decade, and by conservative estimate, $100 million worth of stolen art is still at large. By general agreement the rate of discovery has been dismal (8).

It is difficult for a burglar to sell a world-famous painting such as the *Mona Lisa* by Leonardo Da Vinci because the buyer would be clearly identified as a receiver of stolen goods, and there would be great public pressure on him to restore the painting to the owner. The *Mona Lisa* was stolen from the Louvre in 1911 by an employee, Vincenzo Perugia.

> He was well known to the guards and had no trouble in getting in on a day in August when the museum was closed for repairs. After extracting the *Mona Lisa* from its frame, he hid it under his painter's smock and walked out. The loss was not discovered until the next day. The Paris police searched him and his house, as they did every other employee of the Louvre, but failed to find the painting, although in fact he held it there for two and one-half years. Later, he returned to Italy, judging that the search had been called off, and answered an advertisement put in the press by a Florentine antique dealer, Alfredo Geri, who was mounting an exhibition of old master paintings. Perugia demanded the equivalent of £20,000 and was trapped by Geri, who recognized the *Mona Lisa* at once (9).

The burglar may hold a work of art in ransom, offering to return it to the owner or the insurors for a huge payment and immunity from prosecution. Insurance companies faced with the prospect of a $100,000 payment to the owner are tempted by the prospect of a $10,000 payment to the burglar or his representative. The latter claims to be a public-spirited informant, in no way connected with the burglary, but naturally eager to obtain a reward (10% of the value of the picture) for his services.

Like the kidnapper who threatens to kill his hostage, the burglar may threaten to destroy the works of art if the ransom is not paid. Even in the absence of a direct threat, the risk is present, and a government may intervene in order to preserve the national heritage. When eight Cézannes valued at two million dollars were stolen from a museum at Aix-en-Provence, André Malraux, Minister of Cultural Affairs, warned the police that safe recovery of the pictures was paramount, thereby imposing restrictions upon the police, who had planned to arrest a gang upon suspicion of their involvement. One insurance company rejected a ransom demand and paid out $1,300,000 to the owners, but another insurance agency, despite police protests, offered a reward. The paintings were recovered from an abandoned car.

Lesser known works of art may be purchased from burglars by unscrupulous museums or private collectors in the hope that their possession of stolen goods will pass unrecognized. Sometimes these items are "laundered" by sale through more than one art dealer, so that the final purchaser buying from a reputable dealer has no idea that he is buying stolen property.

It is difficult to identify some works of art and antiques, as they bear no serial numbers. An artist may draw more than one picture of the same scene, and a craftsman may make more than one vase of a particular design. In order to cope with this and related problems, Scotland Yard, the New York Police Department and some national police agencies have formed art and antique squads. These detectives are trained in such special fields as furniture, armor and weapons, porcelain and tapestries.

Graves

For centuries in Italy, tomb burglars or *tombaroli* have been breaking into Etruscan tombs in search of vases, bronze statues and other items that date back to the fifth century B.C. When they locate a burial site, they use an *asta*, a probing device, to locate the tombs. Treasure-hunting tomb burglars operate in many countries, and skilled professionals who earn their living in this manner pass their trade secrets on from one generation to another.

Gold, precious stones and diamond rings in contemporary burial sites attract grave burglars. Burglars broke into the grave of Michael Todd, the motion picture producer who had been killed and badly burned in an airplane crash. They ripped back the lid of his bronze coffin and removed the rubber bag containing his remains, which were found later less than 100 yards from the grave hidden under dirt and tree branches. It is believed that the burglars were under the mistaken impression that a valuable diamond ring was buried with the remains.

In 1978, grave burglars removed Charlie Chaplin's body from a small unguarded Swiss village cemetery. Almost three months later, two men were arrested after they called the Chaplin family lawyer demanding a ransom for the return of the remains of the famous comedian. The telephone call was traced, and the burglars revealed that the body, still in its coffin, was hidden in a shallow hole in a cornfield near Lake Geneva. Several weeks previously a farmer had noticed that some earth was upturned among the furrows in his cornfield but thought wild boars had done it.

Place of Entry

There are several modes of entry into nonresidential buildings including (1) forced entry or entry with the aid of an employee who has left a window unlocked or provided a duplicate key, usually at night or on weekends; (2) surreptitious entry during working hours, with the burglar remaining hidden on the premises until all the employees have left; and (3) entry by imposture and removal of goods during working hours.

Forced entry is usually through a locked door or window, as in residential burglaries, but the back door is more likely to be forced than the front door. Roof entry, which was reported in only 0.2 percent of residential burglaries, occurred in 4.6 percent of retail stores, 4.0 percent of warehouse and plant, 2.4 percent of bank and 1.6 percent of office burglaries (*UCR*, 1961). Other sites of entry include ventilator fans and air ducts.

Burglar alarms are more likely to be encountered in non-residential burglaries, but they do not bother the smash-and-grab burglar who throws a brick through a jewelry store window, grabs a handful of valuable items and is on his way in seconds. Some burglars inactivate or avoid burglar alarms, while others check to see whether the alarm system is effective by shooting a marble through a window with a slingshot or by other means. "If I wasn't sure the burglar alarm was hooked up or not, I would jimmy the door or shake the window real hard or something like that, and that should set the burglar alarm off, and then I would go a block or two and watch to see if the patrol was coming."

Once inside the building of a single-story shopping center, the burglar can use the crawl space above the ceiling to break into a number of stores or offices. Occasionally burglars will break in by backing a large stolen truck against a building. Stores of cinder block construction are especially vulnerable to this form of entry. Burglars backed a truck into the wall of a liquor warehouse knocking out a hole three feet by five feet.

A forklift truck was used to load 264 cases of expensive scotch whiskey worth over $28,000 onto a conveyor belt to the truck.

During working hours, the bold burglar will walk through areas of many buildings not open to the general public. A telephone receiver hanging from a belt at his waist is sufficient to convince many persons that he is an employee of the telephone company. Uniforms of merchant guard services, public service company or other organizations may be worn as disguise, but a confident manner, without any disguise, is often sufficient to carry the day. A warehouse burglar describes his skill in stealing merchandise during working hours and then driving off with it in a customer's truck:

> I had over eighty warehouses that I studied good. Before I'd go in I'd case the joint out, I would just walk casually around like I am working all over the place. Once in a while they would stop me and say "What are you doing?" I would have these requisitions and I'd say, "I'm filling these up." All of these warehouses have shipping and receiving desks, on top of the desk are the invoices, I would just reach in and grab four or five, put them in my hands, pencil behind my ear and I would walk up and down the warehouse. I'd draw a visual picture in my mind where every car, every truck is, whether there is a guard or not, where the fence is, different avenues of escape. When I took stuff, I'd always load it on a customer's truck. I'd get exactly what I wanted.

Tunnelling into Banks

The eight million dollar burglary of the Société Générale bank in Nice, France in 1976 was by means of a thirty foot long tunnel from a large underground sewer to the bank vault. The tunnel roof was supported by metal stanchions and wooden beams set in concrete. The five tons of excavation and safecracking equipment used by the gang included inflatable rafts, twenty-seven oxyacetylene cylinders and several heavy hydraulic jacks, which were used to move a five-ton safe that stood in the burglar's way inside the wall of the vault. There was even a portable stove to provide hot meals. Electrical power for lights and a portable fan was obtained through a half-mile electrical cable attached to the power supply of a municipal underground parking lot. Tunnelling does not always result in such rich rewards.

In South Gate, California in 1977, a man identifying himself as Mr. Goldman rented a vacant building across the street from the Security Pacific Bank and paid $1,550 cash for three months' rent. A large sign reading "The future home of Goldman Carpet Company, Watch for Grand Opening—Goldman Carpet Company" was placed on the building. Mr. Goldman spent a total of $4,000 in cash for the rent, a telephone answering service, utilities, lumber, new exterior locks, oxygen tanks and acetylene tanks.

During the next two months, six men worked two 12-hour shifts a day inside the building, changing shifts at 6 AM and 6 PM. One Friday evening a burglar alarm went off in the bank building but patrolmen found no entry into the bank. There were further alarms on Saturday but there were no signs of entry into the bank. A bank security guard heard noises and vibrations and on Monday the bank manager discovered a tunnel ending in the floor of the vault.

The tunnel entrance was in the vacant business across the street, starting with a 14 foot deep entrance hole, leading into a 4 foot by 5 foot tunnel shaft which was 115 feet long, coming up beneath the foundation of the bank, making the end of the tunnel 6 feet below the vault floor. The entire tunnel shaft had been shored with timber and plywood. An attempt to break into the vault had been abandoned, and the burglars were $4,000 out of pocket.

Selection of Items

In nonresidential burglaries, money is sought from coin-operated machines, cash registers, hiding places and safes. Electric typewriters and calculators from offices, drugs from pharmacies and general items such as liquor, television sets, clothes, furs and jewelry that are likely to find a ready sale are taken. Sometimes customers will place orders for suits, tires or other merchandise. "Fast Eddie" acquired his nickname because he would take orders for tires and deliver the correct size three days later. One drugstore burglar would call up his friends after he had gained entry and find out what they needed.

Unusual items include *animal sperm* used for breeding purposes; *urine samples,* which were taken from a drug abuse agency presumably because the burglars were attending the agency on a court order, and they stole samples, including their own, to avoid detection of drug traces in their urine; *snakes and wild animals* from zoos; *mercury switches* from thermostats for use in bombs; *baseball pitching machines,* used for batting practice, were taken in the burglary of a Tokyo baseball training center and, with minor adjustments, were used by radical Japanese students to throw firebombs and rocks in political demonstrations.

> Burglars broke into a Denver meat warehouse and removed cardboard boxes that they assumed contained edible beef. While driving the suspect Filbert Maestas to police headquarters, a police officer started to laugh, and Maestas asked him what he was laughing about. The officer replied, "You wouldn't believe what you took from the building . . . you took 1200 beef assholes." Maestas replied, "If I go to jail for stealing beef assholes, I'm really going to be mad." Following his conviction of second degree burglary, he appealed to the Colorado Court of Appeals, claiming that his statement quoted above was improperly admitted in evidence because it was made prior to any *Miranda* advisement. The Colorado Court of Appeals ruled, "In light of the fact that the apparent object of the burglary was edible beef, but the actual fruits of the crime consisted of a portion of the animal's anatomy which is frequently referred to in terms of humorous disapprobation, it is not surprising that the officer was amused. Under these circumstances, there is no basis for us to conclude that the officer's laughter was merely a ploy to trick Maestas into making damaging admissions . . . his statements were voluntarily offered and were not the product of interrogation." The court rejected the appeal (Colo. Court of Appeals 76-269, 1977).

SAFE BURGLARY

Many safes in use today are small and not embedded in concrete so that they can be carried from the scene of the burglary and forced open at leisure in the privacy of the burglar's garage or in some isolated location. Other safes are fire resistant rather than burglar resistant. The consequence is that many safes are opened by burglars who have not specialized in this work and did not break in for the purpose of opening a safe, but ransacked a cheap safe along with the rest of the premises.

A study of 401 safe burglaries in a two-month period in California showed that homes netted safe burglars the highest return for their effort, with an average of $8,146 per home attacked. Restaurants, service stations and schools were the

premises most frequently hit. In these locations one would
not expect to find either the large amounts of money or the
elaborate security measures of a large bank. Indeed, only 27
of the 401 premises were equipped with burglar alarms (2).

Fire-resistant safes are usually lightweight safes mounted
on wheels and are no more than thin steel boxes enclosing
insulating material to protect the contents from damage during
a fire. *Burglar-resistant safes* usually weigh 750 pounds or more
and may be embedded in concrete. They are constructed of
laminated or thick steel and are designed to resist the efforts
of a determined, skillful burglar for a long period of time.
Many modern safes have spring-loaded "relockers" that cause
the safe to lock permanently whenever the safe is attacked
with a sledge hammer or torch.

Equipment

The safe burglar's equipment may include a sledge-hammer,
an axe, punch or drift pins, punches, cold chisels, crowbar,
sectional jimmy, electric drills with steel, carbon, tungsten or
diamond bits; electric saw with carborundum or diamond-
edged blades; an acetylene torch, hose and tank; a 220-volt
electric cutting torch and a burning bar; electric blasting caps
and explosives; cystoscopes, industrial x-ray equipment and
hydraulic jacks.

Special training is needed in the use of some of this equipment. A burning bar, for example, consists of a length of pipe
containing steel or magnesium rods; the oxygen forced through
the pipe comes out under high pressure to burn at 7,000° C.
If water is not applied as soon as a hole is made in the safe,
paper currency inside will be incinerated. An inexperienced
burglar using an oxyacetylene torch will sometimes melt a
piece of the safe door so that it is impossible to open it.

Methods of Entry

The intelligent safe burglar checks to see whether the safe
is locked. Unlocked fire-resistant safes used only for the storage
of records have been broken apart by burglars who did not pull
on the door handle and neglected to read a notice taped on

the outside stating that the safe was unlocked.

Employees using combination safes often turn the dial for less than a complete turn after shutting the safe. This makes it easier for them to reopen the safe and also easier for the burglar, who turns the dial slowly in the reverse direction while trying to pull the safe door open. When he reaches the last number of the combination, the door will open. Before leaving the premises at night, the employee in charge of the safe should turn the dial more than one complete turn so that the safe can only be opened by dialing the full combination.

The intelligent burglar will also check to see whether the combination number has been written on the side of the safe, inside desk drawers or on the inside cover of a ledger book. An enterprising burglar broke into a safe company and obtained from their records the combinations of many safes in a metropolitan area.

Another method of obtaining the combination is to watch the opening of a safe through a telescope from a recreational vehicle parked outside a supermarket or to watch an employee opening the safe from a hiding place in the false ceiling above the safe.

A burglar entered a large supermarket during business hours and hid in a stockroom in the rear of the store. After the store was closed and the employees had left, he stole food and a blanket, which he took up into the crawl space above the false ceiling of the store. He crawled along steel girders and braces to the area above the store office where he drilled a small hole through the fiber-board ceiling directly above the dial on the front of the safe. It was later established that a person could look through this hole and read the safe combination while the safe was being opened by an employee of the store.

The following day the burglar obtained the combination number of the safe, and that night after the employees had left he removed over $7,000 from the safe and returned to his hiding place above the false ceiling. The next day during business hours he crawled back down into the stockroom and left the store. Detectives found a blanket, a soft drink container, flashlight and numerous cigarette butts above the store office. There were two different locations where he had defecated during his long period above the false ceiling.

The same burglar is believed to have hidden along with an accomplice above the cashier's cage of a large department store. Several planks had been laid across ceiling supports to provide a safe platform. The burglars had taken sandwiches and milk to the hiding place and, after drinking the milk, had used the milk cartons to urinate in. When the burglars overheard comments by store employees indicating that they had been heard moving about, they broke through the false ceiling and held up the employees at gunpoint, escaping with over $26,000.

Methods of forced entry of safes include:

RIPPING OR PEELING. The burglar uses an electric drill or brace and bit to make a hole in a corner of the door away from the hinge. The hole is enlarged by use of a larger drill, and then a wedge or cold chisel is used to enlarge the opening. If the safe has more than one steel plate, then each layer is peeled back one at a time. Sometimes a notch is cut in the safe above the door and a pry bar is used to rip the door plate off. This is one of the most popular methods.

PUNCHING. A sledgehammer and a drift pin or center punch are used to knock the combination dial off the safe. Then the spindle of the lock is knocked in so that the back of the lock falls out.

CHOPPING. A cold chisel is used to open the bottom of the safe, usually the weakest part of a fire-resistant safe, and a pry bar is used to break in.

BURNING OR TORCHING. An oxyacetylene torch is used to burn the metal around the dial, which is then removed, or a hole is burned in the corner of the door. Burning bars are also effective.

DRILLING. High-speed drills are used to drill the bolts out of the bolt mechanism of the safe. A four- or six-inch core drill used in construction to drill through reinforced concrete can also be used to drill a large hole in the wall of the safe so that the burglar can put his hand in the safe and remove the contents.

SPECIAL TECHNIQUES. Industrial x-ray equipment can be used to find the numbers on a combination lock. A cystoscope, a tubular instrument fitted with a light to enable surgeons to examine the urinary bladder, can help burglars manipulate the tumblers. The dial of the safe is removed, and a hole is then drilled to permit introduction of the cystoscope.

COMBINATION OF METHODS. It may be necessary to use several methods to overcome the various types of obstacles in modern safes. Thus, torching may be interrupted by a torch-resistant copper plate, stone chips may break drill bits or a lead screen or plastic tumblers may defeat x-ray equipment. Burglars who were unable to open a small safe placed it on railroad tracks; it was knocked forty feet down the tracks but remained unopen, and the train was not damaged.

SAFE BLOWING. At one time safe blowers were elite members of the safecracking profession, but their ranks have dwindled due to the introduction of the acetylene torch to cut through metal and also to the construction of relatively burglar-proof safes in large banks. Modern large bank vaults are virtually impregnable. In 1962, when the building located at 15 Broad Street in New York City was being prepared for demolition, the task of dismantling the 10 by 20 foot vault of the Morgan Guarantee Trust Company occupied 2,000 man-hours of labor (7).

The vaults in small banks are still vulnerable; recently, burglars in Dade County, Florida, used a timed explosive device containing one and one-half pounds of gelatin dynamite to break into a bank vault and obtain $600,000. Burglars in rural northwestern Georgia were less successful in their attempt to rob a bank by use of explosives. Six sticks of dynamite, each weighing three pounds, were placed around the vault door and detonated. The explosion completely destroyed the interior of the building and caused severe structural damage, resulting in $165,000 in property loss. Yet the vault remained unopened and no money was taken.

CANNON ATTACK. Artillery such as howitzers, antitank cannons and missiles are not part of the weaponry of the average burglar, but terrorist groups with access to these weapons may use them to blow their way into bank vaults. In 1965, a group of nonterrorist burglars used a 20 millimeter cannon to break through an 18-inch reinforced concrete wall at the Brink's, Inc., office in Syracuse, New York. The World War II vintage anti-tank gun and 200 rounds of armor-piercing ammunition were purchased from the Potomac Arms Company in Alexandria, Virginia and shipped to the Railway Express Office at Plattsburgh, New York. The burglars did not attempt to claim the weapon but broke into the storage depot and removed it. The cannon was taken by truck to the Brink's, Inc., office. After gaining entrance to the building, the burglars used mattresses and blankets to muffle the sounds of the weapon and wore breathing masks to protect them from the clouds of concrete dust. They fired 33 rounds at the wall of the vault from a distance of only a few feet, and a hole large enough for a man to crawl through was blasted in the reinforced steel and concrete wall of the vault. They removed $416,000 in cash, checks and securities, but many thousands of dollars were destroyed by the cannon fire.

NOTES

Burglars sometimes leave written notes at the scene of the crime. These notes may be classified as follows.

APOLOGETIC. "Sorry I'm such a muck-up but I guess I don't know what's happening. I pawned your gun and will send you the pawn slip." A youth who broke into a school to obtain the address of a former girl friend left a note, "I am sorry for the mess, you can rest assured I did not take anything."

APPRECIATIVE. "Thanks for everything."

BIZARRE. The following strange note partly made from words cut out of magazines and pasted on a piece of paper was left in a locked apartment storage room, from which an expensive ten-speed bicycle had been stolen said, "Tearful ostrich, want your bike back? No police, witness, trust me, I mean to do well. I'm just a little screwed up in the head, you understand, don't you, Ol' Pal?" The victim had no idea who might have left this peculiar message.

EXPLANATORY. "You can't treat employees the way you do and expect to get away with it."

HUMOROUS. A burglar scrawled, "You're absolutely right" on a placard that was hanging on the wall of the victim's living room. The placard consisted of a quotation from an 1866 opinion of the New York Surrogate Court, "No man's life, liberty, or property are safe while the legislature is in session."

INFORMATIVE. "We could have taken anything we wanted."

"We got you again." "A word from your local burglar. You sure helped me when you left the door open the other night." After taking eight million dollars, burglars left in the vault of a French bank a note stating, "No gunplay, no violence, no hate." Reference to narcotics or marihuana in a note suggests that the burglary is related to a prior drug sale or purchase by the burglar. One such note stated, "Thanks for the grass, no longer a friend."

INSULTING. "Thanks for the stuff, you should put in an alarm, dumb shit."

MISLEADING. Juvenile burglars who stole several packages of hamburger meat and hamburger buns from a fast-food service restaurant attempted to divert suspicion from themselves by blaming Daddy Bruce, the owner of another restaurant. The note stated, "You stole my ribs, I stole your burgers. Bring my ribs back, I'll give you your burgers back. Don't come without my ribs, Daddy Bruce."

OBSCENE. A man who took only a pair of girl's panties left an obscene note and a photograph taken by the man himself of the lower part of his naked body while standing in front of a mirror in a bathroom. The obscene note stated, "I took a pair of your panties but I left a picture of my cock. Hope you enjoy the picture as much as I will jacking off to your panties."

TEASING. Juvenile burglars left this teasing note for the police inside a stolen briefcase, "Trifon copped out on us again. New hide-out located Trifon's house or Sunderson's. Trifon's house bigger, vote———. Sunderson's safer, vote———. Five week period income $12,240. This week vote taken to see who will be boss."

THREATENING. "Don't call the police or we'll burn your house down."

THE BURGLAR'S CALLING CARD

A few burglars make a practice of leaving a bowel motion at the scene of the crime, the criminal's *carte de visite odorante*. The burglar may defecate in the toilet, yet neglect to flush the bowl, but more often he will do it on a carpet, in the bathtub, on top of the bed or on a couch. One burglary victim sold her expensive dining room table, because at every meal her digestion was impaired by memory of the heap of excrement left on her table by her unwelcome visitor.

Some burglars with crude senses of humor leave their fecal deposit smeared on the inside aspect of the telephone receiver. When the startled householder discovers that his home has been ransacked, he quickly grabs the phone to call the police and finds a sticky mess on his fingers. Other burglars, with equally malicious intent, will have a bowel motion between the bed sheets and then neatly remake the bed, so that the unsuspecting householder jumps into bed and into the excrement.

Bowel motion has also been wrapped in lingerie taken from a dresser and carefully replaced. One burglar would leave a toothbrush standing like a flagpole in the pile. The burglar who left a heap of his excrement on the desk of a Denver County Court judge was probably expressing his sentiment toward the judge. A rejected lover broke into his former girl friend's apartment, urinated in his rival's hard hat and set it on the stove. The victim described her apartment as smelling ripe on her return.

The offender may himself suffer from his impulses to excrete during the burglary by having a bowel motion in his pants during the burglary.

> When this urge—indecent exposure, burglary, rape—hits me I have an urge to have a bowel motion. Often in a burglary I stop and have a bowel motion. I had a bowel motion once with my clothes on, I couldn't hold it. . . . I did commit a burglary near the edge of town. I took some stuff. One of the things was a pistol and a little television set, it wasn't very many things. While I was committing the burglary, I had a bowel movement. I had my clothes on and I just couldn't hold it. It happened just as I stepped out of the house, I couldn't hold it. So I went driving down some road that led out of town. I cleaned myself up with a towel that I had.

Burglars will seldom volunteer information regarding this characteristic trademark of their *modus operandi*, and indeed, their victims may clean up the mess and neglect to mention it to the police. Apparently both parties are embarrassed and prefer not to speak about such odd behavior. When questioned

about it, the offender will try to dismiss the subject by saying
"I had to go in a hurry." One man claimed that he did it on a
rug because he was fearful of being trapped in the bathroom.
"Before I go into the house I don't need to go to the bathroom,
I just have to go right then. The reason I don't use the bathroom, I'm afraid they'll walk in and catch me. That's why I
do it in the open on the rug."

In the writer's experience, many of these men are also
rapists or have significant other sexual problems. One rapist-
burglar, who regularly had a bowel motion outside the residence
of his intended victim, describes this urge to defecate and his
puzzlement over it.

> I spotted a girl on the block ahead of me. By the time I got
> to the corner she was turning into her house. I then discovered I
> had to use the restroom. There were no gas stations around so I
> went in back of her house. I dug me a little hole with my hand
> and proceeded to meditate. While I was meditating the light came
> on above me. I was right below a window. When I stood up I
> could see her in the kitchen through the bedroom window.
>
> Every time when I start stalking a girl, I have to go somewhere
> and have a crap. Every cotton picking time. I have to go some-
> where and have a crap. Most of the times the girl would get away.
> That's something I couldn't figure out. I could have went to the
> bathroom two minutes before I start stalking the girl. But as soon
> as I start stalking I have to go to the bathroom. That's the reason
> the dog couldn't catch the rabbit. If I take up this profession again
> I'm going to study up on it and find out why. That's very humiliat-
> ing, you grab a girl, throw her down, you're going to rape her and
> you say, "Hang on a minute I've got to go over to the trees."

Defecation at the scene of a burglary is puzzling. Friedman
notes that everyone has experienced at some time or another
the peristaltic reaction to fright, and one explanation of this
phenomenon is that it is simply the result of the thief's fear
and general nervousness (4). He reports that police investigators lean toward this view because in police circles, burglars
are considered among the most timid of criminals. The story is
told of a burglar discovered by a woman in her New York
apartment threatening, "Madam if you make a noise, I'll
scream!" But, Friedman adds, if nervousness is the cause, why

is it the professional and seasoned burglar who regularly observes the ritual and not the amateur, whom we would expect to be more nervous? He also wonders why the burglar robbing an apartment would choose to defecate uncomfortably on the carpet when normal toilet facilities were only a few feet away.

Explanations of this peculiar calling card have been reviewed by Theodore Reik, who discounts the theory that feces are a visible sign of the criminal's lighthearted impudence and intention to mock authority. Some criminals believe that they will delay their pursuit if they leave their feces behind; to lengthen their respite, they cover their feces with various objects. Popular names for feces in foreign countries (watchman, sentry, night watchman) are cited in support of this superstition. The custom is also attributed to the criminal's superstitious belief that something must be left behind if he is to escape, the underlying conviction being that every crime must be expiated, and he propitiates the gods by making this sacrifice.

Reik maintains that if the custom goes back to superstition, there must be a deeper psychological explanation and suggests that it is an expression of the unconscious impulse to confess (12). The feces, which are part of the person, represent the culprit himself and are left behind for the purpose of self-betrayal. Indeed, on rare occasions identification of intestinal parasites in the feces may lead to conviction of the criminal. Reik cites the case of a dangerous criminal recently released from prison, who defecated at the scene of his crime and cleaned himself with his prison discharge papers. One Swiss thief used a letter from his mother for the same purpose. Self-betrayal may take the form of leaving not feces, but clothing or some other article that can be traced to the offender.

It is difficult to account for the burglar's bowel motion at the scene; none of the above theories seems convincing. One is, however, immediately aware that it is an act of contempt for one's person, and one's home is often assumed to be an extension of one's person. The first thing you teach a dog is not to defecate in the house. This is surely the ultimate anti-social act of the burglar.

BLUNDERS IN BURGLARY

Some burglars seem to be born losers. In an occupation that offers steady employment and rapid advancement in income, they fail miserably, wasting time forcing open unlocked doors, building large muscles cracking empty safes, breaking legs from falling off ladders, cutting tendons while smashing windows, fracturing skulls from falling through skylights, being shot by peevish victims and having their loot stolen by other burglars.

> A burglar kicked out the glass door of a liquor store and took twelve cases of liquor valued at $770 and $30 from a cash drawer. While driving away his car became stuck in mud, and he had to pay a tow truck driver $25. He hid the liquor in a culvert near a park, and when he returned the next day all he found was one broken bottle and an empty cardboard case. A boy in the park told him that he had seen many people walking into the culvert and leaving with bottles of whiskey. He was charged with burglary.

As in the course of any event, mistakes occur, and even the best burglars draw attention to themselves. There is a range of events that leads to disaster. Fate intervenes and the burglar cannot provide for every possible eventuality. How is he to know that there is a child hiding in the upper branches of a tree overlooking the house? How is he to know that the stranger in the bar to whom he tries to sell a television set is the owner of the stolen set? A former employee of a fast-food restaurant hid above the room containing the safe with the intention of using a telescope to obtain the combination. At 5 PM, during the rush hour evening meal trade, he fell through the false ceiling.

Human fallibility intervenes, as in the case of a burglar who was driving away from a mountain homesite, and in the tension of the moment, forgot to shut the gate. A neighbor driving by realized that the horses on the property might run off, and he made a note of the license plate number of the pickup truck. A house burglar who ran from the scene when a neighbor turned on an outdoor light was hiding near some bushes in front of a home two blocks away when he saw his accomplice running across the lawn. He called to him "Psst" and was promptly arrested. How could he have anticipated that a police officer would have the same build as his accomplice and would look like him in the poor light?

The unconscious need to confess may also contribute to the criminal's misfortune. Many offenders somehow create their own mistakes, as in the case of a burglar who wrote a false name on a pawn slip for a stolen article, but in completing the form he signed his own name. Two juveniles were arrested for auto theft, and in the car were found three record books giving the places and dates of various burglaries as well as lists of items stolen. Inexperience rather than an unconscious need to confess was probably the cause of their mistakes.

DISPOSAL OF THE LOOT

Very young juvenile burglars will often give to their friends or throw away those items that they do not want for themselves. More experienced juveniles want cash returns or marihuana for their loot and, like adult criminals, work hand in hand with fences (*see* Chap. 3). Some offenders acquire marketing skills of their own. "Like if I had anything legitimate, I wouldn't know how to sell it. Nobody would buy it. As soon as you tell them it's stolen, it's sort of a magnet. People just draw to it as soon as you tell them it's stolen."

Burglars prefer to dispose of their loot as quickly as possible to reduce the risk of being arrested in possession of stolen property. The goods may be stored in a girl friend's home or in suburban storage units that permit direct access by the customer by use of his own lock and key. The unit is rented under a false name and address. A juvenile burglar stored the proceeds of burglaries on his way home from school in a storage room in the basement of a church. He had obtained the key to the room in a burglary of the church.

Special circumstances demand special measures. About half of the $4.4 million taken in the 1974 burglary of a Purolator Security, Inc., vault was found under fresh cement in the basement of a Chicago home. The money was buried in a seven-foot hole and covered with five inches of cement.

BURGLARY AND RELATED CRIMES

Burglary may be followed by vandalism, arson, robbery, assault, rape and murder. In some cases the burglary is committed for the purpose of committing the additional offense, in other cases the second offense was not planned but was committed upon impulse or following an encounter with an occupant, visitor or law enforcement officer.

VANDALISM. The damage caused by burglars may result in financial loss far exceeding that from the theft of articles. Juvenile burglars removed merchandise valued at over $1,000 from a store and office building but caused damage within the building amounting to approximately $20,000. Windows were broken, fire extinguishers were sprayed in many rooms, printer's ink was spread around and there was widespread destruction of furniture and fittings.

ARSON. Burglars set fires in the hope of concealing their break-ins or of obliterating their fingerprints. Firesetting may also be the act of vandals or of someone motivated by revenge toward the owners of the property. Pyromaniacs or compulsive firesetters derive excitement and sometimes sexual gratification from watching the flames, but they may attribute the burglary and arson to more conventional motives. The burglar who is frustrated in his search for loot may burn the building.

> Well I went into the theater to see two movies and I waited until everybody left and locked the doors and everything and then I went to the locker room to try to find something to break the office door with. I found a chair that had some thin metal on it that would fit in the door to pry the door open, and so, I took the chair and busted the door knob and the door wouldn't open. So I went looking for other things to try to pry it open and I couldn't find anything, so I was pretty pissed off, pretty mad.
>
> After that I went down some steps behind the curtains to a basement and they had some supplies there. I walked around some more and I was getting pretty mad so I lit the curtains in back of the theater and the fire went out. It didn't get started so I kept lighting the curtains and finally they lit pretty good. Then there was a lot of smoke and fire and flames so I left through the side doors and went into an alley. I heard the fire trucks and came back and stayed there for about an hour watching them put it out.

Peter Leonard, age twenty-three, admitted breaking into a

bowling alley at Port Chester, New York, in 1974 and accidentally starting a fire by dropping a lighted cigarette into a box of stuffed plastic toys. The fire spread to a crowded discotheque, and twenty-four persons died in the flames. Leonard was sentenced to fifteen years to life on twenty-four counts of murder and lesser terms for arson and burglary. The sentences will run concurrently.

RAPE. Compulsive rapists often break into the homes of their intended victims. The writer found that almost one-third of 147 forcible rapes in which the offender was a stranger to the victim occurred in the victim's home or apartment.

ROBBERY. About 12 percent of robberies in the United States occur in homes and apartments, but not all of these robberies involve also the crime of burglary.

MURDER. In his study of residential crime in Boston, Reppetto found that 7 of 321 murders were committed by strangers on residential premises, 5 in connection with a robbery, and 2 with an apparent burglary. The motives in an additional 13 murders on residential premises were not identified, but some of these cases involved illegal entry, not necessarily by strangers. Reppetto concluded that the probability of being murdered by a stranger in a home appears remote, on the order of 1 in 100,000 annually for the average Bostonian (13).

The fact that the likelihood of being murdered by a burglar is remote provides little comfort if you happen to be the victim. In 1974, three Maryland prison escapees were in the midst of a burglary of a house trailer on the Alday farm in South Georgia. When the Alday men began returning from the fields, they were systematically shot and killed. Ned Alday, age sixty-two, his brother and his three sons were all killed. A daughter-in-law was raped repeatedly and then slain. The three escapees were convicted and sentenced to death on the evidence of a suspect's sixteen-year-old brother, who pleaded guilty to lesser charges.

REFERENCES

1. Brown, M.: Blighted by burglars. *Sunday Times,* November 27, 1977.
2. California Department of Justice: *Safe Burglaries in California.* Sacramento, 1970.

3. Ferdinand, T. N.: The criminal patterns of Boston. *Am J Sociol,* 73:84, 1967.
4. Friedman, A. B.: The scatological rites of burglars. *Western Folklore,* 27:171, 1968.
5. Hoff, Armand: *The Panther.* London, Frederick Muller, Ltd., 1975.
6. Hohimer, Frank: *The Home Invaders: Confessions of a Cat Burglar.* Chicago, Chicago Review, 1975.
7. Inciardi, J. A.: *Careers in Crime.* Chicago, Rand, 1975.
8. Meyer, K. E.: *The Plundered Past.* New York, Atheneum, 1973.
9. Middlemas, Keith: *The Double Market: Art Theft and Art Thieves.* Westmead, New York, Saxon, 1975.
10. Perkins, R. M.: *Criminal Law,* 2nd ed. Mineola, The Foundation Press, 1969.
11. President's Commission on Crime in the District of Columbia: *Report.* Washington, D.C., U.S. Government Printing Office, 1966.
12. Reik, T.: *The Compulsion to Confess.* New York, Farrar Straus, 1959.
13. Reppetto, T. A.: *Residential Crime.* Cambridge, Ballinger Pub, 1974.
14. Scarr, H. A.: *Patterns of Burglary,* 2nd ed. Washington, D.C., U.S. Government Printing Office, 1973.
15. Walsh, Marilyn E.: *The Fence: A New Look at the World of Property Theft.* Westport, Connecticut, Greenwood, 1977.

CHAPTER 2

THEFT

A thief knows a thief as a wolf knows a wolf.

—*Proverb*

THE CUSTOMER WHO steals items from a convenience store while the clerk's attention is distracted, the shopper who holds up the clerk for the contents of the cash register and the man who breaks in to take merchandise after the clerk has closed the store all commit larceny, but the first offender is charged with shoplifting (larceny-theft), the second with robbery and the third with burglary.

Larceny is defined in English common law as *the taking and carrying away of the personal goods of another with intent to steal the same.* The taking must be without the owner's consent and with the intent to permanently deprive the owner of his property. The person who takes another's overcoat from a rack, thinking it his own, does not commit larceny unless he decides to keep the coat after recognizing his mistake.

The property should be carried away, but this requirement can be satisfied by even short movement of the item. Merely touching a wallet is not sufficient, but if it is removed from the place it occupied and then dropped because its removal has been detected, this meets the letter of the law. A thief may take constructive possession by employing an inanimate agency, for example, bypassing the electricity meter outside his home to steal electricity.

The *Uniform Crime Reports* of the FBI defines larceny-theft as *the unlawful taking, carrying, leading, or riding away of property from the possession or constructive possession of another.* Motor vehicle theft is not included and is counted separately because of the great volume of thefts in that theft category. Larceny-theft does not include thefts that are part of a robbery or burglary, embezzlement, confidence games, forgery and check fraud.

In the *Uniform Crime Reports,* larceny-theft includes the following categories:

1. Pocket picking
2. Purse snatching
3. Shoplifting
4. Thefts from motor vehicles
5. Theft of motor vehicle parts and accessories
6. Theft of bicycles
7. Theft from buildings (open to the public and where the offender has legal access)
8. Theft from coin-operated device or machine

Statistics on these various offenses, as well as on other crimes, including total number of offenses, rates per 100,000 population, changes in rates, regional distribution, dollar loss, clearances by arrest and other factors are published each year in the *Uniform Crime Reports.* There is no uniformity in the state statutes on the definition of various crimes, and the *UCR* definitions sometimes are not in accord with state statutes. For example, state statutes might interpret thefts from motor vehicles as burglaries.

The following forms of theft will be reviewed in this chapter:

1. Motor vehicle theft
2. Theft by employees
3. Theft from buildings (no unlawful entry)
4. Computers and theft
5. Shoplifting
6. Theft from vending machines and parking meters
7. Pocket-picking and purse-snatching
8. Bicycle theft

MOTOR VEHICLE THEFT

In 1975, for the first time in the United States, over one million motor vehicles were reported stolen within one year. The theft rate was 1 of every 130 registered motor vehicles. Although less than 15 percent of motor vehicle thefts are cleared by arrest, approximately 80 percent of stolen vehicles are quickly recovered because they have been taken for temporary use. Vehicles are also stolen for resale, for stripping, for removal of cargo and for use in other crimes such as armed robbery.

Joyriders

Four out of five stolen cars are taken by joyriders, mainly youths without cars of their own, who need a ride home, want to spend the evening driving around town or wish to impress their friends through a delinquent act. They favor cars left unlocked with keys in the ignition or older-model cars that can be "hot-wired" without difficulty or started with a screwdriver inserted into the ignition.

High-performance sports cars have a particular appeal for youthful offenders. Some will steal only their favorite make of car, but many are careful to choose older-model conventional cars that are less likely to attract police attention.

The cars are usually abandoned after only a few hours use within several blocks of the joyrider's home. If the car runs out of gas, if the motor fails or if there is an accident, the car will be left at the scene. Experienced juvenile joyriders keep a vigilant eye for any indication of suspicion on the part of police officers. The moment a police car makes a U-turn, they will jump out of the car while it is still moving and run. In a chase, a common maneuver is to turn a corner suddenly, stop the car and run between buildings. The longer the delay before attempting to flee on foot, the greater the risk of arrest as additional police cars become involved in the pursuit, and their presence in the area makes escape on foot more difficult.

Joyriders seldom vandalize the car or remove accessories, but they will steal items of value found on the seats or in the glove box and trunk.

Professional Car Thieves

The thief who steals a car for resale or stripping may operate alone, but usually he is a member of a gang that specializes in these crimes. A large well-organized gang includes a management team, a sales team, spotters, car thieves, mechanics and sometimes a salvage lot operator.

MANAGEMENT TEAM. This may be limited to the gang leader and his lieutenant. The team leader knows all members of the gang but may try to prevent members from knowing one another in order to reduce the damage that can result from betrayal by an informer. The leader's income far exceeds that of any of his assistants, and he may even keep his lieutenant on short rations.

SALES TEAM. Members of this team are responsible not only for selling stolen cars on hand but also for obtaining orders from customers. Thus, if a dentist wants a grey Lincoln Continental with air conditioning, a "spotter" will be instructed to look for such a vehicle. The salesman, like his legitimate colleagues, may have to persuade the customer to accept a car that does not meet all his requirements. Many doctors, dentists, airline pilots and other well-to-do persons who would not otherwise break the law are willing to buy a late-model luxury car at a discount price. There may be no mention of the fact that the car is stolen, but this is usually clearly understood or strongly suspected by the purchaser, who is careful to ask no questions.

Many of these salesmen are gregarious people with a wide range of acquaintances, and they spread their nets widely in search of purchasers. Taverns, golf clubs and other places where men gather provide the opportunity for sales talk. Satisfied customers will pass the word on to their friends, and the able salesman has a long list of cars "on order."

THE SPOTTERS. It is not easy for women to break into a male-dominated profession, but a number of women, usually wives or girl friends of members of the gang, have been employed as "spotters." They drive up and down the highways and byways in search of vehicles suitable for resale; late-model luxury cars (Cadillacs, Lincolns, Chryslers, Mercedes and so on), expensive sports cars (Chevrolet Corvettes), four-wheel drive vehicles, pickup trucks, motor homes and semitrailer truck tractors. When the vehicle selected for theft is worth $20,000 or more, the spotter will make an extra effort to select the ideal time and location for the theft by following the owner to determine his driving habits. Many drivers follow the same routine each work day.

Spotters tend to pass by vehicles that have many accessories, especially exterior accessories, installed by the owner, because of the danger that the owner will later be able to identify his vehicle by the holes he drilled to install a gun rack or other special items. Vans with a customized paint job, for example, a mountain scene on the outside, seldom attract the car thief because of their distinctive appearance and the cost of re-painting.

THE THEFT TEAM. Car thieves employed by organized crime are highly skilled young men who can break into and steal a car in less than a minute. The thieves dress appropriately for the type of vehicle in order to avoid arousing the suspicion of the police. A scruffy-looking person is out of place in a Porsche, and men in business suits do not drive Mack trucks. It has been said that juveniles are often employed as car thieves because they will almost certainly be only lectured and released or placed on probation if arrested in possession of a stolen car. Most gangs, however, employ men in their twenties and, for the most part, when arrested in possession of a stolen vehicle, they do not reveal information about their superiors.

Entry into a locked car is gained by sliding a "slim jim" between the edge of a door window and the rubber insulation, and then using the instrument to raise the lock button or lever. Once inside the car, the thief screws a slam hammer into the ignition lock on the steering column. The slam hammer is an instrument for pulling out dents in the body work of vehicles, but car thieves use it to pull out the ignition lock, which is immediately replaced with a new lock that the thief carries with him. These locks and their keys can be purchased without difficulty from automobile parts agencies. The removal and replacement of the ignition lock can be done in thirty seconds or less.

In older-model Ford pickup trucks with the ignition lock in the dashboard, the electrical wires can be unplugged from the back of the ignition switch and plugged into a replacement switch previously purchased, along with keys from a Ford dealer. Lock picks, master keys and duplicate keys are also used by car thieves. If the ignition key code number is known, a punch device can be used to cut a blank key for use. Expert car thieves do not use the "hot-wire" technique because it takes too long.

Gangs seldom use the dodge of taking a new car on a test drive, making a duplicate key and then returning at night to steal the car from the dealer's new car lot. If the salesman insists on being present during the test drive, it is easy to palm the key for a brief moment and make an impression in modelling material. Later, the salesman is asked to bring the car to an expensive hotel so that the prospective buyer's wife can look at it. When the salesman arrives at the hotel and asks for the prospective buyer at the desk, he learns that no one of that name is staying at the hotel. He returns to the parking lot and discovers that the car is missing.

THE PROCESSING TEAM. Skilled mechanics are responsible for disguising the stolen vehicle and giving it a new identity. These men may be employees in a small repair garage where their work on stolen cars is a part of their regular duties. They may, however, be employees of a large legitimate car repair agency who moonlight, working at night for the gang in a small private garage.

They may work on as many as five or more vehicles in one night, stripping all of them to their frames and then rebuilding them. These vehicles almost invariably are of the same make, so that the mechanics are working on cars that they have been trained to repair and can do their work very quickly, an essential requirement in order to avoid arrest in possession of a stolen vehicle. So long as the vehicle has its original vehicle identification number, it is a danger to the gang.

The Salvage Switch Operation

This operation is designed to provide a new vehicle identification number (VIN) and a new certificate of title for each stolen vehicle in order to conceal from the police evidence of its theft. The vehicle identification number is stamped on the metal frame of each new vehicle by the manufacturer. This number consists of a combination of numbers and letters that usually provides a description of the vehicle (make, series, body style, engine description, year) and the sequential production number.

The VIN is also stamped either elsewhere on the frame

or in some other location known only to the manufacturer and the National Auto Theft Bureau. This VIN is referred to as the confidential VIN, and police agencies can obtain information on its secret location from the National Auto Theft Bureau. It is reported that some car theft rings that specialize in a particular make of expensive car purchase a new model each year and strip it to find the location of the confidential VIN.

The VIN is also stamped on a plate that, in late-model American cars, is placed on top of the dashboard on the driver's side so that it is visible through the windshield from the outside of the vehicle. The VIN plate in older cars, some foreign cars and pickup trucks may be located on the left front doorpost, under the dashboard, in the engine compartment or elsewhere. VIN plates should not be confused with patent and warranty plates, which may be attached to the left door or pillar post or elsewhere. Each year the National Auto Theft Bureau publishes a *Motor Vehicle Identification Manual*, which lists VIN plate locations and helps police officers distinguish VIN plates from manufacturing or parts numbers.

In the salvage switch operation, a vehicle that has been damaged beyond repair and sold to a salvage lot junkyard or dismantling yard is purchased by the vehicle theft ring, along with the certificate of title, for a few hundred dollars. The majority of the owners of the salvage lots are law-abiding citizens, but a few sell their wrecked vehicles for amounts far beyond their true value, knowing that they are being purchased for a dishonest purpose, namely, use in a salvage switch operation.

An auto theft ring may pay as much as $2,000 for a wrecked Corvette and the certificate of title. Wrecked cars may be purchased in many different states, and one gang bought wrecks in New Mexico, Idaho, California, Washington and Oregon. The wrecks were stripped to the frame in one garage, and the frame was then taken to another garage for rebuilding.

A vehicle matching as closely as possible a wrecked vehicle is stolen, stripped to the frame and then rebuilt on the frame of the wrecked vehicle. Thus it receives a new VIN. The VIN plate is also transferred from the wrecked vehicle to the stolen vehicle, which is sold using the title of the wrecked vehicle.

Sometimes that part of the frame of the wrecked vehicle containing the VIN is welded onto the frame of the stolen vehicle. Another switch method is to obliterate the VIN on the frame of the stolen vehicle and stamp on the VIN of the wrecked vehicle. Frame numbers are removed by grinding down, cutting out or welding over in such a manner as to prevent possible restoration of the numbers.

VIN plates are held in place by stainless steel rivets with a rosette head available only to vehicle manufacturers. In transferring the VIN plate, the processing team glues the rosette head in place so that the plate has a normal appearance and will not arouse the suspicion of a police officer making a routine check following a traffic violation.

If the stolen vehicle is for resale in a distant state, no attempt may be made to disguise its appearance. If, however, it is intended for resale locally, some components will be changed to prevent the victim from recognizing his vehicle if he sees it driving down the street. For example, a sliding rear window in a pickup truck is replaced with a single plate of glass, GMC decals on a pickup truck are replaced with Chevrolet decals, a distinctive trailer hitch is removed and a different type of rear bumper is installed.

Stolen vehicles are seldom repainted as this lowers the resale value because purchasers can usually detect a repainting and suspect that the car has been damaged in an accident.

Vehicle Stripping

Another task of the processing team is the complete stripping of stolen vehicles. Vehicle theft gangs either sell their stolen cars or strip them completely and sell the parts to used parts dealers, repair garages, salvage yards, independent truckers and small trucking firms. Within a few hours, the mechanics remove the engine, transmission, doors, windows, windshield, wheels, front- and rear-end clips, grilles, radiator, radio, seats, battery and so on until only the frame and body shell are left. These items are reduced to scrap metal in a scrap-iron mill, dumped in a pool at the bottom of an old quarry or pushed over a cliff into a ravine.

One enterprising gang would carefully dismantle a stolen car by unbolting items, avoiding the use of a cutting torch. The hulk would be left in a street, and eventually the insurance company would sell it to a salvage yard, from which it would be retrieved with the title by the auto thieves, who would reassemble the car they had so carefully dismantled.

Vehicle stripping is very profitable as the parts that make up a car cost much more than the assembled vehicle. Front- and rear-end assemblies are very expensive and are greatly in demand bcause of the frequency of highway accidents involving front and rear damage. Some repair garages and their clients are eager to obtain stolen parts below cost, especially parts for foreign sports cars, as their cost may be as much as seven times greater than for American cars.

Whenever there is a prolonged strike of workers in an automobile company, spare parts become scarce, and it may not be possible to repair some cars. This leads to a rapid increase in the price car owners are willing to pay salvage yards or vehicle strippers for essential parts. A gang may maintain a parts agency in which a proportion of the stock is obtained legitimately from the factory in order to foil any police investigators who are successful in obtaining a search warrant.

Dual-drive diesel truck tractors that sell for $35,000 to $50,000 provide a big income from stripping, as a $12,000 diesel engine finds a ready sale for $4,500. Some independent truckers and small trucking firms are delighted to obtain an $8,000 transmission for $2,000 and to make similar savings on rear ends, cabs and other parts.

Vehicle stripping is also carried out by persons who are not members of large auto theft gangs. A young man who needs a new transmission for his sports car, new tires for his truck or bucket seats for his car may steal a vehicle and remove only the items he needs. The car may be taken to a remote area, perhaps in the countryside where police are not likely to appear in the brief time that it takes to remove the desired items. Minor car stripping involves only the removal of such items as the wheels, tires, battery and accessories.

Cargo Thieves

Trucks are sometimes stolen only for their cargo. After the contents have been removed, the truck is driven a short distance and abandoned. Bold thieves driving diesel tractors will hook up to a loaded semitrailer in the loading lot of a large trucking agency and drive off. They may not know the contents of the trailer, but that is of little consequence, as they will not be out of pocket.

Criminals Using Stolen Vehicles

Armed robbers may steal a car just before the robbery and drive it right up to a bank or supermarket. They are not concerned that witnesses will describe the car to the police because they intend to drive it only a short distance to where their own car is parked. The original getaway car is often abandoned before the description has been broadcast over the police radio. Burglars and other criminals may also steal cars for temporary use during their crimes.

THEFT BY EMPLOYEES

Many office workers take home small items of slight value such as a clipboard, pencils or typewriter paper, but they do not usually take more expensive items such as an electric typewriter. Blue-collar workers also help themselves to inexpensive articles that may be useful at home; the baker takes a cake for his family, the construction worker some lumber to finish the basement of his home and the miner slips a few sticks of dynamite in his luncheon pail ("You never know, it may come in handy some day"). But the baker does not steal one of the company's delivery trucks, and the construction worker does not help himself to an air compressor.

The occasional appropriation of items of slight value from one's employer is so common that such behavior is seldom regarded as criminal. Even when the theft becomes more frequent, the employee tends to regard his acquisitions as fringe benefits of his job, or he uses other rationalizations: "Everyone makes a little on the side, they don't pay me enough, they won't notice it."

The employers themselves sometimes encourage such practices, and Ditton, a sociologist who worked for a time in a bakery, discovered that the idea of theft by employees was introduced by the management; deliverymen are encouraged to overcharge customers when they can, so that they run no risk of the week's takings coming in "short," in which case the shortfall must be made up out of wages (6).

Employers indirectly encourage theft by employees when they turn a blind eye to thefts. Zeitlin mentions the experience of an accountant who audited the books of a corporation and discovered that the office manager was dipping into petty cash to the extent of about $2,000 a year. He reported the fact to the president, who responded, "How much are we paying him?" When the president learned that the office manager's salary was $10,000 a year, he told the accountant, "Then keep quiet about it, he's worth at least $15,000" (16).

Although many employees either do not steal or take only a few inexpensive items, theft by employees can cause heavy financial losses and even bankrupty for their employers. In retail stores employee theft is believed to be a greater cause of inventory shortages than theft by shoplifters. Some employees have greater opportunity to steal because they work as salespersons, cashiers, truck drivers, stock clerks or security officers. A waterfront commission reported that during a four-year period, "More port watchmen were apprehended for stealing cargo . . . than they—the port watchman force—apprehended. Not only do they steal for themselves, they also act in collusion with some truck drivers, checkers, and hi-lo drivers to strip the piers" (14).

In a federal government report *Crime Against Small Business,* Bunn has listed some of the more frequent methods of employee theft (3):

Theft of Cash

1. "Underring" the cash register. The clerk does not give the customer a sales receipt and pockets the money later.

2. Failing to ring up sales. The clerk leaves the register drawer open, puts money directly into the register without ringing up certain sales and takes out the stolen money later.

3. Ringing up "no sale" on the register, voiding the sales check after the customer has left and pocketing the money.

4. Overcharging customers so that cash overages can be stolen.

5. Taking cash from a "common drawer" register.

6. Cashing bad checks for accomplices.

7. Making false entries in store's records and books to conceal thefts.

8. Giving fraudulent refunds to accomplices or putting through fictitious refunds.

9. Stealing checks made payable to cash.

10. Pocketing unclaimed wages.

11. Paying creditor's invoice twice and appropriating the second check.

12. Failing to record returned purchases and stealing an equal amount of cash.

13. Padding payrolls as to rates, time worked or number of employees.

14. Forging checks and destroying them when returned by the bank.

15. Pocketing collections made on presumably uncollectible accounts.

16. Issuing checks on "returned" purchases not actually returned.

17. Raising the amount on checks, invoices or vouchers after they have been officially approved.

18. Invoicing goods above the established prices and getting a kickback from the supplier.

Theft of Merchandise

1. Passing out merchandise across the counter to accomplices.

2. Trading stolen merchandise with friends employed in other departments.

3. Hiding merchandise on the person, in a handbag or in a parcel, and taking it out of store at lunchtime, on relief breaks or at the end of the day.
4. Hiding goods in stairways, public lockers and corridors for later theft.
5. Taking unlisted packages from delivery truck.
6. Stealing from warehouse with cooperation of warehouse employees.
7. Stealing from stockroom by putting goods on person or in packages.
8. Stealing from returned-goods room, layaway and similar places where goods are kept.
9. Making false entries to pad inventories so shortages will not be noticed.
10. Giving employee discounts to friends.
11. Putting on jewelry, scarves or jackets to model, then wearing them home and keeping them.
12. Shoplifting during lunch hour or relief periods.
13. Stealing special "property passes" to get stolen articles out of store.
14. Taking sales slips from training room or supply area to put on stolen goods.
15. Stealing trading stamps.
16. Getting stolen goods through the mailroom by slapping on "customer's own" label normally used to ship out altered goods.
17. Putting "return to manufacturer" label on goods and sending them instead to the employee's own address.
18. Picking up by sales clerk of a receipt discarded by customer and putting it on stolen goods, which the clerk keeps or turns in for refund.
19. Intentional soiling of garments or damaging of merchandise so employees can buy them at reduced prices.
20. Printing of own tickets for stolen goods by marking room employees.
21. Clerks spurring sales by unauthorized markdowns in order to get kickback from manufacturers.
22. Employees stamping own mail with store postage meter.

23. Shipping clerks sending out stolen goods to their own disguised post office boxes.

24. Smuggling out stolen goods in trash and refuse containers.

No list can cover all the ingenious means of theft by employees, but mention should be made of another frequent method. Managers of apartment houses work for several months or even a year and then suddenly leave the apartment house, the city and the state with the tenants' cash payments for one month's rent. Their arrest might seem inevitable, as their disappearance with the money leads to a warrant for their arrest, but many of these offenders are not apprehended before the statute of limitations make prosecution impossible.

Some offenders using false identification obtain work as managers of convenience stores and quickly decamp with the day's receipts of $400 to $500 and with money orders made out to friends. They may only work for one day and then move on to another store belonging to a different chain.

In an unusual theft, a service station employee telephoned his supervisor to report a bomb threat and was told to lock the station and leave. When the supervisor checked the cash register after the police had searched the station for a bomb, he noted the absence of $20 bills; a quick audit showed over $150 missing. The employee did not report for work the next day but later made partial restitution, muttering something about taking the money.

City employees have made up to a $1,000 a day from parking meter thefts. Lax supervision has contributed to substantial thefts by persons employed to empty or repair street parking meters.

A detective using binoculars observed a parking meter repairman who was not authorized to collect money removing coins from meters. The repairman drove to a bar, where he removed a white canvas bag from his car and took the bag to a woman who was waiting for him in another car. The two went into the bar, where the man paid for their lunch and drinks in coins. When arrested, the man stated that he lived with his parents, but a search of the room that he claimed he shared with his brother showed that he did not live there as there were no work uniforms nor other clothing belonging to him. A search of his girl friend's home revealed no evidence, but she later admitted that on hearing of her boyfriend's arrest, she had taken over $160 to her sister's home. She admitted that she used to roll coins in coin wrappings and change the coins for paper bills at several different banks. It was estimated that the repairman obtained $200 a day from meter thefts.

THEFT FROM BUILDINGS

This category includes thefts from such places as churches, restaurants, libraries, public buildings and other public and professional offices during the hours when such facilities are open to the public. In the *Uniform Crime Reports*, this category does not include shoplifting and thefts from coin-operated devices or machines within open buildings. Theft from a structure accompanied by a breaking or an unlawful entry (trespass) without breaking is classified as a burglary (*UCR*).

A common ploy is to distract the attention of an employee, for example by telling him that the pop machine is not working. While the employee is checking the pop machine, the thief commits his crime. An accomplice may keep the employee busy while the theft takes place as in the following examples.

A girl drives into a parking lot, tells the attendant she needs help in locating an address, then asks him what he is doing that night and invites him to sit in her car. While he is in her car, the girl's accomplice commits the theft.

A man walks into a gas station on a cold day, states that he has just called a cab and asks if he can wait inside the station. His partner drives alongside the station and complains that his car is overheating. If the service station attendant for any reason starts walking back inside the station, the partner will try to prevent this by saying "Check my oil, check my oil." In the meantime, the man inside the station is busy committing a theft.

COMPUTERS AND THEFT

Computers can be used by thieves to steal property. The president of a telephone equipment distribution business stole $1 million in equipment over a three-year period from a telephone company in California by placing orders with the company's computer. He knew the computer's secret entry code and used a telephone to place his orders for equipment, which he picked up in a truck disguised as a telephone company truck.

The shipments were not missed because he also picked up the bills of lading. He was found guilty of theft and served two months in jail. On his release, he obtained work as a consultant for a computer security firm.

In a case of pension theft in Canada, an employee of an insurance company changed several deceased insured persons' account numbers to his own to collect their pensions. He was caught when a staple in a punch card forced manual handling, which revealed several cards with the same number (11).

Thieves can steal computer programs; for example, an employee of the Texas Instruments Automatic Computer Corp., photocopied forty-nine computer programs belonging to the company. He attempted to sell these to Texaco, one of the company's clients, for $5 million. The matter was brought to the attention of the authorities, and the defendant was brought to trial. During his trial, the defendant argued that since he had photocopied the programs, no original documents had been stolen and thus no property had been taken. The defendant, however, was found guilty, and the court held that the programs were in fact property. The U.S. Court of Appeals upheld the conviction (1). He served five years.

Thieves can also steal information from computers. Theft of information may take two forms: (a) theft of output data; and (b) theft by interception. The former may involve the copying of mailing lists, printouts, programs and other computer-related data. The latter may involve the interception of valuable and confidential data while in the transmission or reception stage (1). In Chicago, 3 million customer addresses were stolen by three night-shift computer operators. In another case, a man was suspected of trying to sell listings of new customers. The list was estimated to be worth $37,000 on the address list market (11).

Many cases are reported of theft of computer services. This is usually by an employee or by someone who knows the secret access number and can communicate with the computer by telephone. In California, a federal grand jury charged two men with stealing perhaps millions of dollars of computer time from the Illiac 4, the world's largest computer, which is owned by the Defense Department. Although the indictment listed computer time and storage in excess of $100, experts said that for $100 you could probably use the Illiac 4 computer for one one-thousandth of a second.

SHOPLIFTING

Shoplifting, the ten-finger discount, is thought to cost retail stores $5 billion each year in the United States. Estimates of losses from this crime in department stores range from 2 to 6 percent of their inventory each year. Some small stores have much greater losses, which may force them out of business. It is often difficult to determine the loss from shoplifting, as it is not possible to tell what percentage of inventory loss is due to theft by employees. It has been suggested that internal theft can be as great as or greater than theft by customers.

In the *Uniform Crime Reports,* shoplifting is defined as *the theft by a person other than an employee of goods and merchandise exposed for sale.* This violation assumes that the offender had legal access to the premises, and thus no trespass or unlawful entry is involved. This category includes thefts of merchandise displayed outside a building as part of the stock in trade, such as in department stores, hardware stores, supermarkets, fruit stands, gas station and so on. In 1977 the average value of goods and property reported stolen by shoplifters was $39. Women spend more time shopping than men, and women figure more prominently than men in shoplifting statistics.

Types of Shoplifters

AMATEURS. Amateurs steal items for personal use rather than for resale, and the majority of these offenders can afford to buy what they steal. Shoplifters come from all walks of life, and many of them do not see themselves as thieves; rather, they think they are breaking some technicality in the law, much as a driver who exceeds the speed limit considers that he is doing what everyone else does. In fact, not everyone shoplifts because shoplifting always involves a victim, in contrast to speeding.

Burglars are usually from the poorer neighborhoods, but the amateur shoplifter is often from an affluent section of the city. Furthermore, shoplifting is one crime in which older people figure prominently. A study in England showed that the peak age among British women shoplifters was fifty-one to sixty (7).

Shoppers tempted by goods on display and the absence of store personnel, frustrated by a long wait for attention from a salesperson, or angered by overcharging may steal on impulse. The ease with which the theft is accomplished encourages further thefts. The amateur usually begins by taking small items that can be concealed without difficulty, but increasing practice leads to greater variety in the choice of articles. Meat is expensive these days, and at first, the lady of the house is satisfied with a small package of rib eye steaks, but before the year is out she may have graduated to standing rib roasts or a whole turkey for Thanksgiving. If the thief is detected early in her shoplifting career, the shock may be sufficient to stop further thefts. But a successful pattern of thefts is not so easily discouraged.

Some amateurs steal only essential clothing or household items, others take luxury items that they can ill-afford or that they feel guilty purchasing from their salary or household allowance. Sometimes the item is of slight value, and the gain comes mainly from getting something for nothing or from the thrill of a forbidden act.

Many of the older women shoplifters examined by Gibbens appeared to be suffering from depression. He gives the following description of a typical case.

> She is a woman of fifty who had a hysterectomy a year before and has not felt well since. She has backaches, headaches, dizziness, insomnia and a persistent sense of depression. She sometimes gets up in the night to turn off the gas or to see that the door is locked. She has no serious financial difficulties, but her husband and children take no notice of her and she feels that life in the future stretches out like a desert. She has been seeing her doctor regularly and receiving tranquillizers, but she has not been to him for three months because she feels she is wasting his time (7).

As Morrice points out, not all female shoplifters fit this description. In some, the theft is precipitated by obvious stress.

In younger women this may be a recent miscarriage, a bereavement or some other kind of personal loss. Sometimes the episode of shoplifting seems to be a way of punishing husband or family by bringing shame to them by association and at the same time gaining their attention and perhaps their concern. Occasionally a woman of good character who is convicted of shoplifting repeats the offense. This may be due to a recurrence of stress or depression or even because she feels the first conviction ruined her reputation for good. One middle-aged lady of the writer's acquaintance who felt neglected by her husband turned to alcohol for solace; but she marked the anniversary of her son's death, year after year, by shoplifting. Another, an elderly shoplifter convicted on three separate occasions despite lengthy psychiatric treatment, finally secured her husband's close attention and curtailed his individual recreational activities because he found it necessary to accompany her wherever she went in order to prevent further repetition of the offense (9).

JUVENILE OFFENDERS. Juveniles often operate in groups and usually steal for use items such as tape cassettes, records, clothing, cosmetics and automobile parts. Both the shoplifting and the items stolen contribute to a status within their social group. Thrill seeking is also a factor in this crime. Very young children may be taught to slip items into their mother's handbags, and when caught, the mothers show an outward display of anger and distress that protects them from suspicion.

NARCOTIC ADDICTS. Addicts who support their habit through shoplifting may be masters of their trade, but many operate without any finesse and may resort to prostitution, burglary, robbery and other crimes to obtain money. Items stolen are sold to a fence or bartered for drugs. When detected, these offenders are sometimes quick to assault store detectives, even female detectives, in order to avoid capture and will not hesitate to use a knife or other weapon in an attempt to escape.

PROFESSIONAL SHOPLIFTERS. These pros earn their living, a comfortable living, from the theft of items for sale to fences and other customers who place orders for specific items. A shopping list may include dresses of a particular size and color that have been preselected by a client. These offenders operate with skill and exercise great caution to avoid arrest. Jewelry and other small items of great value, furs, clothing and expensive leather purses are favored.

A professional shoplifter may earn from $600 to $1,000 a week. One young woman stole three diamond rings valued at $12,000 and an ultrasuede outfit worth $450 in one day. Although well known to the police and to store detectives in large department stores, she is seldom arrested because of her great skill and her patronage of small stores, which have no security personnel. She dresses in the latest fashion, carries a large amount of money in her purse to create the impression of wealth and is an excellent "con artist."

COMPULSIVE SHOPLIFTERS. Compulsive shoplifters are said to suffer from kleptomania, a personality disorder associated with an impulse to steal, but these persons are more often encountered in print than in person. One often hears of the very rich woman who continually steals items for which she has no use, often of slight value, from department stores, but experienced detectives can seldom recall examples. According to the cynic, rich persons who steal suffer from kleptomania, poor persons who steal are thieves. One encounters shoplifters whose thefts seem to be related to some psychological turmoil in their lives, but these persons can hardly be described as suffering from kleptomania (*see* Chap. 4).

Techniques of Shoplifting

There may be no attempt at concealment; the shoplifter simply picks up something in the store and walks out with the item in his hand, or a woman tries on a hat, looks at it in a mirror and then walks away wearing it. The very boldness of the theft and the confident manner of the offender do not arouse suspicion. "Two men in the Midwest entered a department store, picked up a canoe, and walked out with it over their heads. They were arrested when they returned to the store to pick up the paddles. Another man, working alone, picked up a large overstuffed chair from the furniture department and carried it to an elevator and out of the front door of the store (*FBI Law Enforcement Bulletin,* December 1965)."

Another trick is to engage a TV salesman in discussion just before his lunch hour; when the salesman leaves for lunch, the thief walks out of the store carrying a TV set. He has a rolled-up piece of paper intended to resemble a sales receipt in one hand, and as he passes any store employee, he comments on the excellent service.

More often the shoplifter tries to conceal both the act of theft and the item he has stolen, by one or more of the following techniques. He steals when there is no salesclerk in the vicinity, when the salesclerk is busy with other customers or taking care of various duties just after opening time or just before closing time. An accomplice can distract the clerk's attention by talking to her, appearing to faint, faking a heart attack or staging a fight. A small fire will distract everyone's attention.

> One professional cleared the ground for herself by acting the part of a disagreeable, fussy, bargain-hunting shopper. Consequently, salesclerks, who knew her type vanished on seeing her. Furthermore, she changed her dress and hairdo frequently and tried never to steal the same merchandise two times in exactly the same way. Her disagreeability as well as her ability to alter her appearance, the store detectives agreed was a major factor in her success (4).

Another method of escaping the eyes of any store official is to take several items of clothing to a changing room and then return only two items to the clothing rack. Cameron describes the case of a very short woman who would conceal herself behind clothing racks that were about five feet high.

> About half an hour before closing time in the store, she selected the merchandise to be taken and firmly pinned the skirts and jackets she had selected to the hangers so they would not drop off in transit. Then just at the closing hour, she returned to the selected merchandise and put the suits (hangers and all) inside her bulky coat and left the store with the lingering crowd of shoppers. The final operation of stealing the merchandise took only seconds to complete and was done so adroitly that store detectives watched her on three occasions before they were finally sure that she was a thief (4).

The item stolen is immediately hidden either under the shoplifter's clothing or in a handbag or other container belonging to the shoplifter. Occasionally, stolen items are slipped inside

a packaged item, such as a shirt, which is then purchased from
a salesclerk. Very small items such as a diamond ring can be
concealed in one's hand. Indeed, the ring may be stolen right
from under the eyes of the salesclerk. Like the conjuror who
distracts the attention of his audience through movements of
one hand while doing something with his other hand, the shoplifter is able to steal a ring without the clerk being aware of it.

Special clothing includes booster panties tightly fastened
above the knees to retain objects dropped inside at waist level
and coats with special pockets, booster hooks to hold merchandise and slits to enable the thief to slip his hand outside the
coat without being seen. Women can enter a store flat-chested
and leave with a large bust or in an apparent advanced stage
of pregnancy. Underneath a loose-fitting overcoat, the offender
can wear several dresses or carry concealed merchandise. The
shoplifter may even wear new shoes out of the store and leave
his old shoes in a dressing room. Items have also been hidden
under wigs, hats and scarves. Loose-fitting boots are another
good hiding place.

"Crotch carriers" walk out of a store with stolen items held
under their skirts, between their thighs.

> Their loot may be anything from two cans of coffee, a canned
> ham, a turkey or a roast, and cartons of cigarettes to clothing,
> phonograph records, and even a typewriter in a case! Their mode of
> walking may give them away, as they, necessarily, walk slowly,
> pigeontoed and with a shuffle.
>
> To be able to carry such loads between the thighs takes skill
> and practice, as in fact one young woman attested. She admitted
> upon arrest that in order to prove her skill in "shoplifting school,"
> she had to be able to place three phonograph records between her
> thighs and walk out of a store without dropping or breaking them.
> Another shoplifter admitted that she practiced walking with a tele-
> phone directory between her thighs to strengthen the muscles (*FBI
> Law Enforcement Bulletin*, December 1965).

Shoplifters use all manner of containers to hide stolen items,
from baby buggies and umbrellas to cartons of popcorn and
specially constructed booster boxes. The latter are boxes that
have a hinged top, bottom or side. They may take the form of a
gift-wrapped box or a parcel tied with string and ready for

mailing, but one side can be quickly opened and a stolen item placed inside the box. A spring returns the flap to its original position and the ribbons on the gift box or the string on a parcel match perfectly at the join.

Popcorn containers are particularly suitable for small heavy items of jewelry, which quickly fall down below the top layer of popcorn. Stolen items may be rather sticky when retrieved or smelly when removed from a diaper bag, but after all, this is a small price to pay for expensive merchandise.

Some shoplifters carry with them an electronic calculator and add up the cost of their loot to make sure that they do not exceed $200 or whatever sum makes the theft a felony rather than a misdemeanor under state law. Occasionally, articles are paid for, but the price tickets may be switched with those of less expensive items in the store so that the purchase remains a bargain.

Shoplifters who steal items for the purpose of returning them to the store to obtain a refund may also steal items that have been purchased by customers. A woman who had purchased merchandise worth over $130 put down her purchases while looking at some clothing on display. A shoplifter stole her purchases and within an hour obtained a full refund from another branch of the store. She gave a false name and address and could not be traced.

The shoplifter may betray herself through her vigilant surveillance of the salesclerk. While trying on an expensive string of pearls, she may arouse suspicion because she uses a store mirror, not to check her appearance, but to watch the movements of the salesclerk. Store personnel watch for customers who bring into the store a bag that bears the store's label. They may be returning merchandise for credit, but they may also be shoplifters who hope to give the appearance that they have paid for items they later slip into the bag.

Upon arrest, the professional will usually protest her innocence; the amateur may also claim innocence but will often acknowledge her guilt and seek to excuse her conduct.

> I have never shoplifted before and can offer no explanation for
> my behavior, except to say that I was feeling very depressed over

some family problems and the amount of studying I have to do. Also, my husband was out of town, and I was feeling very lonely. I have been studying very hard for the last few weeks and have been feeling very tired and depressed.

I got home (from the supermarket) and the eggs were broken and the milk was spoiled. I went back and took the steak because I felt it was time I got something back.

THEFTS FROM VENDING MACHINES
AND PARKING METERS

It has been estimated that nationwide rings of professional thieves specializing in thefts from vending machines and parking meters cost vending machine companies and municipalities millions of dollars each year. In Denver, over a weekend, thieves obtained about $6,000 from approximately 600 parking meters by unlocking the meter vault and removing the entire meter bank. The cost to the city was estimated to be approximately $50,000. This included the stolen money, new banks, new locks and man-hours for replacing this hardware. Suspects were arrested; their method of operation is described below by Captain Donald B. Mulnix of the Denver Police Department. He refers to these crimes as burglaries because in Denver, as in some other jurisdictions but not in the *UCR*, these thefts are classified as burglaries.

The two suspects arrested were part of a loose-knit gang of vending machine burglars which have been in operation for several years. Members of this gang have backgrounds in locksmithing and are capable of designing and machining their own lock pick tools and cutting keys. Apparently their method of operation is to make extended trips throughout the United States in pairs. When they arrive in a target city, they make the rounds of businesses which have vending machines and loot all of the coin boxes.

The "Burglar's Buddy," a lock pick for a tubular type lock, is the most used tool. In addition to looting the machines, they also write the lock code number of the machines they burglarize on a scratch paper. With this seven-digit number they can return again at some future date and save time in picking the lock by presetting the "Burglar Buddy" to this code or by cutting a key.

It appears that this gang may work during normal business hours posing as collectors. They carry large coin bank bags, and the speed in which they can open these machines makes their activities appear normal. From some of the evidence recovered it appears they may be dumping the coins into two and one-half or five gallon metal cans. While on a trip they may be shipping these cans back to a confederate marked "machine parts" or something similar. Apparently it is no problem to turn hundreds of dollars in change into currency. Our investigation revealed that most banks will do this as a customer service, and such transactions are not unusual and do not attract the suspicion of the bank.

The gang apparently obtained meter keys to the Denver parking meters by cutting off three meters at various locations in Denver. After breaking them open the locks were removed, and a member of the gang had keys made by a locksmith in Boulder, Colorado. He told the locksmith that he managed laundromats in some apartment houses and had lost his keys for the coin boxes. After he obtained the keys the gang returned to Denver.

They burglarized the meters by working in pairs on each side of the street. They would casually walk along during the early evenings and pretend to be loitering around a meter. The door would be unlocked and the meter bank taken out and dropped into a large purse or laundry bag when no one was looking. The operation took a total of ten hours. Information indicated that members of this gang had recently taken a trip through several western states and had stolen several parking meters. They intended to have keys made for these meter locks and then make a return trip to those cities and loot their meters.

POCKET PICKING

It takes no great skill to pick the pockets of a wino stretched out in a drunken coma on the sidewalk of skid row or of the intoxicated convention visitor excited by his encounter with an attractive prostitute. There will always be criminals quick to take advantage of any adversity that renders a victim helpless. When a businessman in San Antonio, Texas suffered a heart attack while dining at a motel and collapsed on the floor, patrons rushed to give him artificial respiration. He was pronounced dead; when police looked for identification they found none. His wallet, stripped of money and credit cards, was found in a restroom twelve feet from where he lay dying.

The highly skilled pickpocket belongs to a vanishing breed rather than an endangered species, for the police have never been a serious threat to this type of offender. The apprenticeship is long, and only the more talented acquire the necessary physical dexterity for "dipping" and the mental adroitness for selecting suitable victims. Today's crook in search of ready money would rather grab an old lady's handbag than spend the time learning how to remove a wallet without the victim's awareness.

One would not expect to find talented pickpockets in Denver, Colorado or Topeka, Kansas, but in London and some other large capital cities, these men still flourish. Usually they work as a team in crowded airport terminals and railroad stations. They also accompany carnivals and circuses.

> At a bus stop, they usually stand well back from the queue, sizing it up. Police say eyes are the surest give away, being directed at waist level, looking for "leathers" (wallets) or "pokes" (purses). Selection of the "mug" (victim) is left until the approach of the bus. . . . Next step is to isolate the mug. The "stall" jostles through the crowd rudely so he is positioned directly in front. As the bus pulls up he plays for time. "Are you going to Buckingham Palace?" he may ask the conductor, his foreign accent covering the crassness of the question. In the crush behind, teammates two and three have come alongside the mug, pushing to prevent him moving his arms. Now the "hook"—the slippery fingered operator whom the others protect at all costs, for he (or quite often she) is the one with the talent—swings into action, closing in behind the mug while he is helpless (12).

At stock car races, fireworks' displays and air shows, the victim's attention is concentrated on the exciting event, and he is less likely to notice a pickpocket at work. Public hangings of pickpockets in England used to provide an ideal opportunity for other pickpockets, so much so that they would seize the opportunity despite the risk of playing a feature role themselves on the gallows.

The offender's accomplice can distract the victim's attention by stepping on his foot, pushing him to one side or making obscene comments or suggestive remarks to the victim's wife.

In selecting victims, the pickpocket looks for signs of affluence:

> This can be established by many indications: the use of certain trains or certain accommodations aboard ship. Purchase of expen-

sive seats in theatres or movies. Entertainment of expensive guests in night clubs, on dude ranches and at sport resorts. Registration in expensive hotels. It can be established by carefully watching booking-offices in banks, travel bureaus and railroad stations. Finally there is that general impression of self-assurance, ponderosity, unconcern, and good humor—sometimes anxiety too—that is presented by people who have much money in their pockets. We do not give much thought to these things. But the experienced pickpocket, no doubt, has a distinct feeling of the reflex left by a full purse, on the mood and the gait of the individual. People with money walk differently from those without money; and there is a distinct difference in the way they move their arms, and inspect shop windows and restaurants. There are other evidences. Promptness of payment, e.g., in agricultural sections of the country when cattle or crops have been sold. The farmer released for short festival periods from work often displays an explosive inclination to waste money and to enjoy the wasting (8).

The man with a well-filled wallet keeps an eye out for shady characters, so the pickpocket dresses well, but not ostentatiously. He quickly passes on his loot to an associate so that if the victim complains to the police or chases him, nothing belonging to the victim will be found in his possession.

PURSE SNATCHING

This form of theft is defined in the *Uniform Crime Reports* as *the grabbing or snatching of a purse, handbag, etc., from the custody of an individual.* If more force is used than is actually necessary to snatch the purse from the grasp of the person, then a strong-arm robbery has occurred. Many of these crimes are committed by juvenile offenders, who are especially active after the mail delivery of social security checks.

BICYCLE THEFT

The majority of bicycle thieves are juveniles, and the relatively few adult offenders are usually just eighteen years of age. They seldom bother with one- and three-speed bicycles, preferring ten-speed machines that they steal for use, for resale or for stripping. It is easy to find purchasers at flea markets or on the street, and many youths are quick to pay ten dollars for an expensive cycle without asking any questions.

The ten-speed gear mechanism is the part of the bicycle that is most likely to break down, and bikes are often stolen for this mechanism. Bolt cutters are used to cut through bicycle locks. The front wheel is often taken because of the ease with which it can be removed from a bike that has a wire lock securing only the frame and rear wheel.

As persons who purchase bikes often throw away the bill of sale, neglect to note the serial number or mistake the model number for the serial number, it is difficult for the police to trace such bicycles when they are stolen. In those cities requiring bicycle licenses, the serial numbers of all licensed bikes are kept on file. Bicycles without a metal license plate can be impounded and checked by the police. License plates are often stolen in order to avoid license fees, but the police may check the license files to see whether the bike matches the license number.

CHOICE OF ITEMS

Items favored by thieves have already been reviewed under the various categories of theft. In general, the professional criminal prefers cash and items that can readily and with slight risk be sold for cash. Organized crime groups have profited from the theft of stocks, bonds and other securities. Between 1965 and 1970, stock exchanges and large brokerage houses were overwhelmed with paperwork, which facilitated the theft and disposition of securities.

Organized crime groups have also been involved in the widespread theft of airline tickets, which have been sold in bars, restaurants, boutiques and similar places. In 1974, Pan American Airways bought back about 2,000 stolen airline tickets for over $50,000. The blank airline tickets were numbered, and the numbers of the stolen tickets are routinely posted at ticket counters in airports, but in practice, agents are often too busy to compare incoming ticket numbers with the list of those believed stolen. Pan American said that if all the tickets had been used, the cost to the airline would have been at least $2 million.

The energy crisis and the increased cost of electricity have contributed to the theft of electricity. The New England Electric System noted a rise in "unaccounted for" electricity, the difference between the amount produced and that sold or lost in the lines. In 1972 the company missed 0.8 percent of its production. By 1975 the figure was 1.8 percent, and the difference was worth $6,600,000. Thieves realize they would be caught if their meter recorded no usage, so they disable the meters for the middle two weeks between the meter reader's monthly visits, or they install jumper wires so that the meter records about 30 percent of the electricity used. Some of the tampered meters are at private homes, but about 75 percent are at restaurants, supermarkets and other places of business.

Customers of self-serve gasoline stations sometimes drive away without paying, and much time is wasted by those police departments that act as collection agencies for oil companies. When the attendant has recorded the license number of the car, the identity of the owner can be obtained. If the owner denies the theft and denies loaning his car on that date, the detective must obtain a picture of the car owner from the bureau issuing driver's licenses and then must show the attendant a group of photos to see whether he can identify the thief. After the thief has been identified, he usually pays the few dollars he owes to the gas station owner, who then refuses to prosecute.

Medical records of patients involved in litigation or insurance claims have been stolen from doctors' offices and from the medical records departments of hospitals for sale to attorneys and insurance companies. A former employee of a national private investigation firm pleaded guilty in 1976 to charges of theft following a long investigation by the Denver District Attorney regarding theft of confidential medical records. Undercover investigators asked the company for the medical records of a person (who was another employee of the District Attorney's office), and the company obtained for them a copy of this person's medical records from a local hospital. In advertisements the detective agency stated:

1. Have you been denied medical authorization by a client?
2. Does the claimant's attorney withhold medical information from you, or submit only "partial" medical records?

   If either of the above is true, let us develop the true medical picture. We have specialized in background medical investigations for over two decades. . . . We have access to sources which enable us to thoroughly analyze the background of the client . . . a complete review of the hospital charts for accurate information on the patient's history, x-rays, emergencies, outpatient experience, costs, etc.

Copies of medical records can be obtained by theft, for example, by an accomplice who works in the hospital as a medical records librarian or as a filing clerk. Records can also be obtained by criminal impersonation, that is, by posing as a member of the clergy, as a doctor's secretary or as a doctor. A common technique is for a person in a white coat with a stethescope to appear at the medical records department in the middle of the night and irritably demand the records of a patient, falsely claiming that he is being readmitted.

The theft of books is more common in England than in the United States. In a study of shoplifters in London, Gibbens found that only one woman stole a book, but between 50 and 60 percent of the men stole books, nearly always without taking other objects (7). Smith comments that the bookseller laments the passing of the old order, when scholars were gentlemen, books had an honest provenance and browsing was not so much an invitation to larceny as a civilized pleasure of urban life (13).

The theft of books from libraries is becoming a major problem, and as early as 1970, the librarian of a medical school in Philadelphia announced that the costs that year for replacing books and journals "missing" would be an estimated $7,500 to $10,000, or 10 percent of the annual acquisitions budget. Thieves will steal not only the book, but also the card on the book from the card index. Librarians can conceal their thefts in this manner.

Libraries with collections of rare books attract thieves who sell these books to collectors. Often, librarians are not aware of the value of some of their older books and take inadequate steps to protect them. Howard Nixon, Deputy Keeper of Printed Books at the British Museum, has commented: "In the old days we assumed people would not steal books. Now we have to assume that they bloody well will. In entering the British Museum nowadays they search you to make sure you haven't got a bomb, and as you leave they search you to see you haven't got a book."

Godfrey Smith reports the case of an American doctoral student at Newcastle-upon-Tyne who had been given special privileges that enabled him to steal books and resell them to the trade for $18,000. In court, the student admitted telling the dealer they were a collection his grandfather had made: "I wanted to establish my family as best I could, and wanted scholars to quote these books as coming from the family collection. In America everyone is ancestor crazy. All I was trying to do was to tidy up my own family image. I've done no more than many of my fellow countrymen have done" (13).

Amateur thieves steal street signs for display in their homes or fraternity houses. Over 700 street signs are stolen each year in San Francisco, and the favorite signs are those of streets that are tourist attractions.

REFERENCES

1. Bequai, August: *Computer Crime.* Lexington, Massachusetts, Lexington Bks, 1978.
2. Brickell, David, and Cole, L. S.: *Vehicle Theft Investigation.* Santa Cruz, California, Davis Publishing Co., 1975.
3. Bunn, V. A.: Business management for crime prevention. In *Crime Against Small Business. A Report of the Small Business Administration.* Washington, D.C., U.S. Government Printing Office, 1969.
4. Cameron, M. O.: *The Booster and the Snitch: Department Store Shoplifting.* New York, Free Press of Glencoe, 1964.
5. Chilimidos, R. S.: *Auto Theft Investigation.* Los Angeles, Legal Bk Corp., 1971.
6. Ditton, Jason: *Part-Time Crime.* London, Macmillan, 1977.
7. Gibbens, T. C. N., Palmer, C. and Prince, J.: Mental health aspects of shoplifting. *Br Med J,* 3:612, 1971.
8. Hentiz, Hans von: The pickpocket. *J Crim Law,* 34:11, 1943.
9. Morrice, J. K. W.: *Crisis Intervention Studies in Community Care.* Oxford, Pergamon, 1976.
10. O'Hara, C. E.: *Fundamentals of Criminal Investigation,* 4th ed. Springfield, Thomas, 1976.
11. Parker, D. B., Nycum, S. and Oüra, S. S.: *Computer Abuse.* Menlo Park, California, Stanford Research Institute, 1973.

12. Rocca, Tony: London: a dipper's paradise. *Sunday Times,* May 29, 1977.
13. Smith, Godfrey: The fine book thieves. *Sunday Times,* June 17, 1973.
14. U.S. Department of Justice and of Transportation: *Cargo Theft and Organized Crime.* Washington, D.C., U.S. Government Printing Office, 1972.
15. Walsh, D. P.: *Shoplifting: Controlling a Major Crime.* London, Macmillan, 1978.
16. Zeitlin, L. R.: A little larceny can do a lot for employee morale. *Psychology Today,* June, 1971.

CHAPTER 3

THE FENCE

*Both are thieves, the receiver
as well as the stealer.*
—Phoclides, *Sententiae*

A FENCE IS someone who buys and sells stolen goods. This may be his only occupation, but the majority of fences also own or operate legitimate businesses that provide a cover for their illegal activities. Despite the saying *No fence; no thief*, thieves would continue to thrive even without the help of criminal receivers of stolen property. Nevertheless, fences provide a valuable service for burglars, robbers, shoplifters and other thieves.

Fear of arrest while in possession of stolen goods and a need for ready cash prompt thieves to dispose of their loot as quickly as possible. It is easy to sell the occasional television set, but the busy burglar who breaks into twelve to fifteen homes a day has many more to peddle, and a truckload of shoes or women's sweaters is quite beyond the marketing skill of most criminals. Furthermore, the offender who is well known to the police cannot risk selling his loot on the streets. Although the fence may not pay high prices for stolen goods, he asks no questions and seldom betrays his clients to the police.

The fence may be much more than a middleman responsible for distributing goods from the thief to the buyer, as he may also actively assist burglars by providing information on attractive targets and by introducing them to criminals with special skills in lock picking, safe blowing or circumventing burglar alarms. Further services include provision of bail bond and legal aid. He may also select, equip, finance and control burglars who break into targets of his choice.

Fencing is a $7 billion a year industry in the United States, yet fences are seldom arrested and rarely convicted and do not usually receive long prison sentences. Indeed, they may be placed on probation following conviction in court. Persons intent on a career in crime could not choose a more lucrative yet relatively risk-free criminal occupation, but some measure of talent is required for success.

JONATHAN WILD

A remarkable Englishman, Jonathan Wild (c. 1682-1725), provides a model, apart from his premature death on the gallows, for those interested in joining the profession. Wild, a notorious organizer of criminal bands on a scale that would make most bands of today (except those involved in gambling, narcotics and prostitution) seem ordinary, was an original thinker and a shrewd, capable executive. His career has captured and engaged the pens of Fielding (2) and Defoe (1).

While learning a trade in London, he was imprisoned for several years for nonpayment of debts and on his release, he took advantage of his knowledge of crime and criminals by becoming a receiver of stolen goods. Recognizing that substantial rewards could be obtained by returning stolen property to its legitimate owners, he set up business as a recoverer of stolen goods. He acted as an agent for victims of theft and burglary by placing advertisements in papers offering rewards for return of stolen property, *no questions asked.* Thieves were quick to return their plunder to Wild because they received a commission based on the price paid by the victim for recovery of his property. Wild also formed a corporation of pickpockets, thieves and burglars and divided London into districts with gangs in each district. His "lost property office" was so busy that he had to open two branch offices, and some victims would pay as much as half the value of their property. Goods that were not claimed were disguised so that they could be sold, and several experts were employed to make alterations to watches, rings and other jewelry.

The stolen goods were stored in several warehouses, and Wild even purchased a ship to carry plunder for sale in Holland.

On the return trip, the ship carried contraband linen and liquor, which were smuggled into England to avoid payment of excise duties. His employees were dependable because most of them were criminals who had escaped following a sentence of transportation to the colonies, and if reported to the authorities, they would be retransported or hanged.

Those burglars and thieves who did not cooperate with Wild risked his vengeance. Under the provisions of the Highwayman Act of 1692, a reward of £40 was paid to anyone who captured a thief and provided evidence that led to his conviction. Wild, with the aid of his assistants during his fifteen-year career as a fence, captured over 100 felons.

"He was the first criminal to become a 'celebrity' known to everyone in town, a good neighbor, a prominent citizen who petitioned for the Freedom of London, and a donator to charitable causes; the first to keep books like an accountant and to understand that crime is a business, and that it needs the same care, attention and planning that all businesses need if they are not to fail; the first to employ respectable lawyers on permanent retainer in order to outwit the courts with their own jargon; and the first, a quality much admired at the time, to use science in the art of detection" (3).

Such was his public reputation as a thief taker that in 1723, the Privy Council sought his advice on controlling crime, but within two years Wild's reputation was destroyed, and public opinion turned against him. His most serious mistake was in becoming a public figure. Truly successful crooks should remain anonymous.

Jack Sheppard, a young highwayman who became a public hero overnight following an audacious escape from Newgate prison where he had been held in manacles and shackles, publicly revealed Wild's skulduggery and treacherous behavior. Following Wild's arrest for helping the captain of his ship to escape from custody, unfavorable reports of his activities were published, and witnesses appeared who were willing to testify against him. Following conviction on a charge of receiving money for the return of stolen property, he was executed in 1725.

FENCING ACTIVITIES

Basically, the fence is a businessman whose income depends on the scope of his operations and his skill in marketing. Like the buyer for a chain of department stores, he needs to know the demand for various items, and he should have a talent for anticipating changes in fashion that affect the purchasing habits of customers. His profit margin is related to his ability to purchase goods at the lowest possible price and to sell them at the highest possible price yet retain a satisfied clientele. If he strikes too hard a bargain, burglars and customers alike will take their business elsewhere.

He tries to convince the burglar that items are less valuable than might be expected. He is like the owner of a used car lot who tells a car seller that his convertible will be difficult to move off the lot, "Rag tops are out, they depreciate too quickly, this is a bad time of the year to sell them." At the same time he tells a customer, "These cars are hard to come by, everybody wants a convertible, it puts the price up but it puts your resale value up too, this is just the time to buy one."

In like manner, the fence tells the burglar that there is a seasonal demand for an item, and in the absence of a quick sale, he will have it on his hands for another year; that the wholesale price is only 40 percent of the retail price; that customers are not interested in cameras without attachments; that there is no electrical cord for the welding machine; that the market is flooded; that a new model is coming out shortly; that the diamonds are only imitation diamonds and so on. In his book *The Professional Fence*, Klockars gives an entertaining and informative account of one fence's bargaining techniques (4).

The fence will often pay no more than a dime per dollar retail price. Items such as color television sets and electric office typewriters are usually purchased for a standard price, and there is little or no haggling. Unusual items that will be hard to sell may draw as little as 1 percent of the retail value, but items for which there is great demand may be purchased for 25 percent or more of their retail value. Fences sell goods at prices substantially below their market value, but fences who operate stores sometimes sell new items at their usual retail price, whereas fences without businesses tend to sell new items at one-quarter to one-half of the retail price. Clothing such as fur coats may be offered for a very low price because the item is not exactly what the customer wants. The fence may hint that the item is "hot," whether or not this is correct, as this tends to convince customers that they are obtaining a real bargain.

Like other businessmen, the fence is responsible for transporting, storing and advertising his goods. His reputation spreads by word of mouth, and many fences have an unusually wide range of friends and acquaintances. Obviously he cannot advertise in newspapers that he is dealing in stolen goods, but he can advertise removal, salvage, fire and discount sales. His limited capital has to be used to best advantage, and he extends credit more often to his customers than to his thieves. Like other businessmen, he has to protect his property and may resort to burglar alarms. As the character of his suppliers is not always beyond reproach, he may conceal from them the location of his main warehouse.

Unlike honest businessmen, the fence has to avoid the arms of the law, and he is keenly aware that in order for him to be convicted of receiving property, the district attorney has to prove (1) that the property was in his possession, (2) that the property was stolen and (3) that he knew it was stolen. Statutes may also require proof that he received the property for his own gain or without the intention of restoring it to the owner.

To avoid arrest in possession of stolen goods, the fence may require burglars to leave their loot at a "drop," which may be a house, garage, warehouse, trailer or truck rented or registered in the name of someone other than the fence. At the "drop," steps are taken to eliminate, as far as possible evidence that proves the property is stolen. This is preferably done beforehand by the burglar. Sales tags, identifying marks or serial numbers are removed, precious stones are reset and other means are used to disguise the property.

To prove that he did not know that the goods were stolen, he draws up a bill of sale in which a reasonable price is paid for the merchandise, and he makes out a check in favor of the

burglar, being sure to use a fictitious name. He asks the burglar
to endorse the check, which is sent to the fence's bank. His
explanation is that the man from whom he purchased the
merchandise wanted a cash payment so he cashed his own check
to pay the man. This smoke screen makes it difficult for the
district attorney to charge him with receiving.

In practice, many fences do not bother to remove identifying
numbers because the stolen goods are in the hands of a customer
before the burglary detective has been assigned the case, and
that customer is unlikely to come under police investigation.
For example, an otherwise honest citizen who purchases a "hot"
television set will keep it in his home, where it is most unlikely
that anyone will check the serial number. The fence may not
even see the stolen property, quickly arranging for its sale to
another fence.

The fence takes care to preserve the anonymity of those
criminals who provide his livelihood, but if he faces arrest
himself, he may bend his own rules and be willing to make a
sacrifice. Such is his distaste for life behind bars that in return
for his own continued freedom, he will give detectives information to enable the arrest of some unworthy burglar who has
betrayed his trust by selling him shoddy merchandise, by refusing to break into a choice target or by taking his business to a
rival fence.

Relatively few fences are charged with receiving stolen
property, and even fewer are convicted because of the difficulty
in proving the four elements of the offense.

1. The property must be "received." It is not, however, necessary
   for the fence to touch with his own hands or even to see the
   goods. It is sufficient if the goods are delivered into his control.
   Some states, however, attach a penalty for intentionally receiving goods believed stolen, even if not actually stolen. This
   permits prosecution of the fence who purchases goods from an
   undercover police officer after having been told that the goods
   were stolen, when in fact the goods were not stolen.
2. The property must have been stolen and must retain its
   character of stolen property at the time it is received.
3. The property must be received with knowledge of its stolen
   character. The fence is very unlikely to admit knowledge of
   the stolen character of the goods. "Accordingly, the circum-

stance that the buyer paid an unreasonably low price for the goods, that the seller was irresponsible (e.g., he had a reputation as a thief or burglar), that the transaction between the buyer and seller was secret, all point toward the buyer's guilty knowledge of the property's stolen character. Furthermore, the fact that the fence knowingly received other stolen property from the same thief, or even from another thief, at about the same time as the receipt of the stolen property in question can be introduced as evidence that the fence had guilty knowledge that the property in question was stolen" (6).

4. The property must be received with wrongful intent.

Another problem in the prosecution of fences is that the police are very dependent on the use of informants, who are usually younger persons of poor reputation with long criminal records. They do not make a good impresison on the jury, whereas the fence is so often a middle-aged businessman with no prior criminal record, and he is supported in court by respected, influential character witnesses.

In a sixteen-month study, a research team from the College of Business, Colorado State University, collected data on 250 fences in Colorado and obtained detailed information on 70 fences who were known to law enforcement personnel in the Denver market area. (This group does not represent a random sample of all fences in this area.) It was found that the fence is likely to be a white, middle-class, middle-aged male with no prior arrest record for major crimes who generally derives less than one-half of his income from fencing. More than 1 in 8 of these 70 fences earned over $100,000 a year; about half earned $50,000 or more and about one-quarter earned $15,000 or less per year.

Fencing is more prevalent in bars and restaurants (22%), secondhand and antique stores (20%) and in auto-related businesses (15%) than in other types of businesses. The most frequently observed price being paid to thieves for stolen goods was from 10 to 25 percent of retail value.

CLASSIFICATION OF FENCES

Type A.	Fully covered business specialist	20%
Type B.	Fully covered business generalist	14%

Type C.   Partly covered business fence   13%
Type D.   Noncovered business fence   23%
Type E.   Individual fence   30%

The definitions and examples given below are taken from *The Design of Anti-Fencing Strategies* by Roselius and his associates (5).

Fully Covered Business Specialist

Fences in this group own or manage a business, handle stolen goods compatible with their legitimate product assortments and limit their stolen goods dealings to a narrow assortment of items. Generally, these businesses are regarded by customers and competitors as legitimate enterprises. Many of the stores of this type are small businesses, but some are well-known chains of stores that have achieved prominence in their respective fields. Some Type A fences are marginally profitable businesses that depend on stolen merchandise to achieve adequate profits for survival, while others are highly profitable enterprises. Some of the details of the case examples have been slightly modified to protect the anonymity of the fence.

Example 1

One Type A fencing operation is a small jewelry store, owned and operated by a forty-two-year-old businessman who is a highly respected member of the local business community. His shop specializes in Indian jewelry, silver and gold rings and accessories and watches. The legitimate portion of the operation is only marginally profitable, and the fence has elected to deal in stolen property to supplement the store's revenue. Each week the fence receives from teenagers small jewelry items that they have shoplifted from stores outside the immediate trading area. These thieves deliver the merchandise directly to the store, which is located in a small shopping district. Although some bargaining over the price the fence will pay occurs, a general price expectation is held by both the fence and the thieves. This price paid to the thieves varies between 10 and 20 percent of the retail value of the merchandise delivered.

Like many Type A fences, the jewelry store owner does not have a criminal record. Furthermore, the fence does not engage in criminal activities other than placing an occasional bet on a sporting event. Even his illegal fencing activity is limited, as stolen goods only account for approximately 5 to 10 percent of the total merchandise sales.

The store's patrons are often unwitting buyers of stolen property and include both local residents and tourists. While these customers vary demographically, most are white and middle class. They pay full retail price for the merchandise and deal with the fence as they would with any other business-man. The fence takes checks and credit cards and issues receipts.

Unwilling to jeopardize his business by dealing with untrust-worthy thieves, this fence deals with only six local teenage thieves, and he refuses to buy stolen merchandise from other potential thief suppliers. The six thieves are generally pleased with the arrangements with their fence—they trust him, know that he will pay a "fair" price and will not question them too carefully about the origin of the goods. They do not expect the fence to help them out if they get into trouble. Instead, they prefer that the fence remain silent under all circumstances.

While law enforcement personnel are aware of this fencing operation, they have not devoted the resources necessary for building a court-admissible case. Furthermore, no opportunistic confession helpful in convicting the fence has come from the thieves. Presently, the general police policy is to allow the fence to operate on a limited basis and press for a prosecution if some fortuitous event should bring the necessary evidence.

Example 2

A second example of a Type A fence is the owner of a small but quite profitable chain of retail tire stores. He limits his dealing in stolen property to tires stolen by two excellent warehouse thieves. The dealings between the fence and the thieves are straightforward, with the fence meeting regularly with the thieves to state the kinds, sizes, price ranges and number of tires he wishes to buy. After the stolen goods are delivered to one of the stores, they are redistributed to other the thieves find their stolen goods arrangement highly satis-within 24 hours after receipt of merchandise. The fence and stores in the chain. Payment to the thieves is by company check factory. The fence has a reliable source of quality merchandise that is purchased at a price allowing him to lower his cost of goods sold, thus increasing his profitability. In turn, the thieves have a sure and secure outlet for the items they steal. They perceive the price they receive as fair in light of the quantity that the fence will accept and the low probability that this fence will contact the police.

Recently, one of the thieves was apprehended by the police and confessed that the owner of this small chain was his fence. When the police contacted the alleged fence, they were welcomed by him, with accompanying claims that he had no idea that the thief supplier could possibly be selling stolen merchandise to him. The detectives were invited to inspect the premises, and the fence produced cancelled checks with the name of the thief on them. The fence claimed that the supplier (the thief) worked for a tire company, and that he, as a legitimate businessman, just assumed that all the dealings were proper. When the police reviewed the case for possible prosecution, they concluded that it was simply a matter of the thief's word against the merchant's regarding the question of knowledge that the merchandise was stolen. A prominent businessman with only one minor arrest in his distant past was being challenged by the accusation of a thief with a long criminal record. The district attorney concluded that the probability of winning a case against the fence was very doubtful, and no formal charges were brought against him.

Example 3

A third Type A fence is the operator of a small television repair shop. His location in a lower-income retail district affords him rich opportunity to keep in contact with heroin addicts congregating in the bars around his establishment. He has spread the word that he will pay cash or narcotics for stolen portable color TVs that they deliver. Because he does not pay top price for stolen goods, the addicts frequently sell goods elsewhere. But, when they need money in a hurry and have a stolen television, they often strike a deal with the TV shop fence.

Unlike the two previous examples, this fence is engaged in

numerous other illegal activities including gambling, narcotics and prostitution. He has been arrested several times and convicted twice during the last ten years. Nevertheless, his total income is low, and he struggles to keep his business open, with fencing income accounting for less than half his total income. His chronic financial problems have resulted in another fence financing part of his operation. These two fences exchange stolen goods, with the financing fence typically faring better in the exchange process.

The stolen goods are displayed in his shop, sometimes with serial numbers removed. The fence's customers are neighborhood residents, who buy the sets at a slight discount from regular market price.

Dealing with many thieves and announcing general willingness to buy stolen property increases vulnerability. Not surprisingly, this fence was recently convicted after a burglar provided damaging information to the police. Subsequently, television sets represented as stolen were sold to the fence by an undercover officer. The fence plea-bargained and was convicted.

Fully Covered Business Generalist

Like Type A fences, stolen property operators in this group own or operate a business and handle goods compatible with their legitimate product assortments. The main point of differentiation is that they have businesses that are "naturally" able to handle broad ranges of stolen products. Included in this group are pawnshops, secondhand stores, antique shops, auctions, salvage or scrap yards and general merchandise establishments. Law enforcement officials frequently regard these types of businesses as major sources of fencing problems, and many laws have been passed on state and local levels to regulate their activities.

Example 1

One Type B fence in the study area owns and operates a pawnshop located in a lower income level retail district of a large city. Although long regarded as a major fence by police officials, he has only been arrested twice and never convicted of a serious crime. His total current income exceeds $100,000 per year, mostly derived from stolen property dealings.

His humble-appearing place of business has been a major contact point for thieves of many types. Currently, seventy-five thieves are regular suppliers. They know that while the fence drives a hard bargain, he will take almost anything they can deliver, including clothing, furs, sporting goods, legitimate and illegitimate drugs, jewelry of all types, coin and stamp collections, tools, automotive parts, commercial and other photographic equipment, stereos, televisions, portable consumer optics, transportation electronics, office equipment and furniture, small electric appliances, antiques, musical instruments, and guns. This is only a partial listing of items the fence deals in, as he is willing to take in virtually all marketable stolen goods.

The brevity of his criminal record is surprising in light of the size and duration of his stolen property operation. His other criminal activities are numerous, according to reliable sources. Among his associates are major organized crime figures who provide numerous potential outlets for goods that cannot readily be handled in his establishment or that pose a high risk. The fence also engages in narcotics selling on a peripheral basis. He has been known to participate in gambling and loansharking activities.

Less than half of the stolen goods handled by the fence are sold directly from him to the ultimate buyer. Most of the property is collected at his establishment or at drops, then transferred to other resellers in the market area or sometimes in other parts of the country. His direct customer clientele includes lower-income Anglos, blacks and chicanos and generally lower-income individuals. The price is often negotiated, resulting in end prices somewhat below current market prices. Although the customer does not know the precise origin of the goods, he may suspect that the goods are stolen.

The thieves deal directly with the fence or one of his two trusted employees. Most of the items come from residential and commercial burglaries. The prices paid by the fence to his suppliers range from 5 to 25 percent of the market value of similar legitimate items. Cash is the usual means of payment, and frequently the transaction is recorded on invoices. Virtually all supplying thieves supply other middlemen as well. The fence does not offer services to thieves such as a lawyer, burglary equipment or vehicles for them.

Although he has been subjected to numerous surveillances and investigations, his operation has not been seriously curtailed. His skill in concealing potentially damaging evidence is almost legendary. Furthermore, he has assisted police in the investigation of thieves and other criminals when it is to his advantage, particularly when he faces possible law enforcement problems of his own.

In his later years, the fence grows considerably more cautious, as his retirement is anticipated in the near future. According to plans, his trusted employees will perpetuate the business, and he will continue to serve as advisor and share in future profits.

Example 2

Another example of a Type B fence is an auction run by a fence who lacks the skills and finesse of the previously described pawnshop operator. The result was a fencing operation that lasted only four years and produced annual profits of less than $25,000. Factors contributing to his demise were (1) his inability to move stolen property quickly, (2) his failure to develop a network of secure and trustworthy thief suppliers and (3) the general carelessness in disguising his operation. Two thieves finally sppplied sufficient information for execution of a search warrant that netted the evidence required for a successful prosecution.

This fence's suburban customers purchased stolen goods ranging from Indian jewelry to office equipment sold through the auction. Most were unsuspecting buyers who bought merchandise as they would in any similar legitimate establishment. Frequently, the dealer would sell food items and professional equipment and supplies (including dental supplies) to small retail establishments or individual professionals. On at least one occasion, valuable jewelry items were sold to other fences in the Denver market area.

The thieves supplying the fence varied in number and type

during the four years. The typical number of thief suppliers
was fifteen to twenty during any one period. Goods originated
mostly from shoplifting, minor hijacks and commercial and residential burglary. The fence and thief dealt on a direct, face-
to-face basis, with the fence paying cash for stolen goods. The
fence also introduced thieves to potential accomplices.

This fence's criminal record includes six arrests and two
convictions. He occasionally associated with known organized
crime members but operated independently during most of his
fencing career, although he was marginally associated with
gambling and narcotics sales. Sometimes he would participate
directly in burglaries.

Example 3

A third example of a Type B fence is the owner and operator
of a sizable antique establishment. This occasional fence deals
with less than a dozen thieves and does so with considerable
discretion. The fence never acknowledges to the thief that he
suspects the goods are stolen. Payment is made by check and
receipt of merchandise is logged, thus enhancing the credibility
of claims of no knowledge that the goods were stolen. By
adhering to this cautious program, the fence has avoided any
prosecution.

His middle-class customers pay normal retail prices for the
merchandise and do not suspect that the antiques or non-
antique used items are stolen.

The thieves receive general information from the fence regarding the types of items most desirous to the fence. The
price to be paid is subject to intense negotiation, but sometimes
the fence will pay almost full wholesale prices for highly
marketable items.

Example 4

A fourth example is a salvage dealer who has been in the
fencing business for more than twenty-five years. While con-
centrating his fencing efforts on stolen metals such as copper,
brass and aluminum, he also takes many other stolen items.
Both his legitimate and illicit dealings are profitable, and he
has a total annual net income in considerable excess of $50,000.

Numerous thieves in the study area dispose of their goods through him. The price paid to the thieves is often equal to the prevailing legitimate market price, but often when the thief has very hot merchandise, the price is below market value. Most of the stolen goods are shipped by the fence to smelters and other scrap dealers.

While law enforcement personnel have long been aware of his operation, no case has been filed. Problems with tracing goods to the specific theft act and proving that he had knowledge the goods were stolen have not been overcome. Another possible factor is the fence's willingness to assist police in apprehending thieves. On several occasions he has given leads on thieves and occasionally testified that the thieves delivered specific items to his establishment.

Partly Covered Business Fence

Type C stolen property dealers own or operate businesses and handle some stolen items that are compatible with their legitimate merchandise lines and store image and some items that are not. The Type C fences studied in depth operate boldly in the stolen property marketplace and might be appropriately described as the "wheeler-dealers" of fencing. Capable of handling wide ranges of product types and quantities, most have many contacts with potential outlets for stolen property. Most participate in various criminal activities other than fencing, and many have associations with major organized crime figures. Their numerous illegitimate activities contribute to the high total profitability of their operations.

Example 1

An owner of a suburban jewelry store is a twenty-five year stolen property system veteran who does a sizable volume of illegal business. His fencing career began modestly as a teenager when he began peddling stolen goods to friends and bar and tavern patrons. Now he operates a modest-appearing jewelry store, selling to both wholesale and retail accounts. Jewelry items and precious metals account for all of his legitimate sales and a major portion of his fencing. In addition, he deals in stolen products such as guns, furs, collections, office equipment, consumer electronics and automobile registration papers, which are not directly compatible with his store image. This combination of activities yields a net income of approximately $40,000 to $45,000 per year, coming mostly from fencing.

Like most other Type C fences, this businessman has been arrested several times. His record includes two theft-receiving arrests and as many convictions. His criminal record, however, does not fully reflect the scope of his illegal activities. He has been heavily involved in gambling operations, slightly involved in narcotics selling and partly involved in the financing of a prostitution operation. While not generally regarded as a major organized crime figure, he frequently associates with major individuals in the organization. Several of these individuals are major fences.

Twenty-five to thirty thieves constitute this fence's stable of regular and reliable thieves. The thieves are a diverse group, including narcotic addicts, nonaddicted professional thieves and major shoplifters. The stolen goods come from robberies, commercial and residential burglaries and shoplifting. Telling thieves where they can pull fruitful thefts is a major function performed by the fence. His information is obtained from appraisal reports done for customers and from casing stores and residential locations.

Thief suppliers contact the fence in person and by phone to negotiate prices and to determine time and location of delivery. Payment is usually in cash, and generally the thief does not receive a receipt or invoice. While highly productive and skilled thieves have some power in the price-bargaining process, the fence usually has the greatest influence on the price paid. The fence knows merchandise values thoroughly and is able to make quick payment. This ability to pay cash is particularly valuable in dealing with narcotic addicts, who frequently need money immediately. Trusted thieves usually deliver merchandise to the store, while others may drop the merchandise at other locations. After receipt, the fence removes stones from identifiable jewelry objects and alters or melts many gold and silver pieces. Nonjewelry merchandise is typically delivered to a drop location where necessary alterations to goods are made. This merchandise will be stored at the drops and sometimes at the fence's home until the fence finds an individual buyer or sells the items to another fence.

The typical purchaser of this fence's stolen property is a white, middle-class individual. Stolen jewelry items are usually sold at regular retail prices. But if the fence assesses a customer as trustworthy and possibly interested in buying other stolen nonjewelry items, he will offer him lower prices on the goods that are incompatible with his normal store image. Usually, a customer is not told directly that the items are stolen, but persons buying nonjewelry goods have cause to suspect the illegal origin.

This fence also sells to legitimate jewelers and other fences. Frequently, he is unable to move particular items of stolen jewelry through his own operation quickly, so he sells them at wholesale prices or less. He deals regularly with about a dozen jewelers, and at least two are fully aware that most of the items sold are stolen. Large precious stones are frequently purchased at very low prices by organized crime members who have extensive connections with jewelry fences throughout the country. Nonjewelry items are sold to area fences who have done business with him for years.

Recently, a thief informant provided information sufficient for obtaining search warrants for examining the fence's place of business and home. None of the stolen goods found were traceable to specific burglaries. All indications are that his fencing operation continues at its normal pace.

Example 2

Another Type C fence earns practically all of his $50,000 net income from fencing. His used car business provides only a partial cover for his marketing of stolen autos, trucks, consumer electronics and guns. He procures the items from six thieves, three of them being employees of his own business. Frequently, the fence specifies the exact types of vehicles to be stolen, a key determinant being his possession of auto registration papers. Stolen autos and trucks are substantially modified and then driven by employees to fences both inside and outside the state. Consumer electronics and guns are sold to individuals in the area as well as shipped to fences on the West Coast.

Arrests and convictions on two theft-receiving charges sent him to prison but did not interrupt his total business. Another fence he had trained and financed filled the void so that connections with out-of-state fences were maintained.

Example 3

The third Type C fence example operates an automobile parts business that partially covers his fencing of auto parts and accessories, consumer electronics and office equipment. This fence has a long criminal record as a burglar and fence and has recently been a direct participant in major thefts. His four regular thief suppliers are highly productive, from where he received most of his annual $60,000 net income. The customers are evenly divided between individuals and area businessmen, who use the goods rather than resell them. Contacts are made with buyers at his business or via telephone. He was recently arrested and convicted for burglary.

Noncovered Business Fence

Like the previous fences described, Type D fences own or operate legitimate business enterprises. However, the distinguishing difference between them and the other fence types already cited is that Type D fences deal in goods not directly compatible with their legitimate product line. For example, a fence who sells stolen television sets in a bar is a Type D fence. A business resource base (the bar) provides contact with both customers and suppliers, but because the televisions are not directly compatible with the normal liquor and food product line handled by the bar, the business needs to have a special or separate marketing program for its stolen goods.

Example 1

One of the "toughest" bars in the study area is a major center of fencing activity. Located in a predominantly lower-income minority area, its patrons include major heroin-addicted burglars and semiprofessional thieves. The owner of this establishment sells narcotics, manages one or two prostitute establishments and accepts gambling bets. The bulk of this bar owner's net income of more than $50,000 comes from fencing.

For the last eight years, this fence has been buying and selling stolen property from the same location. He was arrested twice during that time but never convicted. His business has grown with the help of some organized crime money, and today he can handle large quantities of stolen property. He is willing to buy almost any type of stolen item if the price is right. Most frequently handled items are televisions, guns, stereos, auto tape decks, typewriters and jewelry.

Individual bar patrons are heavy buyers of stolen goods, but they must be "known" to the fence and his employees if they are to qualify as potential buyers. Contact and negotiation of the sale are done in person at the bar and occasionally by telephone. Sometimes, customers take their purchases out through the bar's front door, but more frequently, stolen items are picked up in the alley behind the establishment or delivered to the buyer's auto.

Because of the relatively high profitability of selling to individuals, this fence sells goods directly from his bar whenever possible. Other fences are used when goods are easily traceable or if inappropriate for the fence's clientele. For example, a case of spark plugs or a very expensive jewelry piece would probably be sold to another fence. Many of these other fences are bar patrons owning businesses or peddling merchandise individually. Sometimes the other fences are linked to an out-of-state organized crime figure who finances part of their fencing/bar businesses.

Most of the stolen goods come to this fencing operation directly from thieves. Thieves negotiate prices in the bar, a frequent rate being 20 percent of the retail value of the item. Goods may then be delivered to the rear of the bar or to a drop or may be exchanged at some mutually agreed upon location. Thieves receive payment in either cash or narcotics. If thieves are arrested, they receive no legal or bond services. Strong, probably justifiable, fear of retaliation from the fence keeps arrested thieves from assisting police in his arrest. Recently, however, an addicted thief did provide information for a search warrant that was executed. Nothing stolen was discovered, as the fence knew the police were coming.

Example 2

Another Type D fence is the owner of a recreation center featuring pinball machines, billiards tables and a snack bar. His clientele includes many local teenagers who often spend their evenings "hanging out" at his establishment. The fence engages in some small-time marihuana selling and occasionally peddles harder drugs, including cocaine. But the major portion of his income comes from his legitimate business activities, with fencing providing only about 10 to 15 percent of his total net income of $20,000 to $30,000.

The suppliers of his stolen goods are teenage males who are amateurish thieves pulling minor burglaries or engaging in shoplifting and car prowls. Many are only occasional thieves; determination of who is a regular supplier of stolen property is difficult. During a sixty-day period, twenty to thirty individuals may supply the fence with an assortment of merchandise. The most popular items are tape decks, prerecorded tapes, portable color televisions, stereo equipment and automobile accessories such as hubcaps and radios. Frequently, the thieves are willing to accept as little as 5 to 10 percent of the items' retail market value mainly because (1) the thieves do not have contacts with other fences, (2) they do not want to bother with locating prospective individual buyers or (3) they need a few dollars in a hurry. One amateur thief sold a $900 stereo unit to the fence for $30. In some cases, the fence will purchase stolen items without any cash outlay, but instead gives the thief and his friends a "free" evening of billiards.

Customers are often patrons of this recreation establishment. Other buyers are friends or acquaintances of the fence or may have received notice by word-of-mouth that they might be able to buy stolen goods at low prices there. Average prices are 50 percent less than retail market value. Items are purchased for cash, and no receipts or checks are used. Virtually every purchaser knows the goods are stolen.

This fencing operation has been active for three years.

Neither the fence nor his involved and knowledgeable assistant has a criminal record. The business is still perpetuating.

Example 3

A third example is a major organized crime figure who during his twenty-five-year criminal career has participated in the movement of several million dollars' worth of stolen goods. He owns a bar and makes most of his contacts there or on the telephone located in the establishment. Fencing is only one of several illegal activities he is engaged in. Others include gambling, loansharking and organized narcotics selling. Most of his income in recent years has come from illegal gambling operations and loansharking.

Goods moved by this fence and his associates are in every product category. Quantities range from truckloads to individual items. To facilitate this movement, the fence maintains several drops for thieves, although the goods are rarely physically touched by the fence himself. The details are handled by lower-ranking criminal associates.

The key ingredient of this large-scale operation is the network of fencing contacts built by the fence. Outlets include grocery stores managers, appliance retailers, jewelers, auctioneers, etc. Many are located in the state, but sizeable out-of-state shipments are made regularly. Some goods are on store shelves within hours after the theft. Although most sales are made to other fences, most of whom operate businesses, some sales are made to trusted customers, including prominent citizens residing in the study area.

The fence and his agents procure merchandise from both thieves and other middlemen. From 50 to 100 thieves are regular suppliers. The number of middlemen supplying goods is not known, but the minimum number is 10. Many of these middlemen deal with the fence reluctantly because they often can obtain higher prices elsewhere. However, the web of fencing outlets available through the fence is highly capable of moving stolen goods quickly, and therefore, fences find it expedient to sell goods through him.

Individual Fence

Individual fences buy and sell stolen property, but unlike business fences (Types A through D), they do not own or operate business establishments to aid them in their stolen property activities.

Example 1

One Type E fence began peddling items in local bars and selling stolen goods to fellow employees in a factory where he worked. Building his trade on his general business acumen, gregarious personality and high intelligence, he soon discovered that devoting full-time to fencing was a profitable and challenging business alternative. After working mostly out of his home for six years, he developed a trade netting him $65,000 per year. Basically, his illegal efforts are limited to fencing and some loansharking. Though he procures many goods from narcotic addicts, he avoids narcotic sales because he knows how easy it is to prosecute anyone possessing these items. The scale of his operation has necessitated occasional dealings with organized crime members.

The items this fence handles come from all product categories except automotive vehicles and drugs. He has been known to sell numerous kinds of items such as auto registration certificates, securities, meat, clothing, tape recorders, calculators, coin collections, large appliances, typewriters, paintings, hand grenades and machine guns.

As an independent fence, he developed several techniques for moving stolen merchandise that he employs in various ways, depending upon the type and quantity of merchandise, police pressure and volume of other fencing opportunities. The first technique is the "straight peddle" approach that involves contacting individuals in bars, factories, personal service establishments, such as barber shops, and on the street.

The second resembles the peddle approach in that it involves the sale of relatively small quantities of merchandise per transaction to a large number of customers. The prime customers in this second approach are small businesses which resell the goods. This might be a small television store; office supply store; secondhand or clothing stores, or about any other type of small store. The fence offers these merchants goods, the origins of which are thinly guised. Most merchants have reasonable cause to suspect the goods are stolen.

A third technique is the "customer order" approach, which becomes a major outlet for stolen merchandise as the fence becomes better known. Customers place orders with the fence and tell him to make contact with them when he has the items. For example, an office manager placed an order for ten IBM Selectric® typewriters; a dentist wants an Olympus OMI® single-lens reflex camera; and a sporting goods store wants as many cross-country skis as are available. The fence carefully records these orders in code, consummates each sale when the goods become available. The fence uses ongoing relationships with business resellers, many of whom would be classified as Type A, Fully Covered Business Specialist, or Type B Fully Covered Business Generalist. Several of these relationships have existed for most of this middleman's fencing career. Dealings are candid and straightforward, although there is usually some bargaining over price. The buyers usually pay cash for the goods despite the high prices of some of the merchandise.

A fourth approach is the sale of stolen goods through organized crime members and affiliates. This fence usually tries to avoid using these channels whenever possible because the selling price is usually less than market value.

A few miscellaneous methods of reselling stolen property need mention. One is the sale of goods through classified ads in newspapers. A favorite style is "Must move to California immediately. Selling television, stereo, furniture, etc." This fence also used, "Must move immediately" advertisements to announce an open house or apartment sale. Sometimes he would rent an apartment just for a weekend sale of stolen items and display all types of merchandise. When he sold a stereo set, for example, he would then go to his car or to the basement of the apartment building and bring up another set. He would also rent space at flea markets to move some of the items.

Virtually all stolen items obtained by the fence are received directly from thieves. Many suppliers are narcotic addicts and are in quick need of cash for drug purchases. Other thieves also desire a quick transaction for cash. These factors necessitate the fence's ready access to substantial sums of money. Frequently he will carry several thousand dollars in cash on his person. The more trusted thieves are allowed to deliver goods directly to the fence's home or an apartment he maintains.

Other thieves will deliver to a location selected by the fence for an occasional exchange of goods. If the items are delivered to a drop, the fence will quickly move the property to another site in order to avoid having the goods restolen by the supplying thief or one of his associates.

Sometimes the fence will render the services of facilitators to perform special services for him. For example, a gunsmith will be used to remove serial numbers from firearms, or a jeweler may switch stones on a valuable piece of jewelry or alter the pieces so that identification is difficult.

All of this activity sums up to a sizeable individual fencing operation that resulted in only three arrests and one conviction as he continues in his illegal operations.

Other Examples

The other Type E fences examined employ variations of the general marketing approaches used by the fence just described. One uses the "straight peddle" approach by obtaining his stolen goods from narcotic users and reselling them to small retailers. Another buys goods from all types of thieves including shoplifters and then resells the items through organized crime figures and their associates. Another meets weekly with bicycle thieves to discuss his product needs. After receiving stolen bicycles, he ships them to various college campuses for resale. Finally, one fence-burglar simply buys a few stolen items from burglars with whom he "pulls jobs" and sells these items in local bars.

REFERENCES

1. Defoe, Daniel: *The King of the Pirates.* New York, Jenson Society, 1901.
2. Hall, Jerome: *Theft, Law and Society,* 2nd ed. Indianapolis, Bobbs-Merril, 1952.
3. Howson, Gerald: *Thief-Taker General: The Rise and Fall of Jonathan Wild.* London, Hutchinson, 1970.

4. Klockars, C. B.: *The Professional Fence*. New York, Free Pr, 1974.
5. Roselius, Ted, Hoel, R. F., Benton, D. A., Howard, M. K. and Sciglimpaglia, D.: *The Design of Anti-Fencing Strategies*. Fort Collins, Colorado State University, 1975.
6. Walsh, M. E.: *Strategies for Combatting the Criminal Receiver of Stolen Goods*. Washington, D.C., U.S. Government Printing Office, 1976.
7. Walsh, M. E.: *The Fence: A New Look at the World of Property Theft*. Westport, Connecticut, Greenwood, 1977. Used with the permission of the publisher.

CHAPTER 4

IN SEARCH OF CAUSES

*The causes of events are ever more
interesting than the events themselves.*
—Cicero, *Epistolae ad Atticum*

CRIMINAL CONDUCT, like other human behavior, has complex causes, and it is not easy to assess the role of any single factor. There are many who share Tolstoy's belief that the seeds of every crime are in each of us. Dostoyevsky, in *The Brothers Karamazov*, gives dramatic expression to this theme, "Nobody in the world can be the judge of the criminal before he has realized that he himself is as much a criminal as the one who confronts him," and again, "Everyone pretends to hate evil, but deep down they all like it, all of them."

Those in search of the causes of crime tend to look either within the individual or within society for their answers. Psychiatrists and psychologists examine the offender, explore his relationships with his parents, study his early personality development, evaluate recent stresses and search for other psychological factors that could have contributed to his crime. Physicians may also consider brain injuries and diseases, endocrinal abnormalities and chromosomal disorders in relation to crime. Sociologists stand further back and review the effects of unemployment, overcrowding and other social factors on the incidence of crime. They assess the role of social changes and identify conditions in society that favor the growth of crime.

It has been shown that high crime and delinquency rates occur in slum areas near the centers of cities and industrial areas as well as in newly established districts with transient populations. The demonstration of high crime rates in the presence of social disorganization does not explain why some persons in these circumstances become criminals whereas others do not.

Wolfgang suggests that there may be subcultures of violence in which quick resort to physical aggression is socially approved. He comments that when a blow of the fist is casually accepted as a normal response to certain stimuli, when knives are commonly carried for personal defense and when a homicidal stabbing is as frequent as Saturday night, then social control against violence is weak (13). Social control against burglary and theft is also weak in some of these subcultures of violence, and concerned members of these neighborhoods display bumper stickers reading "don't rip off your brother."

Crimes against property rise in times of economic depression, but the prosperous period following World War II was accompanied by an increase in such crimes. It is tempting to think that social changes such as a higher rate of employment, an improved standard of living and reduction of discrimination will lead to a substantial reduction of crime. Dostoyevsky recognized the weakness of this viewpoint when he wrote in *Crime and Punishment,* "Environment is the root of all evil—and nothing else! A favorite phrase. And the direct consequence of it is that if society is organized on normal lines, all crimes will vanish at once, for there will be nothing to protest against, and all men will become righteous in the twinkling of an eye."

Oscar Wilde has said that, "The criminal classes are so close to us that even the policemen can see them. They are so far away from us that only the poet can understand them." Wilde was uncharitable in his comment on the police, but many persons would agree with him that it is difficult to know the criminal. There are those who say that research on crime has not enabled us to modify either the incidence of crime in our society or the course of criminal behavior in the individual offender. We must admit limitations in our knowledge, but we do know that crime is largely a product of youth and masculinity.

SEX AND CRIME

Wootton has said that if men behaved like women, the courts would be idle and the jails empty (14). Not only in crime, but in general social life, women are more liable than men to

decency and morality, however defined. Women do not figure
strongly in the ranks of burglars, females accounting for only
6 percent of the arrests for this crime in the United States.
Women do account for 32 percent of the arrests for larceny-
theft and are more often arrested for this crime than for any
other crime index offense.

For many years, women have been actively involved in shoplifting, and prostitutes have long supplemented their income by
picking the pockets of their customers. The relatively infre-
quent participation of women in burglary is often limited to
assisting male burglars by acting as informants, lookouts or
decoys. Female employees in businesses or in the homes of
the wealthy have provided information on the location of
valuable items and the most suitable times for their removal.
They may also inactivate burglar alarms, leave doors unlocked,
provide duplicate keys or act as lookouts to warn of the appearance of police.

Attractive young women act as decoys by distracting the
attention of night watchmen, security guards and police officers.
The night watchman who has been seduced by a burglar's female
accomplice is unlikely to reveal the reason for his failure to
detect the burglary in progress. During the time of the burglary,
the woman accomplice may keep the precinct police away from
the scene by claiming that her car has broken down or that she
has been the victim of an attempted rape. Burglars will often
leave a girl sitting in their getaway car to disarm the suspicion
of police officers arriving at the scene of a burglary.

In countries where women play a limited role in society,
they also play a limited role in crime. As women achieve a
greater measure of independence and equality in society, they
not only become fighter pilots and police officers, but also
terrorists and burglars.

AGE AND CRIME

Crime statistics have shown that males between the ages
of fifteen and twenty-four have the highest rate of crime. In
recent years in the United States, males and females under
the age of twenty-five have accounted for over 80 percent of

all arrests for burglary and over 65 percent of arrests for larceny-theft. The incidence of these crimes fluctuates according to the proportion of the fifteen- to twenty-four-year-olds in a given population. Thus, the "baby boom" after World War II contributed to the increase in these crimes in the 1960s. The fertility rate in the United States has since fallen sharply, and this is beginning to cause a reduction in the crime rates.

Some burglars are very young indeed. Eight- and nine-year-old children will join older brothers or friends in their housebreaking activities. Small boys can more easily gain entry through milk chutes or small windows. Young burglars may steal candy, food, toys and bicycles. An eleven-year-old boy set his alarm for 3 AM, and armed with his father's bolt cutters, he broke into a neighbor's garage three blocks away and stole a bicycle to obtain new tires for his own bicycle. A group of young children obtained jewelry and bicycles from home burglaries and threw all their loot into a lake "for fun."

In a series of burglaries in a large apartment building, the police suspected the superintendent or someone with access to his keys because there were no signs of forced entry. The culprit was a twelve-year-old-boy who, armed with a knife, a dentist's mirror and a coathanger, had perfected a method for lifting the peephole slot, inserting the mirror and guiding the coat hanger to disengage the lock system (10).

There is a Persian proverb that an egg thief becomes a camel thief. Some burglars start by stealing from mother's purse, then progress to shoplifting and burglary. No great skill is required to break into a neighbor's house, the likelihood of detection is slight, and the risk of imprisonment is remote indeed for the first-time offender. Providing he is reasonably circumspect and has a good attorney, the juvenile burglar can often remain on the streets despite repeated arrests by the police. These factors surely contribute to the extent of this crime.

Some young persons happen to be burglars only as they go through a phase, a stage or part of the Sturm und Drang of adolescence, and if not caught (although some would say they often turned into criminals) may drop burglary, as they drop promiscuity, swaggering or fad music.

Adolescents and college students sometimes impulsively indulge in antisocial conduct that they regard as pranks rather than as illegal acts.

> We had about half-an-hour to kill, and we decided to look around for something to do. By random choice we came to this hotel, and we were walking around the building when my friend said he had to make a telephone call. On finding an open door we entered a room on the 16th floor, and he made his call. We then decided to pull a prank and order room service. We ordered some food which came to about $12 and started to eat it when the hotel manager came up to our room and took us to his office. We were simply looking to kill some time and wound up doing what we thought was just a practical joke.

Society is ambivalent toward the "pranks of youth." On the one hand it explicitly discourages antisocial behavior, on the other hand it condones some "student behavior" in all its crassness and vulgarity. Fraternity initiation ceremonies sometimes require the students to commit an act of vandalism or petty theft. Student panty raids on sorority houses in the 1950s were enjoyed by all, but student forays occasionally lead to serious infractions of the law. Fathers do not want their sons to "sow their wild oats," but when they do, their behavior is dismissed as "he's turning into a man." Haven't all societies in all times to some extent encouraged such behavior?

Older persons figure prominently in shoplifting, and the peak age among British woman shoplifters was fifty-one to sixty years of age. Although an elderly burglar told a judge, "Old burglars never die, they just steal away," many burglars in middle age or younger turn away from crime. The fire in them dies down; they become more mature and submit to the restrictions of marriage and children by pursuing less eventful lives. By the age of forty the risk of recidivism is markedly reduced in many offenders.

RACE AND CRIME

Although blacks have higher crime rates than whites for a number of offenses, their disproportionate representation in crime statistics has been attributed to sociological factors such as high rates of poverty and unemployment related to discrimination. In recent years in the United States, blacks have accounted for 29 percent of the arrests for burglary, 32 percent for larcency-theft and 26 percent for motor vehicle theft (*UCR*).

MOTIVES

Financial Gain GREED

Financial gain is an obvious motive for burglary and theft. Persons who have no great enthusiasm for steady employment are attracted by less tiresome sources of income. Upon occasion, however, hours of strenuous physical exertion of breaking into a store and taking apart a safe result only in worthless account books and ledgers. Unemployed, drug-dependent persons who must pay large sums of money for narcotics generally turn to shoplifting, till-tapping, burglary and other illegal means of acquiring money, as this is the only way they know to support their habit.

Persons arrested for burglary may give a "hard luck" story such as, "I was hungry and had no job and no money. I had been looking for a job and had spent all my money on trying to find a job. I broke the window with a brick. I went inside to get some money to eat on and to help me look for a job." Sometimes such explanations do not bear scrutiny, as when relatives reveal that good job offers have been refused by the burglar. In the following case, a cleaning woman in a hospital who confessed that she stole a patient's $900 diamond ring to feed her baby used the ring for the down payment on a new car. "I have been having trouble feeding my little girl because I have to pay rent. I work by myself to take care of her. This day I had nothing to feed her, no milk. I did take the ring. I have a baby. People should not leave stuff lying around like that."

Persons who are steadily employed and financially sustaining may steal on impulse without regard for the possible consequences of their theft or burglary. The opportunity to obtain cash or some desirable expensive item with apparent slight risk of detection may lead to an otherwise law-abiding person placing his career in jeopardy. "I saw this radio and I thought it would be cheaper to get it free. I've never done this before. I'm not a criminal at heart." In some of these cases, the person's judgment and self-control have been temporarily impaired by the effects of alcohol, fatigue or emotional stress.

Revenge

Another motive for burglary and theft by persons who have not previously committed crimes is revenge. Chronic law breakers may also upon occasion select specific targets in order to obtain revenge or settle a grudge. Persons who have suffered a real or fancied injustice, whether through loss of a job, rejection by a lover or some other misfortune, may retaliate through burglary or theft.

> I took the firewood from outside the restaurant because I was pissed off at the service and unable to get the manager to come and listen to me.
>
> My reason for doing this was due to my boss beating a friend on a deal they made for some drugs.
>
> He burned out my amplifier and I wanted to get even.
>
> This black poodle was digging up my bushes. I'd seen it before and chased it off several times before. I put it in the bathroom overnight, the next day I took the dog to the Dumb Friend's League.
>
> A young man, following an argument with his girl friend, broke into her place of employment and removed an empty cash register worth $300. "I decided to get even with her so I decided to take their cash register because I knew it would be really hectic for them with only one cash register on Friday, they're really busy on Fridays. I left it where I knew it would be found, but I was hoping it wouldn't be found for a couple of days because she works the cash register and she would really be busy. I knew there was no money in it, they clean it out every night. I didn't want money I just wanted to get even with her."

Envy

The burglar who destroys items within a home may have as one of his motivations envy of others who are wealthy or who appear to have a happy contented family life. Reference has already been made to the youthful burglar who, on seeing family pictures including the children, would respond by breaking articles in the house. His companion commented, "I guess [he did it] because his mom and dad had such an unhappy marriage. He liked his mom and dad and [was angry when] they were separated."

Another burglar, who was also a rapist, would peep in the windows of homes and fantasize that he was a member of the family in order to fill a void in his own life. He gives a vivid account of the thoughts and feelings behind his theft of family mementoes and destruction of property.

> When I'd break into a home, I would fantasize it was my home, fantasize about the people who owned the home similarly to how I fantasized while window peeping. I think I was trying to share their lives and feel safe too. I felt safe peeping at them, I didn't feel safe being with people and doing things with people. Many times I've spent an hour watching television with a family, watch them eat dinner, read newspapers, kids running in and out, watch women do their housework, watch people entertain and have parties.
>
> I'd fantasize about what work the man did, where they'd come from, what they liked to do, did they fight, were they happy, why were they happy? Why other people seemed happy bugged the hell out of me. I didn't really believe it. The sexual thing came in there, watching women disrobe, get ready for bed, bathe, I used to be anxious to see what they did when they were alone.
>
> When I'd break into a home, I would take things; I realize now I was taking things of sentimental value, mementoes and other items which could not easily be replaced. I would take the object, feeling very strongly at the time that I would have what the owner had, always to experience bitter disappointment later and find the sentimental object was empty to me and I would throw it away. Sometimes I'd knock things over, lamps and, at the time, I thought it was accidental. Sometimes I'd destroy things. Looking back on it, I think I was striking back at people, they had things I didn't have (8).

Excitement

Excitement is surely another attraction of burglary and theft, but is there not excitement in noncriminal life? It is exciting to be a cop, or a fireman, or a tightrope walker, or a lion tamer, or a parachute tester, or a spy, or a stunt man, or a high construction worker, or a demolition expert. These occupations, however, have tiresome requirements, such as regular hours of work, which do not appeal to everyone.

Most of us lead rather dull, drab lives, but the criminal is unlikely to die of boredom. Anais Ninn put it very well in her diary; she wrote that people jump into crime to bring the blood to life when they are bloodless. The successful offender has to be alert and vigilant at all times. In robbery, the offender confronts his victim at a time and place of his own choosing, catching his victim by surprise, but in burglary the victim may catch the offender by surprise.

The householder who does not respond to the doorbell creates the impression the house is vacant; the police officer on a stake-out and the employer who stands silent watch over his premises must always be in the mind of the burglar, who can never be sure whether he will come face-to-face with someone ready to do battle. The unknown can hold more fear than the known, and the suspense, which may be unpleasurable at the time, adds spice to life, as any mountain climber will verify. "To me it was always the excitement more than the money. I never felt bad if there wasn't any money. The most exciting part was going in—the entry. You know going in there in the dark, when you didn't know for sure what was waiting. Oh, man, opening the safe, I would sweat so hard my clothes would be wringing wet just as if I had done a hard day's work (11)."

Stott refers to a pattern in juvenile delinquents of excitement seeking as a means of escaping from a haunting anxiety. In his efforts to keep his anxieties from intruding into his conscious mind, he seeks an endless succession of new sensations. A youthful burglar was driven by the compulsion to blot out the traumatic memory of his mother's death by a pattern of hectic, irresponsible hyperactivity that was superimposed upon an otherwise well-adjusted personality. Full of life, this youth was continually on the go and always on the lookout for adventure. The unconscious avoidance remained active six years after the death of his mother; asked if he ever thought of her, his face crumpled up just as if he might cry, but without apparent emotion, he said, "There is too much to do, there's no time to think (9)."

Sexual Excitement

A few burglars report a sexual thrill at the time of the burglary or restoration of sexual potency following the crime. An intelligent young burglar with excellent prospects in life was asked if he had ever thought of going straight. He replied, "When I'm on a burglary, it's damn nearly as good as having a woman for me." Heirens, the former University of Chicago student who committed more than 500 burglaries and three murders, had an erection at the sight of the window through which he was to enter; he ejaculated as he went in.

The discovery of an artificial penis beneath the mattress of an armed robber and burglar led me to question his wife about his sexual performance. She revealed that he had difficulty in performing but was often potent after he had committed a crime. The man confirmed her statement.

Guttmacher contends that burglary (the offense of breaking and entering, the very words suggest the possible symbolism) is far more likely to be a forerunner of rape than homosexuality, voyeurism, exhibitionism or any other type of sexual offense. One-third of the rapists in his study had been previously involved in burglary (3).

Some burglars masturbate at the scene of the crime. Others steal women's underclothing, which they take for their own personal sex use. Burglars have been arrested at the scene dressed in women's underclothing, and sometimes the underclothing was not obtained in that burglary. Burglary or theft for the purpose of obtaining women's shoes might not appear to have a sexual basis, but these offenders sometimes confide that they need these shoes to obtain orgasm.

Fetishism refers to *the use of a shoe, female underclothing, raincoat, or lock of hair to obtain sexual gratification.* So called "braid cutters" will snip off a lock of hair from a girl on the street or in an elevator. A forty-two-year-old male described how when he was four years old, he used to obtain pleasurable excitement from swinging on his mother's foot. In later life, he had a compelling desire to touch the feet of women with whom he might be associated, for example, the chambermaid in a hotel. Sexual satisfaction was only attained when a foot was visualized (1). Another of Batchelor's patients described his irresistible urge to purchase women's shoes and slippers (he had accumulated a considerable quantity), which he had to fondle and kiss before he attained complete sexual satisfaction.

Quite remarkable stocks of shoes are accumulated by some burglars. One man had hundreds of shoes, old shoes, new shoes and shoes that had been cut up. Some shoes had glue or paint on them (he was known to sniff both glue and paint). Another burglar had so many shoes in the trunk of his car that he could not close it. His mother reported that he had a garage-full at home. His only explanation was, "I just like shoes."

A youth burglarized a school to obtain the address of a girl (leaving a note that said he was "sorry for the mess and you can rest assured that I did not take anything") and then attempted to steal a car to take the girl to a concert, stating that "there was no intention or forethought to raping anyone."

Sexual factors have been cited as contributing to kleptomania, which is characterized by compulsive, repetitive, senseless thefts, usually by women. The term has been criticized for invoking a social judgment on the part of the psychiatrist. It has been suggested that repetitive thefts by poor women are regarded as criminal acts, whereas repetitive thefts by wealthy women are seen as senseless, and hence, the result of a mental disorder, kleptomania. There is some justification for this criticism, as psychiatrists upon occasion have incorrectly applied the term to "well-to-do" female thieves whose thefts are certainly not the result of a neurotic-compulsive urge. Women on welfare may compulsively and repetitively steal items that are of no value to them. Nevertheless, caution should be exercised in the use of the term *compulsive*. How often do we find ourselves doing something with no apparent forethought? A little intro-spection reveals that our daily lives are passed through with unexplained actions that in no sense can be explained as com-pulsive behavior.

Wittels mentions a shoplifter whose description of her experi-ences comes as close to a description of sexual orgasm as any seemingly nonsexual act can. "When I have taken an object in a department store, I thrust it in my bosom, under my blouse, hide in the next doorway and wait with my heart beating. When I see that I have not been noticed, I feel a wild triumph, a lust the like of which nothing else can offer." Wittels comments that stealing is the sex life of kleptomaniacs, and as a rule they have no other (12).

In support of his viewpoint, a woman of forty, who constantly reverted to thievery, reported that she was sexually excited whenever she stole and that she even experienced orgasm at the moment she accomplished her theft. During sexual intercourse she became frigid; while masturbating, she would imagine she was stealing (2).

Halleck notes that a crime may have a symbolic unconscious meaning to the offender, and in some instances the choice of the object to be stolen or the person it is to be stolen from is deeply influenced by unconscious factors. He describes the following example in which the stolen object symbolized erotic love.

> A seventeen-year-old girl was referred for psychiatric examination after she had been apprehended for shoplifting. She had stolen only pens and pencils from local bookstores. During her interview she talked quite freely about her problem. Raised by exceedingly strict and religious parents, she had always tried to adhere to her faith to the best of her ability. After having had but few experiences with the opposite sex during high school she entered a large university, where she was greatly stimulated by new opportunities for sexual contact. After a short period of time she began to "go steady" and to engage in heavy petting. She felt both erotic stimulation and affection and was convinced that she wanted to marry her boyfriend as soon as possible. Her boyfriend did not share her enthusiasm for matrimony. One night she decided to offer herself to the boy, entertaining the secret hope that she would become pregnant and force him into an early marriage.
>
> After several hours of heavy petting she invited her boyfriend to have intercourse with her. He refused, stating that he was worried about impregnating her. The patient was frustrated and mortified but said nothing. When she later discussed the incident, she repeatedly said, "I couldn't understand how he could possibly refuse me." The next day she went out on her first pen-and-pencil-stealing expedition. When she stole, she was continually troubled with what seemed to her an absurd thought. She kept thinking

she had to take these items and put them in a box. When questioned, she revealed that she recently had learned that the word "box" was a vernacular equivalent to vagina.

This girl's story sounded almost like a caricature of a Freudian case study. The author seriously considered the possibility that she was pulling his leg. Yet her extraordinary naïveté and her obvious frankness testified to her veracity. Furthermore, after a few interpretations of her anger at being rejected and the similarity of phalluses and pens she seemed much relieved. Out of curiosity, the author asked her to come in one year later and found that she was still in school, unmarried but relatively content. She had done no further shoplifting (5).

Power

Those who feel weak and powerless may attempt to gain a sense of strength and mastery over others by playing the role of a tough criminal. They boast about their exploits, but may try to reduce the risk of confrontation with a victim by confining their crimes to burglary and theft. A gun gives them real power, and sooner or later they get up enough courage to engage in armed robbery.

A petty thief and small-time burglar felt like a million dollars after he found a handgun in a burglary. He had a long history of juvenile delinquent behavior, and at fifteen years of age, he held court in a donut shop as the self-proclaimed leader of a group of children much younger than himself. He offered ten- and eleven-year-old children advice on how to commit burglaries and tried to convey the impression that he was a tough hardened criminal.

Psychiatrists and psychologists who had interviewed him at intervals over a period of several years noted the contrast between his outward display of rebellious truculent behavior and his underlying fearful dependent passivity. I met him when he was twenty-one, following his arrest on charges of armed robbery, kidnapping and murder. He was only five feet, six inches in height and had a Nazi swastika tattooed on his left arm. He mentioned his approval of the Nazis as "clean efficient people, get the job done, no bullshit." The Nazi emphasis on ruthless aggression and power has a special appeal for those who are weak and fearful.

He played the role of a tough guy who was not to be

trifled with. He boasted of his many fights in which he had injured ten to twenty persons. "They say I ruptured a guy's spleen." He told me he was going to murder his stepfather. He said of his companion in the robbery and murder, "If I'd wanted to kill him, I'd have wasted him too." Referring to another psychiatrist he said "I just about slugged that bastard."

Apparently concerned that I might not have gathered that he was a dangerous person, he threatened to kill me if I pushed him too far. One day when another prisoner was threatening to attack me, he shouted encouraging comments from his cell, thereby adding to a rather sticky situation. Later I explained to him that he was capable of better behavior.

The next day he apologized, saying "I feel much better because you got mad at me yesterday and put me in my place. I respect you now, you told me to fuck myself yesterday, only you used nice words." This was a turning point in the psychiatric examination, and for the first time, he was able to talk about his tough outer shell and his inner feeling of weakness. "I talk bad shit like I'm a tough guy, I ain't, I'm scared of everybody."

When he talked about the murder, he made many references to his power over his victim. "He would do anything I told him to do." Unfortunately the victim did not do everything he was told to do; he was shot nine times.

Proof of Manhood

Many primitive societies have puberty rites that prepare the adolescent youth for the responsibilities of manhood. These rites usually require the youth to undergo some painful experience to prove his courage. In the United States, these formalized rites are not available, and youths may attempt to prove their manhood through some act of daring such as burglary or robbery. This is more likely to occur in a subculture of violence or theft where such behavior is more likely to arouse respect.

Need for Attention

Most people welcome attention, and some, if they cannot get it through civic accomplishments, will do so through acts of notoriety. (It is better to be wanted by the police than not

to be wanted at all.) Some criminals carry news clippings of
their criminal exploits. A bank robber confided that his one
ambition in life was to appear on the FBI list of ten most
wanted criminals.

Social Protest

Revolutionary groups intent on overthrowing governments
need guns to conduct a campaign of violence and money to
support their cause. Armed robberies, skyjackings, extortions,
kidnappings and, to a lesser extent, burglaries are features of
urban guerrilla operations throughout the world. Burglaries of
sporting goods stores and army storage depots provide firearms
and ammunition.

Burglaries of mining and construction bunkers provide explosives that are used in the construction of bombs. Large mines
are able to store explosives in properly secured bunkers, but it
is difficult to prevent burglary at night or on weekends. Small
mines and construction companies may even store explosives in
unlocked sheds and trailers, which present no obstacle to burglars nor even to the simply curious. Theft by employees is
difficult to control, as miners can easily take dynamite home
in their pockets or lunch pails.

Revolutionary movements attract persons who would not
otherwise be involved in criminal activities. The urban guerrilla
sees himself as a patriot, freedom fighter and revolutionary, but
others would describe him as a bandit, outlaw and terrorist.
Although the revolutionary is expected to steal for his organization, there is often the temptation to keep some of the spoils
for himself.

ENCOURAGEMENT BY OTHERS

—The devil made me do it.

Parents, friends, criminal acquaintances including fences and
agents provocateurs among others may provide direct or indirect
encouragement to commit burglary. Three 9-year-old boys told
police that the mother of one of them had coached them in
breaking into a neighbor's home. Another mother took her
fourteen-year-old son with her to assist in the burglary of a

warehouse. The youth had seven previous arrests for burglary, and one arrest for possession of burglary tools. His older brother asked the court for custody to protect him from the influence of his mother.

Even if the parents do not directly encourage their children to break the law, they provide approval for wayward behavior by protecting them from police investigation. A mother said that she was with her son for every minute of the preceding twenty-four hours and that he could not have committed a burglary during this time. Yet her son was seen leaving a neighbor's home with a stolen television set.

Parents who express strong condemnation of unlawful behavior may nevertheless provide indirect encouragement of such behavior through repeated expression of fear that a son or daughter will break the law. The child who is constantly reminded not to steal ultimately may come to recognize that one parent or the other expects him to steal. When these warnings are accompanied by parental behavior that indicates the child is already suspected of having stolen items in his possession, there is an added risk that the child will fulfill the dire predictions. In effect, the child says to himself, "I'm being blamed for it, I might as well do it."

The father may have underlying wishes to perform the very criminal act that he fears will be committed by his son. Behind the fear lies the wish. Through his son's antisocial behavior, the father gains vicarious gratification of his own forbidden impulses. One child in a family of several children might unconsciously be chosen to act out the parents' poorly integrated forbidden impulses. The child selected as scapegoat may resemble a relative with a criminal record or may have incurred parental disfavor through rebellious behavior. An adopted child is a ready choice, as the delinquent behavior can be attributed to heredity rather than some failure of the adoptive parents (7).

A mother became very angry at her nine-year-old daughter, who was detected stealing money from the teacher's desk. Although the mother knew that her daughter had been taking money from her purse since the age of six or seven, she had said nothing, believing that her daughter would "outgrow" it;

besides "it was never serious, so the less said the better." Johnson and Szurek, who cite this example, comment that the mature mother does not anticipate trouble or constantly check up on her child. They add that neither does she dismiss a significant transgression as unimportant; instead, she resolves the problem promptly without anxiety or guilt. She is neither the nagging, checking detective nor the permissive, lax condoner. This mother later told of her own frequent stealing in childhood and adolescence; her mother had always protected her (6).

Socioeconomic class levels may be important. A particular mother may reflect her class morality rather than her own individual morality; in fact, many people seem to have no personal moral code and simply act on the basis of common sayings and popular songs, such as "A woman is a sometime thing," "All's fair in love and war" (She isn't, it isn't), "Everyone does it," "The eleventh commandment" and "Everyone rips off someone else."

The children of permissive, indulgent parents, accustomed to quick gratification of their wishes, may never learn to tolerate frustration. Children of well-to-do parents who can have almost anything that a check can buy do not grow up prepared to face the consequences of financial adversity. When their parents lose their fortunes or pass on (but not their fortunes), they may resort to theft, burglary, check forgery or some other illegal activity to maintain their extravagant life-styles.

Encouragement of burglary and theft may also come from lovers, both heterosexual and homosexual. Fear of loss of love can be a factor, especially in persons who would not ordinarily be inclined toward criminal behavior. Many strange acts are performed in the name of love. "A waitress, accused of theft of money from the restaurant where she worked, said that her boyfriend took the money and disappeared. The detective noticed that one of her hands was bruised and swollen. She explained that her boyfriend would hit her hand with a hammer so that she could obtain drugs for pain from a hospital emergency room. He would use the drugs to get high."

A chance encounter with a stranger in an amusement center, hamburger stand or bar may lead to an impulsive decision to take part in a burglary. The stranger may set up the crime but not take part in the break in himself. He reduces the risk of arrest by parking his car nearby and quickly leaves the scene if he sees the police respond to a burglar alarm or a telephone call from a witness, as in the following example.

> We met this guy who asked us where we were going and we started talking to him. He asked us if we wanted a ride and then we started telling him about the movie and how much it cost to get in and that we had been looking for a job. Then he asked us if we wanted to smoke some marihuana and as we're riding along he asked us if we needed money and he knew a way that worked every time. All you had to do was cut a hole in a roof and we would get $200 or more. At first we said no but then we talked a little more and then he drove by the place and said that there was no way we could get caught. I was pretty high and didn't realize that we were going to do it till he dropped us off. He reassured us that it would be all right and that he would wait for us and we would have to give him a third of the loot.

In the next example, youthful burglars without a car persuaded another youth to drop them off near the home they had selected and then to wait for them. They were seen by neighbors and escaped, but the owner of the car was arrested.

> I was at work and two guys asked me if I wanted to make some quick money and I said "Yes, what do I have to do?" and they said, "Park your car in front of a house and act like your car is stalled and wait there for us." I picked them up behind the store and they showed me the house and where to park the car. I acted like my car was broke and asked a lady for jumper cables. Then I saw the two guys running down the street, so I waited for three minutes and then went back to work.

Friends may also be a source of encouragement to commit crime, and the bonds of friendship may be decisive in overcoming moral scruples. In juvenile gangs, there is sometimes pressure to join in burglary or theft. Lonely, unhappy youths who are unable to make friends at school may find acceptance in a juvenile gang, but the price of acceptance is participation in delinquent acts.

A drug dealer fearful of being trapped by police informants would insist that prospective drug purchasers accompany him in a burglary before he would sell them any narcotics, thereby binding them to silence regarding his illegal drug sales.

Fences sometimes encourage acquaintances to commit burglaries or thefts by promising them cash payment for stolen property. These fences will often provide burglars information on suitable targets.

CRIME AND PUNISHMENT

Deep-seated resentment may be expressed by the son toward one or both parents through indirect expression such as burglary, thefts or other crimes that would bring disgrace on the family, without the offender or his parents recognizing the motivation of revenge as the origin of his crimes. He may speak only in the highest terms of his parents and later express regret that he has brought shame upon them. The parents are not wealthy and have themselves gone without in order to provide their son with a new car every few years and to help him financially.

Their son remains dependent on them long after he should be supporting himself and remains a child who never grows up. He is encouraged to stay at home but is discouraged from marriage, as his parents do not consider any girl good enough for him. Through direct and indirect pressure, the son becomes no more than a puppet who dances to the tune of his parents. This puppet seems unable to resist parental demands and cannot voice his resentment to parents who have done so much for him at such great personal sacrifice. Both father and mother work long hours to finance a college education that goes on for years as the son changes his educational goals to avoid the unpleasant prospect of earning a living for himself. He expresses his resentment in devious ways without awareness of his hostility toward them.

In one such case, a young man selected television stations as targets for burglary. His explanation was that he stole equipment to build his own television station, yet he had more expensive equipment than he could ever use. His father owned a television station and it must have been awkward for him at the annual convention of television station operators to meet colleagues who had been pilfered by his son.

It appeared from the psychiatric evaluation that his father placed a great emphasis on intellectual achievement yet favored a younger son who was mentally retarded. He could recognize this son's handicap and respond accordingly. His other son was handicapped by short stature, but his father failed to recognize and respond to this son's psychological needs for support and reassurance. This son obtained both revenge and attention through his burglaries.

One should be cautious in drawing conclusions from such case examples, as unusual childhood experiences do not inevitably lead to deviant behavior or to psychological disorder.

THE VICTIM'S ROLE

Opportunity makes the thief.

Victims contribute to burglary and theft by tempting the thief. The manager who walks out of his office leaving a bank deposit bag on his desk, the store owner who places valuable merchandise close to the entrance door, the jeweler who leaves expensive watches and rings on display behind a plate glass window after he closes his store at night and the car owner who leaves his car unlocked with the keys in the ignition are all behaving imprudently. It is not chance alone that leads to their victimization.

PSYCHIATRIC DISORDERS AND CRIME

Sociopathic personality (antisocial personality), alcoholism and drug dependence are the major psychiatric disorders associated with crime. In a study of 223 male parolees, Guze found that these disorders were the only ones found more frequently among criminal offenders than in the general population (4). Among 66 female parolees, there was also a high incidence of hysteria, which was usually associated with sociopathy.

The Sociopathic Personality

The sociopathic or psychopathic personality has many faces, and it would not be possible to paint his picture with a few quick strokes of the brush. Often he looks much younger than his years, and he continues to have a youthful appearance in middle age. He may have a quiet but impressive air of authority;

it is not surprising that the sociopathic burglar can gain entrance
to restricted areas without proper security identification. Such
is his bearing and self-confidence that even if officials have
doubts, they are reluctant to question this stranger in their midst.

If he is questioned, his superior intelligence, quick imagina-
tion, sense of humor and remarkable capacity for falsehood
may carry the day. Not all sociopaths are so quick-witted and
have the same appearance and manner. Far from inspiring
confidence, some may arouse an immediate feeling of distrust so
that they are greeted with the wary suspicion usually reserved
for the ingratiating used car salesman.

Even though they may make a good initial impression, they
are social misfits who from an early age prove to be a problem
to themselves as well as to society. They may make friends
easily, but their demanding, self-centered behavior does not
encourage prolonged acquaintances. The devil-may-care attitude
of the sociopath, his witty and devastating attacks on the establishment, his generosity (with other people's money) and his
adventurous life appeal to many persons. Many a young girl
swept off her feet by the sociopath has been subjected to a
kaleidoscopic pattern of marital experiences: unexpected generosity and sudden loss of financial support, as well as devoted
attention and cruel indifference. The children from such a
marriage suffer the same inconsistent relationships.

The sociopath's emotional attachments, whether heterosexual
or homosexual, are often fleeting and superficial. A friendship
of a few days' or even a few hours' duration with some chance
tavern acquaintance of dubious character may result in an
impulsive marriage. His incapacity for love is combined with
great sensitivity where his own feelings are concerned. Rebuff
or injustice may lead to extravagant expression of feeling. Rejection by a wife or girl friend may arouse great resentment, distress
and even attempts at suicide. Yet, reconciliation is quickly
followed by reappearance of inconsiderate, unfriendly or assaul-
tive behavior.

The sociopath's lack of feeling for others may contribute to
merciless physical assaults or even sadistic murders when confronted in a burglary. Sympathy for members of minority groups
may reflect his perception of himself as an outsider. Unexpected

concern for the elderly, the young or the sick may be derived from memories of childhood suffering and defenselessness against exploitation or brutality.

Sociopaths constitute an individualistic rebellious group, intolerant of discipline and of the legal and social restrictions of everyday life. Many of them use drugs and resort to the excessive use of alcohol. The sociopath may boast of his criminal exploits, indeed he may exaggerate them. On the other hand, he may conceal his antisocial behavior, and his family may join in the conspiracy of silence. He may be very convincing in his efforts to escape responsibility for some criminal act known to the interviewer. He claims that he purchased the property from a stranger in a bar and had no idea it was stolen; the victim made a false identification; the detective fabricated evidence to clear the crime; the judge was prejudiced against him. An act of assault is blamed on threatening or insulting remarks by the victim, but closer study shows that the sociopath initiated the verbal conflict that ended in violence.

Speech, it has been said, has been given to man to conceal his thoughts, and the sociopath can conceal unpleasant facts through vague ambiguous statements and clever avoidance of direct questions so that the questioner is not aware that he has been sidetracked in his inquiry. He is not readily detected in falsehood because of his remarkable capacity for conveying an impression of candor and sincerity. Some sociopaths, however, tell the most extravagant and improbable tales.

The lack or apparent absence of guilt or remorse regarding criminal and other antisocial behavior is a striking feature of the sociopath. Even when these feelings are present, they may not be utilized in the control of behavior. Claims that the sociopath has no conscience are not supported by adequate clinical evidence. The conscience may be weak and inconsistent or may exhibit little control over antisocial impulses, but it is never absent. Its function seems to be directed toward making sure the sociopath is punished for his transgressions either through acts likely to lead to his arrest or through his pattern of self-destructive behavior.

Expression of feelings of guilt and remorse, often fleeting, may be for the purpose of avoiding punishment or reducing its severity. Judges are sometimes very responsive to a felon's acknowledgments of error and promises of better behavior in the future, but the sociopath shows slight sense of responsibility and cannot be relied upon to honor his obligations. His impulsivity is such that while free on bond, he may quickly bring to naught carefully prepared plans for probation rather than a prison sentence. One sociopath said that he would write his biography for publication under the title *The Impulsive Years.*

His impulsivity, unwillingness to take orders, absenteeism, irresponsibility and lack of persistence of effort contribute to his erratic employment record. He conceals his frequent job changes, but his poor work record can be obtained by insisting upon a detailed chronological list of jobs with dates of onset and termination. Jobs that include a great variety of activities, independence of action, travel, publicity and other rewards important to the sociopath may be held for many years.

Sociopaths are in many respects immature, and their childlike character includes egocentricity, great dependency on others and a tendency to blame the world for all their misfortunes. Insatiable demands for attention and approval; lack of concern for the welfare of others or alternatively failure to make other than impulsive sacrifices for others; and an all-pervading selfishness testify to the egocentricity of the sociopath. The self-centered behavior may hide for a time behind a mask of selflessness. Apparent modesty and desire to avoid publicity may be carried to such extremes that one is reminded of the nymph who flees only in the hope of being pursued.

Despite the facade of fierce independence, the sociopath remains extremely dependent on others, but he cannot admit this handicap, least of all to himself. Like a child called to account for some misdeed, he points the finger of blame elsewhere. Any failure in life, loss of a job, financial reverse, divorce or arrest for a criminal act is almost invariably attributed to an unjust employer, heartless wife, incompetent teachers, unloving parents or society in general. Curiously, even though the sociopath may have good reason to blame his parents for neglect or childhood abuse, he may persist in speaking of them almost exclusively in loving and grateful terms. This may occur even though he has murdered one of them.

As a rule, sociopaths do not benefit from the type of treatment presently available in mental health centers, and they seem unable to profit from experience including punishment. In their criminal behavior as well as in other walks of life, they show a lack of judgment and foresight that is almost beyond belief. A sociopathic burglar and murderer altered nine out of ten stolen articles so that they could not be recognized by the owner, then pawned only that article he had not bothered to disguise. Yet the sociopath may score well on intelligence tests.

This finding is a little overplayed in the literature. Who would ever claim that high intelligence prevents or protects one from doing stupid things? It so happens that the sociopath's stupidities emerge in the web of crime, whereas mine appear in the web of psychiatry, someone else's in the web of business, or art, or science or law enforcement. Often stupid acts suggest high intelligence. Sometimes one says that only a highly intelligent person could have been that stupid!

Bernard Shaw once said that we judge an artist by his highest moments and the criminal by his lowest. In brief descriptions of the sociopath, listing the abnormal aspects of his character and behavior provides a distorted picture that should be counterbalanced by mention of his capacity, however ill-sustained, for mature behavior. We should be aware that the sociopath's unreliability and irresponsibility do not show themselves in every situation. He is not dependably undependable.

Disregard for the truth is not seen in his every statement. Not all his checks bounce, not all his obligations are neglected and not all his promises remain unfulfilled. Impulsivity does not preclude self-restraint. He may be cruel, but he may also be compassionate. He may be in jail, or he may never have come in conflict with the law.

Sociopathy begins in childhood or adolescence, blooms in early adult life and fades away after the age of forty. Some sociopaths continue their criminal careers beyond this age, but many gradually acquire as they grow older a sense of social responsibility independent of treatment or punishment. All too often the sociopath's life has all the inexorability of a Greek tragedy, although the hero of Greek tragedy is not capricious, self-centered, antisocial, impulsive and irresponsible. These character traits bring their own reward. Fortune may smile on the sociopath for a time, but the blows he sends out against society often recoil on his own head, and his tenuous personal attachments provide little protection when ill winds blow.

REFERENCES

1. Batchelor, I. R. C.: Revision of *Henderson and Gillespie's Textbook of Psychiatry*, 10th ed. London, Oxford U Pr, 1969.
2. Fenichel, O.: *The Collected Papers of Otto Fenichel*, Second series. New York, Norton, 1954.
3. Guttmacher, M. S.: *Sex Offenses*. New York, Norton, 1951.
4. Guze, S. B.: *Criminality and Psychiatric Disorders*. New York, Oxford U Pr, 1976.
5. Halleck, S. L.: *Psychiatry and the Dilemmas of Crime*. New York, Har-Row with Hoeber Medical Books, 1967.
6. Johnson, A. M., and Szurek, S. A.: The genesis of antisocial acting out in children and adults. *Psychoanal Quart*, 21:323, 1952.
7. Macdonald, J.M.: *Psychiatry and the Criminal*, 3rd ed. Springfield, Thomas, 1976.
8. Macdonald, J. M.: *Rape: Offenders and Their Victims*, (3rd Ptg). Springfield, Thomas, 1971.
9. Stott, D. H.: *Studies of Troublesome Children*. London, Tavistock, 1966.
10. Walsh, Marilyn E.: *The Fence: A New Look at the World of Property Theft*. Westport, Connecticut, Greenwood, 1977.
11. Warren, M. A.: Taking the bite out of burglaries. *FBI Law Enforcement Bulletin*, May, 1971.
12. Wittels, Fritz: Kleptomania and other psychopathic crimes. *J Crim Psychopathol*, 4:205, 1942.
13. Wolfgang, M. D.: *Patterns in Criminal Homicide*. Philadelphia, U of Pa, 1958.
14. Wootton, Barbara: *Social Science and Social Pathology*. London, George Allen & Unwin Ltd., 1959.

CHAPTER 5

VICTIMS OF BURGLARY AND THEFT

*He that shows his purse
bribes the thief.*

—*Proverb*

I<small>N MANY CRIMES</small> such as assault, armed robbery and homicide, the victim is almost invariably confronted by his assailant, but in the crime of burglary, the victim seldom encounters the person who steals his property. There are those awkward occasions when the householder returns home unexpectedly or the night watchman surprises the safe cracker at work, but for the most part, victim and offender do not come together at the scene of the crime.

When the thief has a lawful right to be in the location where he plies his trade he may come face-to-face with his victim, but usually he does not stand out in the crowd and his intention is to commit the crime without the knowledge of his victim. Even the pickpocket, who must touch his victim, does so without arousing suspicion.

VICTIM-OFFENDER RELATIONSHIPS

The majority of burglaries are committed by persons who are not known by the victims. Reliable statistics on victim-offender relationships are not available, as so many burglaries and thefts are not cleared by arrest. Despite the incidence of theft by employees, it is likely that the majority of thefts are also by persons who are not known to the victims. In a minority of burglaries and thefts, the offenders are neighbors, relatives, friends or acquaintances of the victims.

L<small>OVERS'</small> Q<small>UARRELS</small>. Boyfriend-girl friend disagreements may lead to retaliation by the rejected party in the form of burglary or theft. Spite rather than profit is the motive. The angry boyfriend may plunder the girl friend's apartment and vandalize her clothing, stuffed animals or dolls and his gifts to her. One boyfriend ransacked his girl's apartment, destroying items of sentimental value, breaking her television, urinating in her bed, pouring tomato juice on her furniture and on leaving without any of her property, nailed her screen door shut. The resentful jilted girl friend may repossess gifts that she had given to her boyfriend and may vent her anger on the man's prized possession, burning or otherwise damaging his car.

On-again, off-again relationships may be punctuated by charges of theft. A man drove a van into the police headquarters parking lot and asked the police to take custody of it. He explained that the van, which contained expensive items, belonged to his rich girl friend, and he was afraid that she would accuse him of theft when she realized that he had left her. This had happened on a previous occasion.

Casual sexual liaisons may lead to theft, as in the case of a young man who met a girl in a restaurant and took her to his motel room. While he was sleeping, she took his wallet and left in his car.

Burglary may also occur, as in the case of a young woman who showed a man she met in a bar the small specialty shop where she worked. She claimed that after they left the shop, he kidnapped her at gunpoint, took her to a motel, raped her and stole her money and the keys to the shop. She also claimed that she did not wake up until the next day because he had placed drugs in her drink at the motel. Her claims of kidnapping and armed robbery were false, because the evidence of witnesses showed that she had been buying him drinks and that she went to the motel willingly. However, her casual acquaintance probably committed the burglary or arranged for someone else to do so using the keys stolen from her while she was sleeping.

PROSTITUTES. Prostitutes have long been known to steal wallets from their clients. In recent years, there has been a dramatic increase in the number of male prostitutes. Wealthy men and older men who prefer not to go to gay bars will pick up young male prostitutes and take them to their apartments.

The prostitute will leave with or return later for such expensive items as stereo equipment. The owner of a penthouse apartment made three auto-theft reports within a month and one burglary report. All the suspects were homosexual prostitutes.

ACQUAINTANCES. Friends are not always what they seem to be. A man who invited a friend to dinner excused himself during the meal and borrowed his guest's car to run an errand. When the friend returned home later that evening, he found that someone had broken into his home and stolen his television set and cash. The following day, the television set was left at a pawn shop by the dinner host.

One evening two young men went to a friend's place of business and started to load onto their pickup truck an old stainless steel bench that had been left outside the business after a remodeling project. They thought their friend no longer had any use for it, and they made no attempt to conceal their presence at the scene, leaving on the lights of their vehicle, slamming the truck doors and so on. The friend, who lived nearby, called the police, and even after discovering they were his friends, he still filed charges against them. He did say, though, that he would have let them go if they had agreed to pay for the bench.

SONS AND DAUGHTERS. Offspring may help themselves to small amounts of money from their parents, but the theft of a television set, other expensive items and jewelry worth hundreds or thousands of dollars is not frequent. These thefts do occur, usually by an adult son addicted to narcotics and in need of a fix. "When I was strung out I stole stuff from anyone I knew." An adolescent or adult son or daughter with a deep-seated grievance toward the parents, often associated with resentment toward a favored sibling, may steal from or arrange for someone else to burglarize the family home. Children who resent a new stepfather or stepmother may steal from that person.

VULNERABLE VICTIMS

Persons who live in high-crime areas are more likely to be victims of burglary. Persons in low-cost housing projects in such areas are sometimes at the mercy of roving gangs of young thugs. These gangs know the movements of residents and can commit burglaries when no one is at home. Any witnesses are quickly intimidated. Both victims and witnesses are acutely aware that the police are seldom in the area, but the gangs are there all the time.

Elderly or physically handicapped persons are ready victims for purse snatchers. Bedridden patients in nursing homes can do little to protect themselves from theft of their rings and other valuables by unscrupulous employees or visitors. One burglar had no hesitation in breaking into a community home for blind paraplegics. When an interstate bus driver stopped to aid a driver who was injured in an auto accident, one of the bus passengers stole a rifle from the involved auto. Looters are quick to steal from persons seriously injured in railroad wrecks or other disasters. Intoxicated persons are ready victims for thieves.

Ideal victims in the eyes of burglars and thieves are those religious groups that do not lock the doors of their mission houses, meet at regular hours for prayers and are reluctant to prosecute persons who steal from them.

Employers are especially vulnerable to theft by employees who are familiar with the operations of the business and the security measures. Stores that place expensive items on open display close to the store entrance makes themselves vulnerable.

REACTIONS TO BURGLARY AND THEFT

Today, in some parts of large cities, you know you are entering the battlefield when you go out on the streets. Areas with high crime rates are commonly referred to as *combat zones* by the police. But most citizens feel safe in their own homes, which they regard as their castles, where no one, neither criminal nor officer of the law, may enter uninvited. William Pitt, Earl of Chatham, in a speech to the House of Lords said it well: "The poorest man may in his cottage bid defiance to all the force of the Crown. It may be frail, its roof may shake, the wind may blow through it, the storms may enter, the rain may enter—but the King of England cannot enter, all his forces dare not cross the threshold of the ruined tenement!"

It is understandable that citizens have a sense of outrage on returning to their home and finding it ransacked. They are shocked by the crude violation of their privacy, and they have a sickening feeling that they will never again feel safe in their homes. Tiny animals will fight to their death to preserve their territory, and persons attacked or threatened in their homes are perhaps more likely to fight than on the streets, where they only have to defend their wallets. A victim of a burglary, in an open letter to burglars, writes of her momentary impulse to resort to violence.

Having spent my childhood in a clean but poorly furnished home, I set out in marriage to make up for this by decorating our abode in an attractive and cheerful manner. My furniture is comfortable and tastefully coordinated; the wall hangings are equally eye-appealing. My housework and leisure time are made pleasant by up-to-the-minute appliances.

If you want all this, boys, you better bring a moving van. Pull it right up to my apartment door next time. No one will notice or question you—or will they?

You already have taken what could be carried away in a sack.

How much did you get for my string of pearls given to me by mother more than thirty years ago? Did the love that permeated them enhance their value?

My late husband's watch was cold metal when you snatched it. He often laid it on his nightstand, and I'd feel the warmth of his body still on it, giving it momentary life.

And that gold wedding band with the Hebrew lettering—King Solomon's lovely: "I am my beloved's and my beloved is mine." How much did that net you?

After the police dusted for your prints, I was left alone, by choice, to try to put myself together. I scrubbed your presence away with soap and water, angry but not afraid.

You did frighten me two years ago when you broke in and took my son's photography equipment and my color television set. It wasn't so much what you took—how can one become sentimental over things that are so easily replaced? What upset me so much was that my secure home was intruded upon. It took me a long time to return to normal and lose the fear that you might return.

And return you did, last week. This time my reaction is not one of fear, but livid anger. I'm mad at the world, at my vulnerability, at a society where even things under lock and key are not safe—and I'm very angry with you!

Did I say I'm not afraid? Yes, I am—not of you, but of myself and the way I shouted to the police—"If you were to find them now and bring them here, I'd kill them!"

Do you know what disturbs me about that threat? I really, really meant it. For one insane moment I was capable of committing a crime. If I'd had a gun, I might have used it, thereby stooping to your gutter level. No, no guns in my house, thank you.

You took my precious possessions and you stole one thing more: my former self, the non-violent, secure, trusting person I used to be. I am sad—depressed—here in my fortress, now secured with double bolts and a burglar alarm" (1).

Appeals to the conscience of the burglar may relieve some emotional pressure from the victim who is crying "is there no justice?" In the face of vandalism and thoughtless theft of objects of sentimental value, such appeals to the burglar are likely to pass unheard. The victim's spirit is not improved by learning from the police officer that the courts are unlikely to impose punishment unless the offender has had prior convictions. Victims would be further upset if they knew how few burglaries are cleared by arrest of the offender.

A family that had left a relatively crime-free rural area, where car doors were only locked on Halloween, on coming to the Denver metropolitan area, suffered so many burglaries and thefts in a short period that the youngest son expressed fears that he would be the next to be stolen.

Some persons are not unduly distressed on learning that they have been victims of burglary and theft, but there may be a delayed reaction of shock and anger. Not everyone is alert to the fact that an unlocked or open front door may indicate the presence of burglars within. They may assume that a member of the family arrived home earlier than expected and left the door unlocked, but the presence of pry marks or a broken lock surely should be sufficient to show the need to leave immediately and seek help. In the following example, a young woman who did not heed the warning signs was maced with tear gas and later threatened by a burglar.

At approximately 7:45 AM, I was about to enter my place of employment, and I discovered that the rear door lock was broken, and I knew right then that we had been burglarized. I entered and turned on all the lights and discovered that our money tray had been placed on my station and it was empty. I went up to the front reception area to call the police. As I turned the corner into the reception area and started to go behind the desk, I saw three men standing on the other side of the desk. They just stood there for several seconds without moving and I was very scared, and just kept looking at them. Two of the suspects turned their faces away from me, but the third suspect just kept staring at me, so I just kept looking at him.

Then all of the suspects started walking slowly around the desk, and I started backing away from them very slowly. I just kept staring at them, and got a real good look at one of the suspects, and I feel that I would be able to recognize him if I ever saw him again. He had very weird eyes, very protruding, appeared to be almost like large bubbles. When they finally got around the desk, he (bubble eyes) sprayed my face with mace. All three parties then walked out the back door, and I called the police. Later that same day, at approximately 7:30 PM, I received a telephone call from a male voice stating "I know you saw me, and I saw you, if you say anything I will see that you regret it!"

RESISTANCE

Victims who encounter burglars and thieves either flee from the scene of the crime or respond by using a weapon, fighting, chasing the offender, calling for help, talking the offender into surrender or at least into halting his crime.

USE OF FIREARMS. Death at the hands of the victim is an occupational hazard of burglary, and one of the burglar's greatest fears is the homeowner who does not answer his doorbell, thereby giving the burglar the impression that the house is vacant, but instead lies in wait with a gun for anyone who breaks in, as in the following example of a burglar who was shot:

The first indication was an early knock on the front door, then the doorbell rang two times. I did not answer. The one that rang the doorbell then went across the street and was talking to several others and was drinking from a bottle. I watched for a while and then two men came across to my doorstep and rang the bell again. I was silent in the bedroom with the gun in my hand.

They began to jimmy the window that was open three to four inches, then I heard the screen rip and the window was then opened wide. The only conversation I could make out or remember was "Wow, a big color (TV), this is too much, get out of the way, Joe, hurry up and open the door." Then one of the men entered the house through the window.

At this point I stepped out and I yelled, "Freeze." He yelled, "——you" and moved. I fired. He moved to the window and as he was leaving I fired two times again. He limped across the street and I called the police.

There is no open season on burglars, and householders who shoot burglars may be arrested and charged in court as in the following example:

Bill Walker and his family were at dinner when a houseguest noticed four persons walk across the street to the bushes in front of Walker's home. Walker's nine-year-old daughter saw them and began to cry. After Walker and his houseguest went outside and did not see anything, Walker told his wife to call the police and obtained his rifle from a closet. When he went outside again he saw three figures carrying a television set from his neighbor's home. The figures dropped the television set and ran.

Worried about the welfare of the neighbor, a woman, Walker knocked on her front door. There was no answer and as he walked to the back of the neighbor's home, another figure confronted him in the darkness, made a threatening gesture and said, "Don't touch me . . . or I'll kill you." Walker shouted at him to stop and fired one shot. The figure kept running. Down the street the police found the body of a high school student who had died from a gunshot wound of the back.

Although many items were missing from the neighbor's home, the prosecutor claimed that the killing was not justifiable as the student had been drinking and because of his drinking was incapable of forming a specific intent to steal, and thus, was not guilty of a burglary and was not a fleeing felon. Walker was convicted of voluntary manslaughter and sentenced to a year in jail and five years probation. A Court of Appeals concluded that the jury should have been instructed that, as a matter of law, the victim had committed a burglary, and ruled that Walker should be given a new trial.

It requires courage and a cool head to apprehend a burglar at gunpoint.

I was in my bedroom lying down when I heard some noise like glass breaking, so I opened my back door to look outside. I heard some noise in the basement apartment next door so I went back to my bedroom to get my shirt and shoes, also my .38. Then I went back out and saw this man running up the stairs from the basement apartment. I told him to freeze and to get up against the wall and spread his legs and arms against the wall. I looked where he came from to see if anyone else was there. He kept trying to turn around so I grabbed him by the collar and pushed him against the wall.

He then kept trying to talk me into letting him go. The landlord's daughter came outside and I told her to call the cops. He kept trying to resist and talk me into letting him go. Then he told me that there is another guy downstairs, that has a gun and he didn't want to get involved in a murder. So I turned him around and faced him toward the stairway. Around this time a couple of neighbors came around and they tried to assist me, and that's when the detective came and put the handcuffs on him.

Many homeowners purchase weapons for protection against burglars, but a firearm can be as frightening to the owner as to the burglar.

A woman heard the door of her home open and thought it was her daughter who was expected home from school. She called to her daughter but there was no answer, and she heard heavy footsteps. At the time she was cleaning a cupboard in which her husband's gun was stored. Although deathly afraid of guns, she grabbed the gun but she had no idea whether it was a revolver or an automatic pistol. She had fired it once but was scared so badly that she had never touched it again until this time. She saw the burglar in the kitchen.

"He was just standing there. I was frozen to the floor. There wasn't a word exchanged. It was like I was hypnotized, it didn't seem like I was looking at him. I didn't know what I would do if he came at me. Finally he ran. I went to the door after he ran out and locked it. He didn't go through the gate, he jumped over the fence. That's when the crying and hysteria began. I found how inadequate I was because I was afraid if I put the gun down it would go off. Even when the police came I could not let go of the gun."

Tragedies have resulted from the use of firearms by persons fearful of burglars. Police officers responding to the scene of a burglary in progress or on a report of a prowler have been shot by nervous citizens. Detectives in plain clothes are more likely to be mistaken for burglars than police officers in uniform, but the latter have also been shot by trigger-happy citizens. A Denver police officer on patrol in the early hours of the morning noticed that a tavern door was open, and he stopped to check the building:

The door was wide open, it looked like it had been left open. I called on the radio, told them where I was and that I had an open door and was checking it out. The dispatcher asked for a cover car. He was there by the time I got back to the door. We got inside and we were checking the basement area. Everything checked OK. There was a door at the top of the stairs, it went to the main part of the bar.

When my head was level with the floor, I pulled on the bottom of the door, which was raised above the floor, a couple of times but it wouldn't budge. I went to the top of the stairs, I was cautious and walked close to the wall. I pulled on the door one more time but it still wouldn't open. I took two steps back and turned and told the sergeant it was locked.

The next thing I heard the explosion, it knocked me down the steps and I told the sergeant I was hit. I was turned sideways, head looking back facing away from the door. I can't say I felt the bullet hit. It was that weird sense that something had happened. I could feel the wetness in my shirt. A few minutes later a burning sensation started. We had no idea who it was. Later I learned it was the bar owner who was sleeping upstairs. He said he'd been burglarized before and had no idea who was in the basement.

It was a .45 automatic, it hit my upper right chest and went down through the liver. I was completely out of it for two days, they removed about a third of my liver. The bar owner was charged with reckless endangerment and the DA took a deferred judgment because he had a clean record. I always thought I was cautious. You're on your toes until you get back in the car. After I got out of the hospital and back to work again, the only thing I did differently was I bought a bullet-proof vest. I wear it faithfully (3).

Some citizens are very reckless indeed in their use of firearms.

A sixty-six-year-old woman reported to police that she watched a man break into her garage, then leave with a battery charger valued at $23. She said that she tried to shoot him when he came out of the garage, but the gun did not fire. The gun was an automatic pistol and she did not know how to use it. The detective explained to her that she could shoot a suspect only if her life was in danger but she said that she intended to learn how to use the gun and was going to shoot the "son of a bitch" the next time he breaks in her garage. Precinct police officers were warned to be very cautious when investigating any prowler or burglar calls at her home because she was armed and dangerous.

Relatives and friends have been shot in mistake for burglars. In Philadelphia, a bus driver returned home from work one morning and was told by his wife that she heard a noise in the basement. Armed with a revolver, he went downstairs to investigate and when he saw movement in a dark corner, he turned and fired, fatally wounding his eleven-year-old daughter. She had missed her school bus and had returned home to obtain the city bus fare.

USE OF OTHER WEAPONS. Knives or blunt objects are also used by victims. A young girl held a thief at bay by waving a bicycle chain. When a burglar kicked open the door of a house, the owner armed himself with a small wrought iron bench, which he used to clobber the burglar as he entered the bedroom. Burglars are vulnerable to attack while climbing through a window.

> About 1:30 AM, a woman, unable to sleep, was drinking a glass of milk in her living room when she saw a burglar pulling on the patio door. The man did not notice her as she was sitting in the room without any lights on. After a few minutes the burglar left the patio door and she could hear him trying to open the front door. She awakened her husband before telephoning the police. Meantime the burglar returned and threw rocks at the glass patio door, then ran a short distance away. He returned and threw two more rocks at the door but the glass did not break. He then attempted to enter through a bedroom window. The husband grabbed him as he was part way through the window, and his wife ran outside and grabbed his legs. The burglar was held in this position until the police arrived.

CHASING THE OFFENDER. This can lead to recovery of one's property as well as arrest of the thief.

> A twenty-seven-year-old woman arrived home to find a large rental van parked in front of her house. The van driver honked his horn repeatedly, and two men ran from the back of her house and jumped in the van. After asking her neighbor to call the police, the woman chased the rental van in her pickup truck. At one stage in the chase, she drove directly at the van, which, at the last moment, swerved off the road to avoid a direct collision.
>
> She followed the van, blowing the horn continuously until the van finally pulled over. The driver said, "OK lady, we'll give you your television set." While the burglars placed the set in her

truck she checked inside the van for anymore of her property. When the burglars tried to drive off around her pickup truck, the van became stuck in an irrigation ditch. She called the police from a nearby house and the men were arrested.

Shoplifters, often regarded as not being dangerous offenders, sometimes are quick to assault department store security officers. Two such officers, one male and one female, attempted to apprehend a man and a woman who had left the store with a man's suit hidden in a baby stroller. The male shoplifter struck the male security officer with his fists, threatened to cut him, and pulled off his belt and began striking the officer with the belt buckle. Both suspects were able to escape in a car.

Victims who pursue suspects should be prepared for action.

> I came home and saw my house in shambles. I got on the phone and called my brother. We followed some tracks in the snow to a neighbor's house. We waited around and we saw some guys in the bedroom. I saw my cameras and binoculars on the bed and went around front and busted in the front door. We went to the bedroom and busted in the bedroom door. We fought with the two guys in the bedroom for about ten minutes. We got all my stuff back and started walking out of the house and I remembered I forgot a camera. I went back into the house and he was loading a 30-30 rifle. I fought with him again and took the gun away from him. The next day a detective called and wanted to know how I got my stuff back.

Persons trained in physical combat do not always succeed in battle. A karate expert saw a man trying to break in his neighbor's patio door and decided to give the burglar a karate kick in the back. The burglar sensed his presence and ducked aside so that the karate expert's foot went through the plate glass, severing his Achilles' tendon.

There is a risk in chasing desperate thieves as a Denver city councilman discovered after he followed two youths who were breaking into his car in front of his home. He caught up with them five blocks from his home and ordered them to drop the police radio which they had stolen from his car. One youth dropped the radio, and the councilman went to fetch it when he noticed the other youth had a gun with a long barrel. Before the councilman could get back in his car, the youth fired three shots, hitting him in the right thigh and left ankle.

Death can come suddenly and unexpectedly for persons who chase burglars and thieves, as in the following example described by a witness.

> About midnight, Jack came down to the apartment and said that someone was stealing my roommate's cycle so we chased him down the street, and Dave drove his cycle down in front of the guy who was pushing the bike down the street. When I got around the corner I heard Dave say, "Don't move." Then I saw the guy pull a knife and move towards Dave and the guy kept on walking. Me and Jack caught him at the corner and put him down on the ground. We didn't know Dave was hurt so I flagged down a truck that was driving down the road and told them to call the police. A girl ran down to us and said Dave was bleeding bad so they got in the truck and went to call an ambulance. When we caught him he said a guy at Billy Jacks (tavern) said he wouldn't take the bike. I got the knife out of his right back pocket and we held him there until the police came.

The eighteen-year-old motorcycle thief later claimed that after the young man threatened to kill him and struck him twice in the head, he flipped open the 4-inch blade of his pocketknife and stabbed the victim in the chest. He felt his hand stop as he hit the victim and he then withdrew the knife. The victim looked at him, went to a kneeling position and then fell over on his back. Death came quickly from the single stab wound in the heart. This description of the stabbing conflicted with that of witnesses who said that the victim stood in front of his assailant with his palms facing outward in a nonthreatening manner and simply told the man to stop right there. The motorcycle thief was convicted of second degree murder and sentenced to twelve to fifteen years in the penitentiary.

No one is better acquainted with the risks of tackling a criminal offender than someone knowledgeable in the ways of criminals. A former armed robber and burglar, who had served many years in a state penitentiary, describes his reaction on surprising an auto thief hotwiring his car. "In my apartment house garage I saw a man sitting in my wife's sports car. I knew the thief would be fighting for his life, I would be fighting for a $6,000 car. It cost me $5 to put the wires back. He had a screwdriver in one hand, channel locks in the other. I told him it was a free ride."

REPORTING BURGLARY AND THEFT

Those victims of burglary and theft who report the crime to the police usually do so promptly. Sometimes the report is made only after the insurance company responsible for compensating the victim insists upon notification of the police. Delay in reporting may be due to delay in discovering the full extent of the loss. If the victim at first thinks he has only lost items of little value, he may not bother to take any action.

> A young woman carried a sack of groceries, which contained her purse, from her car to her apartment. She left the door ajar while she returned to the car for a second package. In this brief time someone entered her apartment and stole her purse in which were her identification cards, charge cards, and checkbook. She did not report the burglary until four days later when forged checks began coming to her bank. She suspected the only tenant at home on her floor on the day of the burglary. Department stores which had accepted her checks identified a picture of this person from a group of police photographs.

Dishonesty in Reports

The problem of false reports of burglary and theft is reviewed in Chapter 6. Reports of genuine crimes may include false statements, for example, the value of property stolen is exaggerated or additional items are falsely added to the list of stolen property. The motive is usually financial gain from an inflated insurance claim or from a greater rebate on income tax payments.

A home burglary is reported, but the husband and wife list only a few items missing. The next day they provide an additional list of stolen items, and the loss goes from $350 to over $13,000. A homeowner may not immediately note how many items are missing, but he is hardly likely to overlook the loss of two large color television sets, the only sets in the home, when he makes his first report to the patrolman. Furthermore, the detective checks with the patrolman who recalls seeing the two TV sets at the time he made the report.

The homeowner who has $1,000 hidden under the kitchen sink is likely to check and see whether this money is missing as soon as he finds out that someone has broken into his home. It always seems strange when persons in difficult financial circumstances take several days, following a burglary report, to discover the loss of large sums of money.

Persons in search of publicity or sympathy may also exaggerate their loss. Employees who neglected to lock the safe or the entrance door at the close of business may be most insistent that they did so. Victims of theft by a prostitute may wish to conceal the casual sexual relationship by reporting the loss of their wallet, but failing to mention the presence of this visitor to their hotel room.

Failure to Report Burglary and Theft

Reference has already been made in Chapter 1 to the study which showed that the burglary rate in the United States is three times greater than that reported in the *Uniform Crime Reports* of the FBI. The problem of unreported burglaries is well known to the police as their investigations often disclose such burglaries. Frequently, billfolds containing identification are returned to the police by the finders, but their theft had not been reported by the victims. A very distinctive watch valued at $3,500 recovered in a raid by a police antifencing unit had not been reported stolen despite its theft from a jewelry store five months earlier.

The national survey of the National Opinion Research Center on criminal victimization showed that the most important reason given for failure to report burglary was a belief that the police would not be effective (2). There is some basis for this belief as police in recent years have been successful in clearing by arrest less than 20 percent of the total burglary offenses reported to them. Lack of concern is a factor in failure to report when the financial loss is slight.

Fear of reprisal deters some victims from taking action when they suspect local youths with a reputation for violence. The victim's involvement in illegal behavior at the time of the burglary, such as illegal drug sales, discourages him from contacting the police. A narcotics dealer, the victim of a $6,000 burglary loss, did not notify the police. Another drug dealer did not report the loss of a package containing a large sum of money, nor did he sue the airline that could not deliver the package because of its theft. Similarly, men involved with prostitutes at the time of the theft of their wallets and other valuables often prefer to remain silent.

Women who are raped during a burglary or robbery may not report any of these crimes because of their shame and humiliation over the rape. Occasionally, the burglary is reported but not the rape. Visitors from another state may not report burglary or theft because they wish to avoid the expense and inconvenience of returning to testify at a trial. Some victims prefer to conduct their own investigations and take personal vengeance on the offenders.

In November, 1978 the FBI, investigating six murders believed linked to a burglary at the home of reputed Chicago crime syndicate leader Antony "Big Tuna" Accardo, searched Accardo's suburban River Forest home. FBI agents said they were looking for clues to the whereabouts of Accardo's houseman who disappeared a few days after he was questioned by a federal grand jury investigating the burglary and subsequent murders. The victims were all professional burglars and several were believed to have been involved in the burglary of Accardo's home. The Federal investigators wanted to determine what was taken in the burglary and why it provoked such swift and deadly revenge, but they did not disclose the results of the search.

Thefts from large businesses by employees may not be reported by fellow employees because they have also been involved in such thefts or they are afraid of or feel sorry for the thief as in the following example:

> In an unusual case, a man sold twenty-five videotapes to a secondhand store and then tried to buy them back the next day. This request aroused the store owner's suspicions and he notified the police. The tapes recorded a three day conference, and one of the speakers was a state legislator who was able to provide information pointing to the owner of the videotapes. Their theft had not been reported to the police, despite the fact that their value was much greater than the cost of the tapes, because they contained the recording of an important training seminar. An employee knew that the only person who could have taken the tapes was a janitor and she had questioned him the day after their disappearance. The janitor, realizing that he was under

suspicion, had attempted without success to buy the tapes back. The employee who failed to report the theft felt sorry for the janitor.

VICTIMS AND THE POLICE

The victims of burglary and theft sometimes contribute significantly to the identification of the offender, either through their independent investigation or because they happen to see their property or overhear some chance remark. The victim of a home burglary overheard the boys in the next house yelling at their mother, then she heard someone yell, "at least I don't take jewelry out of people's houses, get it out of the house or I'll kill you." This information helped the police obtain a search warrant which resulted in recovery of the stolen property.

Another victim of a house burglary was drinking in a bar when a stranger came in and offered to sell him a color television set which was in a car outside. The victim recognized his television set and said that he would buy it, but that he would have to call his brother to get the money. Instead he called the police.

A woman was asked by a neighbor to come and see her new baby. Once inside her neighbor's apartment she saw a television set that resembled one stolen from her home nine days earlier. She checked the serial number on the set and found that it was her set. Her neighbor said her boyfriend had given it to her.

A man discovered that many of his tools were missing from an apartment house storage locker. As his phone was out of order, he went to another apartment to ask if he could use their phone but was told by the man who came to the door that he had no phone. Some of the missing tools were visible on the floor of the apartment so he went to another apartment to call the police. Then he watched, with a shotgun in hand, the thief's apartment to make sure that no one left.

A young woman, about seven blocks from her home, saw a young girl walking on the street wearing a bracelet resembling one that had been stolen in a house burglary. She asked the girl for directions in order to have a closer look at the bracelet, and she noticed that the girl's male companion was wearing a ring taken from her home. After she saw the couple enter a nearby home she called the police.

Three months after a home burglary the victim discovered some of the missing items on display in an antique store. Fifty-eight pieces of jewelry were recovered on a search warrant. Twelve further items were recovered from a bank safety deposit box rented by the store owner.

The victim of an apartment house burglary saw another tenant wearing one of the dresses taken in the burglary. She confronted the juvenile suspect who told her "You're full of shit." Then she made the mistake of going to the suspect's apartment where she was told, "All right whitey, we're going to do a number on you" and she was struck several times, then shoved on the floor. Her head struck a drum set and she suffered an eye injury that permanently impaired her vision.

A burglary victim saw a neighbor youth carrying a crowbar which had green marks on it. Entry into the victim's home had been made by forcing open a door which was painted green, so the victim went to the youth's home where he found his television set. The youth claimed that he had bought the set two months earlier from a stranger on the street, but the set had been stolen only a few days previously.

Some victims, after reporting the crime to the police, take the law into their own hands, telephoning the suspect and impersonating the investigating detective by using his name and title, or calling on the suspect with gun in hand.

In a $12,000 burglary the victim refused to give the detective the name of an employee who might have knowledge of the burglar's identity. Later the victim told the detective that he did not want any further police action as he had gone to the employee's apartment and recovered his property. A friend of the suspected burglar told the detective that the victim had drawn a handgun on entering the suspect's apartment.

Another victim after reporting a burglary to the police did some investigating on his own and found out the name of the burglar. He confronted the burglar in front of a tavern and demanded payment. When this was not forthcoming he tried to force the burglar at gunpoint to get in the trunk of his car for delivery to the police. There was a scuffle and when the burglar ran across the street he fired one shot at him. The burglar filed charges of armed robbery but the two men later agreed to drop charges against one another.

A man suspected of theft told police that his employer "pulled a gun on me and told me that he was going to shoot my ass for stealing those TVs and cameras. I told him 'yes, OK,' and then left the shop." His employer, who made a tape recording of the "confession" for the police, said that he had used a toy gun.

Victims who do not cooperate with the police include persons with negative attitudes toward law enforcement officers ("I don't want any pigs in my house." "The country would be better off without police"), persons who are themselves involved in illegal activity or who for some reason fear the consequences of a criminal investigation.

"A white girl from a wealthy family, who reported the theft of a $500 fur coat from a bar patronized almost exclusively by blacks, told a detective that she would not cooperate further in the investigation because she did not want the police to go to her home as she was fearful that her parents would learn that she had a black boyfriend."

Apparently cooperative victims may in fact be obstructing the criminal investigation. For example, a victim fearful of reprisal by a neighborhood burglar states that the burglar was not included in a group of police mug shots. Yet when she looks at the picture of the burglar who broke in her home she becomes visibly upset and at this time asks "Now what happens if I identify him?" After being told that she might have to testify in court, she states with undue emphasis that the burglar's photograph was not in the group shown to her.

Refusal to Prosecute or Testify

Victims who help the police in their investigation are sometimes unwilling to prosecute or testify. Disgust with repeated postponement of the trial to suit the convenience of the defendant is a factor, especially when the victim has to appear in court each time the case is set down for trial. Lack of confidence in the judicial system also contributes to this problem. A victim in a housing project said he would not be a witness as "I had been one before, and everytime the burglar goes free on probation or some other program, and I end up with broken windows and losing money while in court."

Fear of reprisal deters some victims from prosecution. A department store refused to prosecute a shoplifter for the theft of items valued at $154 unless the home address of the store detective was removed from the police report. Victims and witnesses have good reason to fear harrassment by criminal defendants. A prisoner in the county jail on a charge of burglary telephoned a victim, after obtaining her name through the court records.

> He said this is BD, you don't know me but the police came to my job a few days ago and arrested me and I am here in jail and I want you to help me. I said "I don't know what you are talking about." He said he had been told there had been a burglary at my home and he would be willing to replace anything that had been lost and be willing to pay any amount of money I felt would compensate for any amount of inconvenience this may have caused. I asked where he had gotten my name and phone number, he said from the police.
>
> He said he had a wife and child and they would not have food on the table while he was in jail. I told him my husband was home and I would discuss it with him and he said he would hold. I went to my other phone and called the police. They said it was not possible for anyone to call from the jail. They said they would send a car out. I went back to the other phone. BD was waiting and I told him I didn't believe he was calling from the jail. It was my fear that he was calling from nearby and if I refused to drop charges, he would come to my house.
>
> He again went through the pleading of you can help me get out of here. I will pay you for your inconvenience, whatever amount you say. He said his wife and child needed him at home to earn money for their food. Again I said I didn't, couldn't believe he was calling from the jail. He said he would let me talk to the guard. A man answered hello and said he was an officer at the county jail.
>
> I asked him if he was aware his inmate had called a victim and offered money to drop charges. He said he thought I was the inmate's attorney. I told him how angry I was that this could happen. He said they would mark his card so that it would not happen again. I called his public defender and he said he would see that it would not happen again. That evening BD made another telephone call and again went through requests to drop charges saying he would pay restitution in any amount I wanted. He said the only way he could get out of jail was if I dropped charges. He said he did not burglarize my house or anyone else's

house but he was still willing to pay whatever I would want to drop the charges.

I questioned how he was able to call me again. He said the guards had changed shifts and he told the guards I was his aunt. . . . I hung up and called the detective bureau.

A victim of burglary, when asked if she would be willing to testify on two burglars aged thirteen and fourteen, replied, "Hell no, their mother already told me that she would kick my ass and they threatened to burn me out if I talked to the police." One victim gave as a reason for not prosecuting, "If I leave one night, I'll come home and my place will be torched." Another victim refused to testify because his father was killed in a burglary.

On the day she was to testify in court a woman received a telephone call warning her, "Just remember your kid walks to school." The juvenile suspect had been arrested fourteen times previously for burglary and each case was dismissed because the victim or witness refused to testify. A burglar who was acquitted because no witnesses appeared in court to testify at his trial told a police officer, "I've got a reputation that people know if a guy bugs me I'll kill him." Another suspect told a witness whom he wished to discourage from testifying, "With the court system the way it is, I'll be out in no time and get you."

The day after a witness identified a burglar, he was working in his liquor store when the burglar walked in and poked a finger in his chest. "If I go to jail for this, I'll kill you, I'll blow your ——— head off. You better make sure I get acquitted of this thing. You better tell the judge that I was just walking down the alley, that I wasn't breaking in, or I'll ——— you up and your wife too."

Threats or even assaults on victims may not be revealed to the police, and in these cases the victims give other reasons for refusing to testify. Occasionally, bribes are used to silence a victim or witness. The bribe may be disguised as payment for property stolen, but the amount paid is far above the value of the items taken in the burglary or theft.

The victim's interest in the criminal investigation and prosecution may diminish after his stolen property is recovered. The victim of a house burglary by four juveniles wanted to know if she could drop charges on those juveniles whose parents made restitution.

> When an employee suspected of a $600 theft was arrested in California, the company owner refused to cooperate in extradition proceedings, claiming he could not make a positive identification of the suspect from a photograph provided by the sheriff in California. He said that he had already been paid the missing money by the bonding company and he was not interested in pursuing the matter further.
>
> The company supervisor of a chain of gasoline stations said his primary responsibility was to get back $1,200 stolen by a station manager, and if he was jailed, they would not get the money back. The manager was permitted to return to his job, and the company refused to prosecute him after he agreed to repay the $1,200.
>
> Two days after a warant was issued for the arrest of a family "friend" for the theft of $400, the victim called to say that he had found the money under a pillow where he had left it. This was considered extremely unlikely as the victim had made a very thorough search of his home before calling the police to report the theft. It is likely that the suspect heard about the warrant for his arrest and quickly returned the money.

Those who cannot appear in court with clean hands are often reluctant to prosecute.

> A female social worker employed as a youth counsellor became reluctant to prosecute a thief after the suspect told detectives that she would invite youths to her room, serve wine, smoke marihuana, and have sexual relations with them. She admitted the smoking of marihuana but denied the other activities.
>
> A middle-aged male school teacher who invited young girl students to his home and served them liquor found himself in an awkward position after he accused them of theft. When their parents threatened to report him to the school board he decided to withdraw his complaint to the police.

When the victim's loss in a burglary includes narcotics or marihuana, or when the victim was with a prostitute or a woman other than his wife at the time of the theft, awareness that this information will come to light in court often leads to a decision not to prosecute. Criminals and former criminals often prefer not to appear as prosecution witnesses. Because of this fact these men are especially vulnerable to victimization, as one former offender complained:

> I have a tremendous reluctance to be a part of sending any person to Canon City (penitentiary) because of the personally degrading part of my life spent there, but this is the third attempt to burgle my house this year but the first time I have reported it. It has to stop somewhere because it seems like my reluctance is sensed by prospective owners of my meager possessions. I won't hesitate to report or help in prosecution of any further assaults on my reluctance to jail anyone.

Other persons unwilling to prosecute include some public defenders ("I felt I could not do so in view of the nature of my work"), members of some religious groups such as the Divine Light Mission. ("I would have to know if she's received knowledge from the Guru Maharaji and if she's meditating. If she's just a sister and has not received knowledge, I wouldn't prosecute.")

Other reasons given for refusal to prosecute are the wish to give the thief another chance, a liking for him, or the refusal to believe that a trusted friend or employee could have committed the crime.

REFERENCES

1. Cohen, Fay: Letter to *Los Angeles Times*. Quoted in *Albuquerque Journal*, March 12, 1979.
2. Ennis, P.H.: *Criminal Victimization in U.S.: A Report of a National Survey*. Washington, U.S. Government Printing Office, 1967.
3. Sharshel, D.L.: Personal communication, 1979.

CHAPTER 6

FALSE REPORTS OF BURGLARY AND THEFT

Show me a liar, and I will show you a thief.
—George Herbert, *Jacula Prudentum*

Many victims of burglary and theft exaggerate the extent of their loss to obtain either more money from their insurance company or a greater rebate on their income tax. There are also persons who make false reports of burglary and theft, deliberately, through human error, or because of some mental illness.

THE FORGETFUL COMPLAINANT

Persons who have mislaid items, especially those of great value, on discovering their loss may quickly assume that they have been the victims of burglary or theft. Small valuable items and large sums of money are often hidden by persons fearful of burglars, but they do not always remember the hiding place, especially when they change the hiding place from time to time as in the following example.

A man reported that $840 had been taken from a wallet which was in a sports coat hanging in his closet in the master bedroom. He thought the burglar knew where his money was, and he mentioned that he kept moving the money around so that no one would know where it was hidden. Three months later he called the detective to report that he had found the money in a camera case.

A customer in a store laid her handbag on a counter while making a purchase. Subsequently she realized that a small purse containing her contact lenses and money was missing from the handbag and she reported a theft. The following day she found the purse where she had dropped it between the seats of her car.

Elderly persons with failing memories are especially likely to have forgotten where they left items in their homes. Relatives may take the officer aside to report that the complainant is a forgetful senile, but even without this help the officer can often recognize senility because of obvious mental confusion.

Loss of memory is also a factor in complainants who have been under the influence of alcohol or drugs. Police officers responded to a telephone report of a man with a gun in an apartment. The police had to break down a door to gain entry to the apartment, where they found a man "passed out," but he did not have a gun. The next day this man could not recall what had happened, and when he discovered that the front door had been forced he reported a burglary. "An alcoholic with a poor memory reported the loss of many items in a burglary, which he did not report until three months later. He also claimed that someone had forged his signature on a personal check for over $1,000. Inquiry revealed that while drunk he would give away his property, write checks that were almost illegible and have no memory for these actions. Some of the items he reported stolen had been pawned by him while in a drunken state."

THE SUSPICIOUS COMPLAINANT

Theft of missing property is often suspected after the complainant has noticed persons behaving in a manner which has aroused his suspicion. A hotel guest who had been jostled by two men in the hotel elevator reported the loss of his wallet. Later he found the wallet in another suit of clothes. "A driver for a TV repair service who delivered a television set asked to use the bathroom. Shortly afterwards the homeowner noticed that $27 was missing from her coin purse, and she reported a theft blaming the TV repair service driver. Three days later she notified the detective that she had found the money in her bedroom closet."

THE DELUSIONAL COMPLAINANT

Some paranoid, middle-aged women make repeated reports of burglaries and pester detectives with additional information, speculations regarding the supposed offender, and strident demands for more investigation. Usually there are no signs of forced entry, and the basis for the complaint may be ridiculous. For example, the woman states that she knows a burglar has been in her home because she noticed minute changes in the position of trinkets and scent bottles on her bedroom dresser. No burglar would waste time attempting to replace some trinket in its original position.

Persons with paranoid delusions may make very bizarre reports of burglaries; for example, a woman called the police to report that burglars came into her apartment, shot her three or four times and butchered her body. She had no bodily injuries and contradicted herself regarding the amount of money stolen. Another woman complained that while she was asleep with her socks on, a burglar painted her toenails red, adding "Someone wants to make me look harrassed, it's the Jewish Mafia." Yet another woman complained that burglars had broken into her home daily for five years and had blown laughing gas into her home. Paranoid complainants may also express grandiose delusional ideas of great wealth and high social position.

MOTIVES FOR FALSE REPORTS

Financial Gain

Persons in financial difficulty may attempt to remedy the situation by breaking out a window in their home, reporting a burglary with the theft of items worth thousands of dollars, and then claiming that amount from their insurance company. Some of these rogues become so casual that they make repeated false reports, using the same receipts for television sets and so on to substantiate their losses. Only their insurance companies change. In one case, the complainant did not even bother to wash off the fingerprint powder, which detectives had dusted on the alleged break-in area, before making another false burglary report.

The homeowner who fakes a forced entry through a window is either stupid or too contemptuous of the police when he breaks the window from inside the room so that all the broken glass falls into the garden.

The criminal who specializes in defrauding insurance companies may also set fire to his home or business and then make a claim on his fire insurance company. He will also make false claims for personal injuries from falls in department stores. A group of young female burglars who made a variety of false reports for insurance purposes had a newspaper clipping in their apartment about a man who obtained $46,000 from false insurance claims over four years. One of them had just been paid $9,000 for an "injury" following a fall in a supermarket.

Insurance investigators claim that persons from Arab countries visiting the United States on student visas have collected as much as $5 million in fraudulent insurance claims. The money is used to support the Palestine Liberation Organization and other groups at war with Israel.

Persons who have been genuine victims of burglaries may try to profit from the occasion by padding their insurance claims, as in the following example.

> A twenty-nine-year-old man returned home at 12:15 AM one morning to find that a burglar had forced open the back door of his house. Subsequently, he claimed $2,335 from his insurance company to cover the loss of a television set, a record player, an electric guitar, an amplifier, two custom speakers, 175 records, and other items. It was learned from the insurance agent that the victim had obtained the home insurance policy only ten days before the burglary. He was very insistent on immediate payment of cash for the policy despite reassurance that this was not necessary. Furthermore, he inquired several times about the effective date of the policy and insisted that the policy should go into effect immediately.
>
> In response to inquiries by the detective, he said that he could not recall whether he purchased the television set in Denver or in Kansas City, and he was unable to recall the names of stores where he had purchased other major items. Yet two days later, he gave his insurance company the names of an appliance store and a music store where he had purchased major items. Inquiry revealed that the appliance store had gone out of business nine months before the date of the alleged purchases, and the music store, which kept records of cash sales, had no record of any sale to the burglary victim. Furthermore, the store had never stocked two of the items described by the victim.
>
> It was also learned that the victim, in a bankruptcy petition filed six months before the burglary, had listed household goods in

the value of only $160. These goods did not include the items reported stolen. At this stage of the inquiry the victim complained to the Division Chief of the Detective Bureau about the manner in which the burglary investigation was being conducted. He said that he had reported the burglary in good faith, but the detective, instead of investigating the burglary, suspected him of wrong-doing. He was later convicted of attempted theft by fraud and deception and placed on probation. At his trial, the burglar who had broken into his home testified that all he obtained was a piggy bank and a small radio.

Another source of financial gain from false reports of burglary and theft comes from the reduction on income tax which is permitted for losses from crimes. Often, persons who have claimed such losses have not even bothered to report the burglary to the police, despite the loss of items worth several thousand dollars, which seems rather odd. Another method of avoiding income tax payments involves false reports of burglary to explain the loss of bookkeeping records that the internal revenue service might otherwise wish to see. What use would a burglar have for bulky sales records allegedly stolen from an apartment house storage locker?

To Explain Loss of Money

The husband who has squandered his paycheck on gambling, a prostitute or a drinking binge may claim the theft of his wallet from his hotel room or home. One man who was inebriated had lent a prostitute his wife's car, then made a false report of auto theft after his wife returned from a vacation. The person who is unable to pay his apartment rent or a mortgage install-ment may attempt to obtain the sympathy of his creditor by claiming that his money was taken in a burglary.

In order to avoid revealing to his wife that he was out of work, a man pawned his television set, then claimed that it had been taken in a burglary.

To Avoid Detection

Persons who have been involved in the destruction of their own property or in a criminal act may attempt to avoid detection through false claims of burglary and theft. A husband in a drunken rage after his wife left him, broke the dishes, a large wall mirror, an expensive clock and all the glass in his home. He told police that someone had broken into his home, "probably the kids next door," and that he could not tell if anything was missing because of "the torn-up condition" of the house.

A tenant in an apartment house became enraged when he received a note from his apartment house manager that the title to his car would not be returned until the back rent was paid. He began smashing the furniture causing $600 damage. Later he reported a burglary.

In order to avoid arrest for leaving the scene of an accident in his van, a man told police that burglars had broken into his business and obtained the keys to his van which was parked behind the building. Employees of stores may report a theft to cover their own theft of cash or property.

A burglar, aware that he was suspected of a number of burglaries in the large apartment complex where he lived, reported a burglary of his own apartment in order to throw suspicion on others. However, he made contradictory statements regarding the burglary, and he admitted to his girl friend that he had made a false report. A maintenance man who was in his apartment shortly before the alleged burglary did not see the television set which was listed as stolen.

Another man claimed that he awakened to find his wife dead in bed beside him. Her death was from an overdose of chloroform, and he claimed that he also had been chloroformed, as he said he thought that they were the victims of burglars. He was convicted of conspiracy to commit murder.

To Explain Gunshot Wounds or Other Injuries

Early one morning a man telephoned the police to report that a burglar had tried to break in and when he ran to the dining room the burglar shot him in the arm. Officers found a pistol holster and .38 caliber bullets on the front porch. The glass in the front door had been broken. When they questioned the man's wife she admitted that there had been a family disturbance, and her husband shot himself accidentally as he was coming through the front door. She showed the officers where she had hidden the revolver in her vacuum cleaner. Her husband, who had been admitted to the hospital, said that he was cleaning his gun when it went off. He was embarrassed over shooting himself and that was his reason for reporting a burglary.

To Gain Attention or Sympathy

Unstable, lonely persons upset over a business failure, death in the family or some other stressful event may make false reports of crime to fill the void in their lives. A man who claimed that he was a cripple and confined to a wheelchair reported a burglary of his apartment. However, the manager of the apartment house had never seen any of the items reported taken in the burglary. Furthermore, he was not a cripple, but an alcoholic who started using the wheelchair to gain sympathy after losing his job.

A young woman, recently separated from her husband, was admitted to a psychiatric hospital following a suicide attempt. Within two weeks following her discharge from the hospital she made four reports of crimes against her. These reports included complaints of obscene telephone calls, auto theft and two home burglaries. In one burglary she claimed that the burglar hit her on the face with his fist and told her, "I hate women, I'm going to kill you." He made no sexual advances and left without taking anything. Investigation showed that the burglar could not have left her home in the manner she described. Nothing was taken in the previous burglary. The problem of false reports was discussed with her and she made no further reports to the police.

A research assistant at a University Hospital reported a genuine burglary of his home and estimated that the stolen items were worth almost $5,000. Toward the end of the interview with the detectives he mentioned "almost as an afterthought" that the burglar had taken a microscope case containing a highly contagious spinal meningitis bacillus. The investigators, who were under the impression that the burglary victim was a doctor, issued a public alert requesting the burglar to turn himself in for medical attention, because mere inhalation of the material in the microscope case could bring on serious illness or death. Later the research assistant admitted that he was emotionally upset when he made the report, he was not a doctor and that the stolen material was harmless to health.

A man reported that for twenty minutes he fought with a burglar he discovered in his former wife's home and that he gave up the fight only after he suffered knife wounds. Following police investigation he admitted, "I lied about the break-in. I did it myself, why, I don't know. About the cuts, I did it myself to see if my ex-wife cares. I have been uptight thinking of her, I love her."

For Revenge

Persons intent on revenge—a discarded girl friend, sex rival, resentful employee or angry pimp—may cause or attempt to cause the arrest of the disliked person. Physical descriptions, forged notes and other clues pointing to the alleged burglar are provided to the police. "A service station owner, who complained to police that a customer had refused to pay for car repairs, was told that he would have to seek payment through a civil law suit. The owner, upset over the refusal of the police to take action, a few days later falsely accused this customer of stealing tools valued at $180, while gasoline was being pumped into his car."

Apparently illegal transactions may lead to claims of burglary and theft. A man appears at a small store, gas station or tavern and offers to sell a color television set for a ridiculously low price. The set is in a cardboard carton in his car which is parked nearby. The man does not say that the set has been stolen but conveys this impression by his furtive manner. The purchaser in his eagerness to obtain such a bargain does not check the set. When he discovers the set does not work, he impulsively calls the police to report an armed robbery or burglary.

A man told police that he was watching television with his wife in his living room when he looked around and saw a man taking $80 off his dining room table. He rushed outside and was able to obtain the license number of the burglar's car. When the suspect was questioned, he told detectives, "I've never been near his house. I sold him a funky old TV and he's mad now and wants to charge me with burglary." The man who had reported the burglary, when confronted with this statement said, "Let's just forget the whole thing. I lied to you, the TV I bought was junk and did not work, so I made the report."

For Publicity

In order to obtain free publicity, motion picture actors, striptease dancers and other entertainers will falsely report the loss of jewelry or other valuable items worth $30,000 to $50,000. Substantial rewards are offered for the return of the stolen items or for information leading to the arrest and conviction of the burglar. Newspapers and television stations will often publicize these reports without any check on the likelihood of the complainant owning property of such great value.

CLUES TO FALSE REPORTS

A single clue may arouse strong suspicion of a false report of burglary or theft, but even the presence of several clues may not be sufficient to determine whether a report is true or false. Truth is sometimes stranger than fiction, and reports of genuine burglaries or thefts are encountered which have all the hallmarks of a false complaint. Careful inquiry is especially necessary when:

The Complainant
1. delays making a report to the police.
2. makes the report only after a request by his insurance company or by the internal revenue service.
3. is vague, evasive or uncooperative, e.g. telephone calls and letters from the detective are not answered and appointments for interview are not kept.
4. contradicts himself.
5. reports the loss of valuable items out of keeping with his income or living circumstances.
6. reports a cash loss in a business burglary, which far exceeds the usual amount of money received on that day of the week.
7. reports a cash loss in a business burglary of money that should have been placed in a safe or deposited in a bank.
8. is unable to provide information on valuable items. For example, the brand name, approximate date of purchase and the name of the store or person from whom a color television set was obtained.

9. inflates the value of items reported stolen (common also in genuine burglaries).
10. following the original report, adds a long list of additional items supposedly stolen, especially when something as small as a pocket calculator is noted missing, but the loss of a large television set is overlooked.
11. lists as stolen the identical items that he has listed in a previous burglary or theft.
12. is under the influence of alcohol or drugs.
13. is behind in his rent, involved in bankruptcy proceedings or otherwise in financial difficulties.
14. is senile or otherwise mentally ill.
15. has a criminal record (although burglars can be victims of burglary).

Crime Scene Investigation Shows

1. Forced entry but—
   a. the damage is not sufficient to permit entry.
   b. the window is broken from the inside or pried open from the inside.
   c. the dust is not disturbed at the point of entry, for example, the window ledge.
   d. window screen has been replaced. (Burglars do not usually waste time unless they wish to conceal that a burglary has occurred.)

Note: Burglars who have gained admission through the use of a key supplied by an employee may try to confuse the police by simulating forced entry once inside the building.

2. No signs of forced entry. (A surprising number of persons leave their home or apartment doors unlocked, however, if there are no signs of forced entry the possibility of a false report should be considered.)

Further Criminal Investigation Shows

1. Prior to the burglary or theft report the items reported stolen were—
   a. pawned by the complainant or friend.
   b. sold, for example, at a garage sale to a neighbor.

    c. removed in a rental truck or moving van (information provided by neighbors).

    d. repossessed by a department store.

    e. returned to a rental company.

    f. otherwise disposed of (e.g. traveler's checks were cashed).

    g. reported stolen in a previous burglary or theft report.

2. Items reported stolen are seen in the home when the detectives make a surprise home visit several days after the burglary.

3. The insurance claim is much greater than the loss reported to the police.

4. Complainant has made prior reports of burglary, arson or personal injury and has made insurance claims.

5. Complainant refuses to take a polygraph examination, fails to appear for the examination or appears under the influence of drugs.

CHECKING PROOF OF PURCHASE

Persons who make false reports of burglary and theft may have no proof of purchase, which is not surprising when the complainant obtained his so-called diamond ring from a bubble gum machine. However, some complainants will produce false sales slips for expensive items in order to convince their insurance company that they have indeed been the victims of a burglary. When fraud is suspected, it is necessary to check the sales slip very thoroughly.

1. *The date on the sales slip.* The store may have been closed on that date because it was a Sunday or a public holiday.

2. *The serial number on the sales slip.* This may have been torn off to make it more difficult to check the sales slip. When the serial number is present, a check on the store's original copy may show that it is blank or missing, which suggests that a customer or employee has stolen the duplicate copy and filled it out later. In this case, the date listed for the purchase may not come between or be the same as the dates listed on the sales slip immedi-

ately preceding and following the serial number on the suspect sales slip.

3. *Merchandise listed on the sales slip.*
   a. *Brand name.* The store may not sell the brand name merchandise described on the sales slip, or they may not have had the model listed in stock on the date of the sale.
   b. *Value.* The price listed on the sales slip may not be correct, and the value of the item may be either grossly inflated or, less commonly, too low. On one false receipt, the price of a suit was more expensive than any suit sold by the store. On another false receipt for jewelry, the amount of the sale exceeded the total sales of the day for the whole jewelry department of that store.
4. *Discrepancies.* Discrepancies between a false and a genuine sales slip may reveal—
   a. that the receipt has no cash register validation.
   b. spelling errors—an immigrant from England in making out a false sales slip for a television set betrayed his foreign origin by writing "colour."
   c. the incorrect sales tax.
   d. an incorrect stock number, employee number or store.
   e. the employee with listed identity number was not at work on the date of the sale.
   f. the presence of customer's signature when this is not required in a cash transaction.

SIMULATED BURGLARY-HOMICIDE

Most crimes are reported to the police by the victims, but the victims of homicide seldom have the opportunity to exercise this privilege. Even in death, victims unwittingly may leave some message to indicate the circumstances of their passing.

In Sussex, England, an elderly couple and their two dogs were found bludgeoned to death in their home, which had been ransacked. The intruder had apparently broken in through the back door, as the glass in the door was smashed. The elderly man was killed in the garage and his wife in the living room.

Although the scene suggested a burglary-homicide, there was one discordant factor: The female victim was sitting in an armchair with knitting needles in her hands. If she had heard the glass break, she would not be sitting with knitting needles in her hands. A son, who had recently returned from a visit to the United States had an alibi for the night of the burglary. He recalled having trouble with a vending machine that he reported to the owner. On inquiry, the vending machine owner said that the incident occurred the night before the burglary. In the course of a three-month investigation, detectives went to Scotland to check on the son's financial dealings. After establishing that the son was in need of money, they questioned him for several hours. Finally, he confessed that he had visited his parents to obtain a loan. When the father, who was very wealthy, refused to lend him any money, he killed him, then his mother and the dogs. Before hurrying back to London, he simulated a burglary.

REFERENCE

1. Macdonald, J.M., and Brannan, C.D.: False reports of armed robbery. *FBI Law Enforcement Bulletin*, March, 1973.

CHAPTER 7

CRIMINAL INVESTIGATION

John M. Macdonald and C. Donald Brannan*

It is quite a three-pipe problem.
—Sir Arthur Conan Doyle
The Adventures of Sherlock Holmes
The Red Headed League

IT IS UNDERSTANDABLE that the sheer burden of the overwhelming number of burglaries and thefts with the constant succession of new case assignments for investigation, the problems imposed by the frequent lack of eyewitnesses and the endless paperwork may discourage the criminal investigator. But, understandable as this is, the handicaps should stimulate the detective to respond quickly both to the crime scene and to promising leads, to sharpen his investigative skills and to learn shortcuts in his work.

Above all, he must learn to discriminate between those cases which require his full attention and those which do not merit exhaustive investigation. The impact upon the victim should always be considered. Thus, although the theft of a television set from the home of an elderly widow on a fixed income should be given as high a priority as the theft of merchandise from a business warehouse, the theft of a ten dollar flower pot from the porch of a house is surely different from the theft of stereo equipment worth over a thousand dollars.

Burglars are sometimes less cautious in concealing their

---

* Captain Brannan, Commander Crimes Against Property Bureau, Denver Police Department, is a graduate of the FBI Academy. Nineteen of his twenty-three years in the Denver Police Department have been spent as an investigator or supervisor of investigations. He is a former commander of the Special Crime Attack Team which began as a federally funded project for the reduction of burglaries and is now a permanent unit of the Denver Police Department.

traces when they find little worth stealing, because they assume that the police will not be very thorough when there is only a minor loss of property. Upon occasion, the solution of some trifling crime may result in the arrest of a major criminal. Clearly, the value of the stolen merchandise should not always determine the degree of effort expended by the investigator, and while it may be easy to list guidelines for the investigator, there is always the risk that they will be interpreted as commandments rather than as flexible suggestions for concentration of time and energy.

INVESTIGATION OF BURGLARY

Response to a Burglary in Progress

Patrolmen responding to the report of a burglary in progress should arrive quickly, silently and without being seen. Each patrolman should know his patrol area and adjacent areas so that he can take the quickest route to the scene of the burglary. This requires a day-to-day knowledge of streets closed or obstructed by construction and of the intricacies of one-way streets. Radio reports that the burglar is assaulting an occupant indicate the use of the siren and flashing red lights in the hope that advertisement of the police approach will cut short the assault.

More often, the officers will wish to take advantage of surprise and will attempt to arrive without warning. Thus, in the immediate area there will be no use of siren or flashing red lights. As he drives to the scene the officer will be thinking of the best location for parking in order to take advantage of cover for his police cruiser. He will turn his engine and lights off and turn his radio volume down as he glides to a halt in a parking place not directly in front of the building or home to be checked.

The high speed arrival with the squealing of tires, and screech of brakes, the slamming of car doors and the noisy rush to the building entrance are for television drama rather than for capture of the alert burglar. There is always the chance that the criminal has heard the alert on his police scanner radio and is leaving as the police car arrives. For this reason, the alert patrolman should delay his arrival at the scene rather than allow a suspicious vehicle to leave the area without being checked: The car that is being driven without lights on or with too much regard for traffic safety; the meticulous use of directional signals; a speed well below the legal limit; a car with someone crouched down in the rear seat; an older model car in a wealthy area or indeed any car that is within a block or two of the crime scene in the early hours of the morning. These all deserve attention. A woman driver should not disarm suspicion, as burglars not infrequently use their wives or girl friends to drive the getaway car. Anyone walking down the street carrying a television set or a bulging pillow case should be questioned.

As the officer walks up to the crime scene he takes advantage of any cover, for example, he walks close to a building rather than in the middle of the sidewalk. He listens carefully for dogs barking, which may signal the escape route of the burglar, or for the toot of a horn or a whistle, which may be a warning by a lookout to the burglar inside the building. As he walks alongside cars he should glance inside to see whether someone is hiding in the back seat or whether loot is piled high. A car with its motor running or with a warm exhaust pipe should arouse the officer's suspicion. On a cold night the only car without windows frosted over may well belong to the burglar.

The first two officers to arrive should take up positions at diagonally opposite corners of the building so that no one can leave without being seen. The next officers to appear on the scene will check for signs of forced entry. It is a cardinal error for an officer to enter a building alone without waiting for other officers to arrive. He will only proceed to enter on his own when this is necessary to protect the lives of the occupants of a building. In such an emergency situation, the officer has to make a quick judgment based upon his previous experience and his knowledge of the situation. Delay in confrontation may be the safest response for all concerned, as precipitate action may lead to the seizure of a hostage and possibly end in tragedy.

Crime Scene Search

Until the building has been searched completely, two officers should maintain their positions at diagonally opposite corners of the building. Often vigilance is relaxed when there are many officers at the scene, and the burglar who has been hiding near an exit door is able to make his escape because the officers are inside the building and there may be no one outside to intercept him or give chase.

Officers should shout out a warning of their presence, "Police officers" they may otherwise be shot by householders or building security guards fearful of burglars. Even this warning may not protect the police officer from danger, as an occupant may believe that burglars are impersonating the police. It may be necessary to turn up the police radio or to advise the occupant to telephone the police dispatcher.

There may, of course, be occupants who do not understand such warnings. Dogs, boa constrictors, poisonous snakes and other wild creatures have been encountered by police officers. An officer who saw a stuffed crocodile wisely threw something at it, and when the eyes blinked he beat a hasty retreat. Police responding to a silent alarm in a sporting goods store shot a manikin of a sportsman holding a shotgun.

A systematic search is made of each floor of the building, and care is taken to prevent a burglar from moving into an area that has already been searched. This can be accomplished by guarding stairways, elevators and hallways or by locking rooms that have already been searched. The roof should always be checked as well as rafters, lofts, attics and areas above false ceilings. Police search dogs are invaluable in quickly locating burglars who might otherwise escape detection.

The usual procedure when entering a room or building is to kick or push the door open with sufficient force to strike the wall and anyone hiding behind it. The officer should not stand directly in front of the door, and if he is using a flashlight, he should hold it to one side, as the burglar may fire at the light. Unless there is a special reason for concern, the officer is unlikely to heed the recommendation of the police manual—to enter a room in a crouching position and then move quickly to one side of the doorway.

It is awkward holding a flashlight some distance from one's body while searching a dark room in a crouched position. Some experts have suggested that the officer should hold his flashlight in his left hand, directly underneath and supporting his right hand which is holding his revolver. The officer briefly turns on the light and makes a quick sweep of the room, *with the head of his flashlight pointing in the same direction as his revolver.* It is much easier to aim and fire in this position. The very bright light of a modern police flashlight will momentarily blind the burglar. It has also been claimed that criminals often shoot low in shoot outs so that there may be a disadvantage for the officer to crouch while searching a building.

It is disconcerting to see someone in the dark only to realize that a mirror has reflected one's own image in the beam of the flashlight. A sudden noise from a corner of the basement may be the thermostat turning on the gas jets of the heating furnace. Not just a few furnaces have been shot in mistake for a burglar.

The arrest of one or more burglars should not lead to any relaxation of security measures, as there may be armed and dangerous accomplices still within the building. Those offenders who are arrested should be searched and handcuffed without delay, then kept under guard. An officer, who had a burglar in the back of his police car, left the car briefly to answer the questions of a citizen at the scene; meantime, the burglar was able to slip his feet between his arms so that his handcuffed hands were in front of his body. Despite this handicap, he was able to drive off in the police cruiser, which he abandoned two miles away and then escaped on foot.

The cautious, painstaking search described above is not required in every burglary. Often, the burglary is discovered by householders or employees of a business long after the burglars have departed. Not every burglar alarm is set off by criminal intruders. Electrical short circuits, cats and lawful occupants of a building may activate the alarm. High winds and thunder-

storms can activate a large number of alarms in an area, and it
would be pointless to search all these buildings. In the absence
of signs of forced entry, the search and resetting of the alarms
can be left to the employees of the private security company
which installed the alarm system.

Protection of the crime scene to preserve physical evidence
may be limited to asking the occupants of a home to leave
things as they are until after the police have arrived and completed their search for evidence. Householders, on discovering
that their house has been ransacked, often set about cleaning
spilled food items and returning things to their proper place,
thereby obliterating the burglar's fingerprints and making it
impossible to obtain a photographic record of the crime scene.
At major crimes, particularly if there is a homicide, officers will
be assigned to prevent any unauthorized entry into the crime
scene area. If entry or departure is through a window, care
should be taken to avoid walking on the soil beneath the
window. If for any reason it is necessary to move items during
a search for the burglar, the detectives should be informed,
especially if any such items are likely to be used as physical
evidence.

The Burglary Detective's Checklist

It is seldom possible for detectives to respond to all burglary
scenes as soon as the crime is reported; however, a major burglary
or one that includes a homicide, rape or assault demands immediate response by experts. The detective is usually better
qualified than the patrolman, and his early involvement in the
investigation is obviously desirable. Furthermore, young patrolmen learn much from observing the detective's actions at the
scene. Formal training, no matter how thorough, is less effective
than practical experience under the guidance of a detective.
Burglary detectives will closely examine the following for major
clues:

Site of Entry

The location and method of entry are important elements
of the burglar's *modus operandi*. The point of entry is a likely
site for the recovery of physical evidence such as fingerprints,

footprints and tool marks. The detective will determine whether forced entry was made by direct force, for example, kicking in the door or by the use of tools such as a screwdriver, vise grips or channel locks.

A young man who had access to the key of a storage shed had removed the lock from the hasp with the intent of stealing items from within. But, in order to divert the suspicion from himself, after he opened the lock with the key, he took it inside the shed and smashed it on the worktable with a hammer, however the outline of the lock could be seen on the top of the worktable.

If a window was smashed, did the glass fall inside or outside of the building? Burglars who have been given a key to the building by one of the employees may attempt to conceal their entry through a locked door by smashing a window once they are inside, but the glass will fall outside the building. Persons who make false reports of burglary may also break the glass from inside the house. A man who made a false report of a burglary from his store to obtain insurance had drilled a hole through the door lock. In order to avoid standing in the alley, he drilled the hole from inside the building, then swept the debris into a corner.

If there is no sign of forced entry, the detective will include in his range of suspects—employees, former employees, janitors and burglars known to have lock-picking skills.

Site of Exit

The burglar may not leave the same way he came in, and the site of exit should also be examined carefully for fingerprints and other clues.

Items Moved

Items that have been moved, especially those surfaces likely to show fingerprints, should be fingerprinted. When a house has been ransacked, yet few items have been taken and valuable items have been left behind, the detective will consider the possibility that the burglars knew or suspected there were narcotics or other drugs in the home.

Items Taken

A careful listing of the items stolen may provide clues to the burglar and his motivations. Many juvenile burglars without cars tend to take only cash and small items that they can carry in their pockets and hide from their parents at home. If they have no fence, they seldom take jewelry because of the difficulty in selling these items. Often they will take articles of little value that catch their fancy, such as posters.

Some adult burglars also take only small items that can be carried in their pockets, but unlike the juveniles, they will take jewelry as well as cash. Selection of only valuable items and rejection of cheap or imitation jewelry is a mark of the expert burglar. In a machine shop burglary, the detective discovered that although many tools were stolen, none belonged to individual employees even though identical tools of the same brand belonging to the company were stolen. The burglary was done by an employee who had been fired from his job.

In the burglary of a manufacturing company, only the best and most expensive precision tools worth $6,000 were stolen. Obviously the burglar had expert knowledge and might well be an employee. After the employees were asked to take polygraph lie detector tests, an unknown person rang a neighboring suburban police department to report that there were some stolen tools in boxes near the trash cans by a drugstore. An employee of the manufacturing company who failed to turn up for work the next day, when asked to read the telephone message on the location of the stolen items to a tape recorder, refused to do so. He later admitted the burglary. He said that he left a window unlocked at closing time and later smashed it to make it look like a forced entry.

In the burglary of an office, the drawers of all the desks but one were pried open. An employee who had recently been fired was suspected. The one desk that had not been pried open was used by a friend of this former employee.

Items Destroyed

Widespread destruction of property in a building suggests that the burglars were juveniles. Adult burglars, as well as juveniles, will sometimes use fire extinguishers not simply for vandalism, but to hide fingerprints. Disgruntled boyfriends and ex-husbands may destroy their former partner's most valued possessions and clothing.

Items Brought to the Scene

The burglar may leave behind items such as burglary tools, gloves, socks, cigarettes, cigars, candles, matches, jacket, parole papers, driver's license or other personal belongings he might have brought with him to the scene, including loot taken in an earlier burglary. He may leave behind someone else's driver's license or checkbook in order to provide misleading clues for the detective. When he leaves behind his own driver's license, this may be an accidental loss from his pocket or result from an unconscious wish to be caught.

Any items brought to the scene by the burglar should be preserved as evidence. Tape placed on a window that the burglar broke was preserved. Later, in a search of a burglary suspect's home, similar tape was discovered, and the end of the roll of tape matched perfectly with one end of the tape found on the window glass.

In the burglary of a warehouse, a truck was used to remove over $20,000 worth of merchandise. While being driven either into or out of the warehouse, the truck scraped some cardboard cartons and left orange colored transfer paint on some of these boxes. The truck left tire prints on some very soft pliable rubber moulding. The distinctive orange paint was similar in color to that used on "U-Haul" rental trucks. The opening of the warehouse door was only 10 feet in height indicating that a flatbed truck rather than a large van type truck was used.

"U-Haul" truck rental agencies were checked, and it was found that a flatbed truck was rented on the day of the burglary. There were slight scuff marks on the truck; binding tape similar in size, shape and design to that used on the merchandise from the warehouse was found on the bed of the truck; and the tire tread design matched that found at the scene. The man who had rented the truck admitted loaning it to another person for use in a criminal offense.

The detective should note that sometimes the burglar leaves an unusual visiting card; a bowel motion usually left in some place other than the toilet.

Interviewing the Victim

Victims of burglary may have ideas regarding the identity of the burglar. Often they are quick to name a janitor, door-to-door salesman or an employee who was recently terminated. The detective will want to review the names of persons who have had access to their homes. Ne'er-do-well sons have friends of doubtful reputation who may pay a return visit when no one is at home.

In high crime neighborhoods where the burglaries are often committed by local juveniles without transport, the juvenile burglars, unlike older offenders, will often boast about their activities, and sooner or later the victim will pick up rumors from neighborhood kids regarding the "jerk who did it."

Children asleep at home or at play in the backyard while a burglary is in progress may overhear the burglars and recognize the voices of juveniles from the school they attend.

The detective should obtain the serial numbers of television sets, guns and other items of value. When the victim has no record of such numbers and states that he bought these items from someone he met on the street, but does not recall the person's name, the possibility of a false report should be considered. Suspicion of a false report will be further aroused when the victim is vague; evasive or uncooperative; contradicts himself; reports the loss of valuable items inconsistent with his income or living circumstances; is unable to give information on brand names, approximate date and place of purchase of valuable items; is under the influence of alcohol or drugs; or is senile or otherwise mentally ill.

Interviewing Witnesses—Neighborhood Investigation

Neighbors who saw persons at or near the scene of the burglary or indeed anyone acting in a suspicious manner should be asked the usual questions regarding sex, race, age, height, weight, clothing, glasses, hair length and facial appearance. In addition, the officer should ask, "What was the most unusual feature of his appearance?" or "What was the most striking thing about him?" Such a question makes a person think about the overall appearance of the suspect and often results in eliciting important information not previously mentioned, e.g. the suspect has an ear missing, an artificial leg, gold-capped teeth or a scar running from one eye to the corner of his mouth.

Do not alienate witnesses by demanding identification before attempting to obtain information from them. It is remarkable how often cooperative witnesses will fail to mention vital information such as the license number of a vehicle. Always ask for the license number and if the witness has written the number on paper. The paper on which the number was noted should be obtained by the officer and initialed for later use as evidence. If the witness writes the number on his hand, a photograph should be taken for permanent record. When obtaining a description of the car used, check for special features such as a cracked window, bumper or window decals or a trailer hitch.

It should be remembered that some criminals return to the scene of the crime, and persons who volunteer help or information to officers at the scene may include the burglar.

Review of the Crime Scene

Before leaving the crime scene, the detective will review in his mind all that he has seen and heard. He will be on the lookout for anything unusual, for example, in a rape-burglary in the home of a woman living alone, he notices that the toilet seat is raised, which suggests that the rapist has urinated in the toilet. A search for fingerprints under the toilet seat leads to recovery of the rapist's fingerprints.

Whether or not he has called experts from the crime laboratory, he will consider what pieces of evidence should be sent to the crime laboratory or to the police custodian's office. To satisfy the legal requirements concerning physical evidence the investigator must be able to—

1. identify each piece of evidence, even months after he collected it.
2. describe the exact location of the item at the time it was collected.
3. prove that from the moment of its collection until it was presented in court, the evidence was continuously in proper custody.

4. describe changes that may have occurred in the evidence between the time of its collection and its introduction as evidence in court (1).

The important role of the crime laboratory and further review of the crime scene are provided in Chapter 8.

The Area Search

Officers will follow tracks away from the scene. In wintertime when there is fresh snow on the ground the tracks can often be followed for a considerable distance and may lead directly to the burglar's home. In one case where there were many tracks near the scene, a detective, who was a skilled elk hunter, noticed that the tracks from the home included another mark in addition to the footprints. This turned out to be the cord of a television set, which was dragging in the snow. With this additional clue it became possible to distinguish the burglar's trail from other tracks in the snow.

Distinctive footprints at the point of entry or exit should be photographed, but a radio description may be sufficient to lead to the burglar's arrest by officers searching the area as in the following examples:

Officers responding to the scene of a burglary found well-worn tennis shoe prints on the ground by a broken window. The prints had a diamond pattern with the figure 9 in the center. Other officers found a car in the next block with the key in the ignition and the driver's door open. There was snow on the other cars around but not on this car, and alongside the car was a tennis shoe print well worn with the figure 9 in the middle. The officers watched the car, and fifty minutes later a man walked up to the car, looked around and then got in the car. When the officers approached the car he lay down on the front seat. Although he said he had been at a friend's house he could not give the location. He was wearing the tennis shoes with the above described pattern on the soles and was identified by a witness who saw him running from the scene of the burglary.

In another burglary there were two distinct sets of footprints at the point of entry, gymnasium shoes and hiking boots. Alert officers questioned two young men wearing these distinctive shoes several blocks away and obtained quick confessions. Even when the burglars confess it is still a good practice to take photographs of the footprints at the scene and of the shoes.

Burglars leave many kinds of trails. One man included in his pillowcase of loot a carton of milk from the refrigerator and drops of this milk betrayed his progress down an alley. Restaurant burglars in Greenwood, Indiana fled with $1,105, most of it in small change from a wishing well in the restaurant lobby. The owners saved this money for charity, and it was carried away in a suitcase, a 50-pound lard can and several pillowcases. One bag had a hole in it, and there was a trail of pennies, nickels and dimes that led to a Greenwood motel. A cab driver took the burglars from the motel to a downtown Indianapolis motel where one of the pillow-case money bags was torn open and the contents were dumped on the sidewalk.

Garden gates left open, and the barking of dogs may indicate the burglar's movements. If officers checking near the scene see the same car drive by more than once they should stop the car, as it may be the burglar's accomplice cruising the area. License plates in a residential area may all show letters indicating the same county of registration. Cars with license plates from another area will arouse the officer's suspicion. License plates and vehicle identification numbers can be checked with the National Crime Information Center (NCIC). NCIC is a nationwide computerized information system established as a service to all criminal justice agencies. Through the use of computer equipment located at the Federal Bureau of Investigation Headquarters in Washington, D.C., the NCIC system stores vast amounts of criminal justice information that can be instantly retrieved and furnished through an NCIC computer terminal to any authorized agency.

It is most important when searching a burglary scene and the neighborhood *to look up*. In a bulletin prepared by the Contra Costa County Sheriff's Department from information provided by the Monrovia Police Department, a burglar has described his observations on police searches and he emphasizes the importance of police looking up.

When I was discovered, and the police started moving in, I would go up the nearest tree and get on a flat roof. Police look under everything, but, for some reason, they never look up. When I had to flee an area on foot, I never used streets or alleys. I would go over fences and hedges for blocks, always paralleling the streets being searched. When I had to cross a sidestreet to continue my flight, I would wait and listen first. I could usually figure that all of the cars on a call would go to the source, and then fan out. This gave me a big edge. It takes about ten minutes to go ten blocks on foot without running. I could be three or four miles away in my car without breaking any traffic laws. If I figured the car I had was too hot, I would dump it and get another one. You can always tell the progress of a police search by the noises . . . tires squealing when the cars make u-turns; backing out of driveways in making a turn; and so on. You can hear this for several blocks in a quiet neighborhood. I never worried about foot searches, as policemen seldom leave their cars. I knew, too, that I was willing to tear and soil my clothes going through brush and over fences. I figured they weren't too hot for it with those uniforms.

In observing officers shaking down an area, it appeared to me that they did not really expect to find anyone, that they either thought it was a phony call, or that I was long gone. They made motions like they were searching, but . . . they didn't LOOK. They passed a flashlight beam across me numerous times, but they didn't see me. Of course, my dark clothing helped. When the immediate search was over, I would count them off as they left, I knew one of the officers had waited behind, and I stayed low. Eventually, the car would return and, when I heard the other officer enter it, and the car leave, I would figure the coast was clear and come out of hiding. I once hid in a closet above a wardrobe for eighteen hours in a vacant house. Several officers had searched the house, but none looked in the closets. The officers were the same way about loot I had hidden. They seldom spotted it because, I guess, it was too obvious. They would park a car at a curb and walk right around the bushes that I had the stuff under. It wasn't really hidden . . . just stuck there awaiting my pick-up later. Of course, I did lose some this way because some guy would happen to see it.

Police helicopter pilots are in the advantageous position of being able to look down on burglary scenes and the neighboring area.

Chopper 2 covered a silent burglar alarm and on arrival at the scene we found that the parking facilities were deserted, except for an area in front of the Bear Valley Inn and for a small silver car parked in a darkened area facing east. On our second pass around the roof of the building, this vehicle was observed leaving the parking space and travelling east in the shopping center. We continued to check the roof, keeping this vehicle in sight.

When we were satisfied that a roof job had not occurred, we switched our full attention to the car. The vehicle left the shopping center and when the driver was fully aware that we were on to him, he turned out his lights and began evasive action. He ran stop signs, parked and then pulled away from the curb, anything to lose us. Radio sent three cars to assist us and the suspect was apprehended in his vehicle. The door that was broken in was located near the place the car was parked before it moved away.

The Follow-Up Investigation

The detective, from his knowledge of any burglars who are using the same method of operation in the area where a burglary was committed, will have in mind one or more suspects. He will ask the crime laboratory to compare the fingerprints of these men with any fingerprints recovered from the scene and will show police photographs of these men, together with photographs of other known burglars, to any victims or witnesses who saw the burglar. If there is only one suspect, his photograph will be included in a selection of seven or eight photographs of persons of the same sex, race or ethnic group and of approximately the same age, weight and height. If the suspect has not previously been arrested, it may be possible to obtain a copy of the photograph taken by the local motor vehicle department for his driver's license. Photographs of juveniles are often available in school annuals.

Selection by the victim or witness of the suspect's photograph from a group of photographs will raise the question of whether a warrant should be requested for the suspect's arrest. Decision will be based upon many factors including the detective's assessment of the reliability of the eyewitness's identification of the suspect and the presence of special features in the *modus operandi* that tend to link the burglary with the suspect. The detective may delay a decision until he has completed his search for further evidence.

If the suspect is already in custody, he will be placed along with seven or eight persons of similar physical characteristics in a line-up before eyewitnesses to the burglary. Photographs should be taken of this line-up to counter any later suggestion of unfairness of the procedure by the defense attorney, who should always be notified of and invited to attend the line-up procedure.

If eyewitness identification is supported by physical evidence, such as fingerprints of the suspect from the scene of the burglary, the detective will request a warrant for the suspect's arrest and will also consider whether to apply for a warrant to search the suspect's home or business. Often a suspect, following his arrest, will sign a search waiver. Refusal to do so may not be through fear of recovery of evidence pointing to his participation in the burglary, but because he may have narcotics or other illicit drugs in his home.

When the address of the burglary suspect is not known, it is not sufficient to request the fugitive detail to look for him. The burglary detective himself should make every effort to trace the suspect through the following sources of information:

Police contact cards on the suspect. These cards may list his home address, a description of his car and license number, as well as the names of persons who were with him at the time. On the daily police bulletin his photograph, name and other information from the contact cards (as well as other sources) will be summarized. The description of the suspect, his car and license number may be sufficient to lead to his arrest. Police contact cards on his associates should also be checked.

Arrest record. This record will provide information on prior arrests, and in the case of local arrest records it is easy to check the offense reports for information which may aid in his arrest, e.g. home address, names of wife and associates, names of arresting officers and detectives who may have further information on him.

Traffic tickets. These may also describe his car and list his home address.

Telephone and public service company records.

Employee and apartment house application forms. These may list the names of prior employers, persons who are willing to provide character references and other information that may lead to the suspect.

Penitentiary and reformatory lists of recent releases or escapes. Penal institutions usually keep records of visitors and their home addresses, as well as other information that may lead to the arrest of the suspect.

Parole and probation officers.

Patrolmen and detectives who have a good knowledge of criminals on the streets.

Other sources. Detectives often will establish good relationships with persons in a position to provide information, for example, credit bureaus and criminal informants (see the following section on Interviews).

Interviews

Even though the detective may have interviewed the victim at the scene of the burglary, it may be helpful to talk to him again after he has had time to reflect on the crime. The victim may think of possible suspects, obtain information from neighbors or discover some new evidence. He may recall recent visitors to his home or office, for example, that two months prior to the burglary a contractor repaired his furnace.

In the burglary of a warehouse or other business, the owner should be requested to provide the names of employees and recently discharged employees whenever there is reason to suspect an inside job. The reasons might be that there are no signs of forced entry, or a window is broken from the inside of the building, the alarm system has been inactivated, the burglar's awareness of the combination number of the safe, the secret hiding place of money or the recent arrival of a valuable shipment and repeated burglaries over a period of several months. The detective will be interested in those employees known to be in financial difficulties and will single out those persons with police records or from families with crime involvements. Employers may forget to mention, among their employees, the janitorial service responsible for cleaning the building.

Stolen Property

Property taken by the burglar often provides the vital link that leads to his detection. The detective will list on NCIC the serial numbers of stolen television sets, typewriters, firearms and other articles with registration numbers. Whenever a suspect of any crime is found in possession of such articles, or pawn tickets for them, the officer will check their serial numbers on NCIC to see whether they have been reported stolen in a burglary or theft. Even if the numbers are not on NCIC the items may have been stolen. There are several reasons for this: (1) the victim of a burglary may not have kept a record of the serial numbers of his possessions so he will not be able to provide the numbers to the police; (2) the victim transposed figures or made other mistakes when he provided the serial numbers to the police with the result that the wrong number has been listed on NCIC; (3) the burglary may just have occurred and it has not yet been discovered either by the victim or by the police. (Even though the victim does not have the serial numbers, he may be able to recognize his property from scratches, alterations or other special features.)

Photographs of unusual items of great value will be published in the daily police bulletin, and if photographs are not available, a brief written description will be provided. One such picture of stolen jewelry was recognized by a janitor's son who was in the police building with his father. He had seen the jewelry in the possession of a school friend, who was later arrested and admitted to three burglaries. These photographs should also be distributed to antique stores, second-hand stores and pawnshops.

In those cities where pawnshops and second-hand stores are required to keep a record of all transactions, detectives on the pawnshop detail may call on these stores to obtain copies of these records, which include not only serial numbers, but also the name and physical description of the person who pawned or sold the article, together with the response to the question, "How long have you owned the article?"

Clerks will check all serial numbers on NCIC, and if an item comes back as stolen, detectives will check with the owner of the store to obtain further information on the suspect. The record of the transaction may contain sufficient information to locate the suspect, and if he claims that he bought the item from a stranger in the street seven months earlier, he may have to explain his possession of an item that was stolen in a burglary the preceding week.

Victims sometimes will look for their property at local flea markets, which are usually only open on weekends.

The use of stolen checks or credit cards may lead to the arrest of the burglar or some other criminal who paid him for the items. Credit card companies should be notified promptly of any loss to enable the arrest of persons who attempt to use stolen credit cards. Even if the loss has not been reported, alert store employees may notice some clue that may arouse their suspicion.

> A clerk in a clothing store noticed that the signature on a sales receipt did not match the signature on the credit card, so she called the manager who asked the customer for his driver's license. When the customer said he had no identification on him, the manager called the credit card company and obtained information provided by the applicant for the card, including his prior places of employment and the first name of his wife. After the customer gave incorrect answers to these questions, he said that he had an expired driver's license in his car and he would get it, but he did not return. The victim of the burglary in which the credit card was stolen said that he recognized the description of the man who attempted to use the credit card as the brother of a friend. The suspect had a record of prior arrests for burglary and theft.

Informants

Most persons in society look down upon the informer as a Judas who betrays others for his own benefit; nevertheless, successful law enforcement to some extent is dependent on the help provided by persons who are themselves criminals or the associates of criminals. Many major crimes have been solved with the help of these persons who know of underworld activities.

The motives of informants include *avoidance of punishment*. No one likes to go to jail, and many a burglar has escaped punishment by providing information to the police. As a reward for information leading to the arrest of another offender, the police arrange for withdrawal or reduction of criminal charges. They are often willing to do this when the other suspect has committed a more serious crime or has been unusually successful in avoiding arrest and conviction.

The informant will try to obtain the best side of the bargain and will give as little information as possible while extracting as many concessions as possible in return. His information may be a mixture of truth and deception with more promises than facts. He will attempt to wheedle information from the detective then offer back the same information with some embellishments of his own.

He plays a dangerous game because he escapes relatively civilized punishment for his burglaries at the risk of arbitrary and cruel punishment for his betrayal of colleagues who do not extend legal safeguards, such as the rights to an attorney and to an appeal to a higher court. A thirty-year-old burglar was stabbed in the chest by another reformatory inmate because he was known to be an informer. Fearful of another attack on his life, he escaped from the prison, but was later recaptured. He gave this account of his experiences:

> It all started about two years ago when the police picked me up and threatened me with a lot of charges if I didn't help them. They had me in a corner, they had cases on me. They told me they'd give me a flyer to another state, let me go out of state, they never did. They wanted me to introduce this agent (to a fence) so they would trust him. He posed as my friend and I took him in a pawnshop. He went back later and arrested the pawnshop guy for receiving stolen goods.
>
> They knew it was me, they've got a contract on me. They tried to kill my wife, somebody shot at her in front of the house. After that I kept moving to my mom's, to my aunt's. A lot of guys were pressuring me, they knew I was an informant. They'd say, "You're going to get yours." A couple of people would say, "This guy's after you."
>
> I'd stay away from people, I wouldn't go to the gym, I wouldn't go to a movie. When I'd go to work I'd make sure no one was behind me. I had one friend but after he found out about me, even he wouldn't talk to me. It's getting to me. I'm too weak. I can't stand up to them. If I get sent back to the joint, I'm just going to hang it up. I just can't see myself going through it again. I'm not going to let anybody kill me, I'd rather do it myself.

Whenever judges adopt a policy of long severe sentences, there is an increase in the number of informers. The younger man without family ties is less likely to become an informer than the older chronic offender who faces a long prison sentence. If he is married and has young children, he knows that a ten- or fifteen-year prison sentence will mean that his children will grow up without knowing him. The temptation to inform on his accomplices or other criminals becomes much greater.

Jealousy and revenge. Whenever a burglar leaves or is unfaithful to his girl friend or wife, he runs the risk that she will respond by betraying him to the police. An accomplice who does not receive his fair share of the proceeds of a burglary or who has been cheated in some other manner may gain revenge by providing information to the police, but he will take care to conceal his own contribution to the crime.

Need for attention. Some criminals and their associates seem to be motivated by a need for attention, even if the attention and friendliness has to be sought from a police officer. Not all officers are able to establish long-term relationships with informants, and those that do so are often willing to expend much time and energy needed to preserve these relationships with persons who may be very demanding.

Obligation. Other informants are motivated by a sense of obligation arising from some favor by a law enforcement officer, for example, an officer who helped the family of a burglar while he was confined in a penitentiary. Gratitude for past favors may bring unexpected rewards.

Financial gain. Few police departments have substantial amounts of money for the payment of informants. Some federal law enforcement agencies have provided regular income for good informants, and occasionally newspapers, victims or the relatives of deceased victims, offer considerable rewards for information leading to the conviction of an offender who has committed a major crime, often one involving loss of life or great financial loss.

Elimination of competitors. No businessman welcomes a successful competitor, and a pimp who finds his income threatened by another pimp may attempt to put him out of operation by reporting to the police burglaries and thefts committed by his rival's girls.

Family pride. Law-abiding parents concerned over a son's burglaries may provide confidential information to the police in the hope that the son's criminal career will be cut short.

Protection of informants. Although textbooks on criminal investigation provide information on police record-keeping systems designed to protect the identity of informants, most officers prefer not to keep any records. No matter what steps are taken to restrict police access to these records, there is always the risk that an informant's name will reach the wrong person. There is also the risk that some day a court will subpoena these records. Many officers do not reveal names of their informants, even to fellow officers, partly for security reasons and partly because they wish to keep the informant for their own use. This latter position is not entirely selfish, for as in some other occupations, one man cannot serve two masters.

Officers who wish to obtain a search warrant or an arrest warrant on the basis of information provided by an informant need not disclose the informant's identity providing they establish his past reliability or independently corroborate the information. Care should be taken not to list the informant's name on any documents filed in court or in evidence provided at trial, as this can lead to threats upon his life, physical assault or murder of the informant as in the following case:

> The defendant, in a federal court case involving counterfeit checks, learned the names of two informers, a nightclub dancer and her boyfriend, from a copy of the affidavit for a search warrant. That same day he let out a contract to have the two informers killed for $500 a person. That night the hired gunman picked up the dancer at the nightclub and forced her at gunpoint to go to his home. Here his nerve failed him, and when the defendant in the check offense case learned of this he went to the gunman's home with the gunman's sister, and all four drove to a mountain park near Denver.
>
> The defendant hit the informant a few times and accused her of snitching. She continued to deny these accusations and he shot her. He then handed his gun first to the gunman's sister and then to the gunman, who both shot the informer. The body with six bullets in it was dumped down the hole of an outdoor privy. A few days later the gunman hid in the apartment of the victim's boyfriend and killed him with two blasts of a shotgun.

Surveillance

When reliable informants report that a burglary is going to occur at a warehouse or other building, arrangements can be made to keep the target under surveillance. If a very active burglar has successfully avoided conviction in court, detectives equipped with radios using a special channel and cars that do not resemble the conventional unmarked police cars can keep the burglar under surveillance during his working hours. There is seldom manpower available for these special assignments.

Chemical Surveillance

A "double staining" powder can be obtained that leaves a purple or violet color on the skin of anyone who touches it. This color cannot easily be washed away, and even if it is not visible after washing it will show up under a black light as bright orange in color. Whenever employees are suspected of stealing money, this powder can be used to catch the offenders as in the following case of a burglary:

> The owner of a restaurant reported to police that money kept disappearing from his safe. There were no signs of forced entry either into the combination safe or into the locked room containing the safe. The four employees who had keys to this room all passed polygraph tests. In order to catch the burglar, the detectives placed over $100 inside a special money bag after recording the serial numbers of each bill. Double staining powder was then placed in the bag, which was shaken before being left in the safe.
>
> The manager locked the safe and set the dial at twenty-five so that he could tell if anyone tampered with the dial. He also placed a match in the locked door jamb and checked the door at regular intervals. At 8 PM he found that the door had been opened and that someone had moved the dial on the safe. At this time the hands of all employees were checked, and the stain was found on the hands and clothing of an employee who admitted taking the money out of the safe.

VEHICLE THEFT INVESTIGATION

The Theft Report

When a citizen calls the Denver Police Department to report that a car has been stolen, a clerk in the Auto Theft division takes the information and then checks to see whether the missing car is in the police pound or is wanted by the police department. The clerk also checks repossession records to see whether the car has been repossessed because of the owner's failure to make payments on a car loan. If these methods prove futile, the next step is to request the precinct patrolman to call on the complainant and complete a vehicle theft report.

One of the first tasks of the patrolman will be to determine if the vehicle has been stolen. The motorist who cannot find his car may jump to the conclusion that it has been stolen. When he is not sure where he parked it or if when taken to the location in a police car he is unable to show the exact parking spot, "It was somewhere along here," then his difficulty in recall may be due to the fact that he was intoxicated when he parked the car and actually has no memory of where it is.

The driver who has been in a hit-and-run accident may falsely claim that his car was stolen in order to conceal his involvement in the accident. Leaving the scene of an accident is more likely to occur when the driver has no insurance or is under the influence of alcohol. Similarly, a burglar, robber or rapist whose car has been identified at the scene of the crime may later report that it was stolen. He usually will not want to talk to police officers and will probably ask a friend to make the report for him. Furthermore, attempts to speak to him directly frequently prove unsuccessful because he knows he will face questioning either about his crime or about the alleged auto theft. The car may have been seized by the police prior to the report of its theft.

Discreet inquiry may reveal that the owner who has reported the theft of his car has failed to make several loan payments, and this should prompt questioning of the bank or loan company to see whether they have repossessed the car. In Denver and some other cities, loan companies and tow truck companies are required by city ordinance to report any vehicle repossessions within thirty minutes, but this requirement is not always observed promptly.

Car rental agencies are sometimes quick to report that a car is stolen simply because the renter has not returned it on the date previously agreed upon. If the renter has provided a valid credit card number, the car rental agency can probably be assured of payment, and an officer who stops the car should not jail the driver without further investigation. Some state laws require that a registered letter be sent to the renter before the car can be reported as stolen.

In family fights and boyfriend-girl friend disagreements, one partner may report a vehicle stolen with the intent of causing the arrest of, or otherwise embarrassing, the other partner. Yet, no reference may be made by the complainant to this disagreement. The patrolman should be alert to any mention or discussion of a recent divorce or family squabble. It is helpful to ask who has keys to the vehicle and who has permission to use it. If the car has been taken by someone who has permission to use it and if that person does not abscond with the car, theft cannot be charged.

Vehicle theft report forms usually list the information which should be obtained by the patrolman. This includes—

location, date and time of theft;

year, make, model, body style, color and general condition of the vehicle;

license plate number, state of issue and VIN (vehicle identification number);

transmission: automatic, four-speed, three-speed, other;

special equipment: air conditioning, stereo, tape deck, bucket seats, magnesium type wheels;

dents, scratches, missing parts, broken windows, decals and other identifying features;

legal owner, insurance company, liens;

personal property left in vehicle.

Follow-Up Investigation

The detective should telephone the victim to see if he has any additional information such as a neighbor's description of a strange car in the area or a local youth seen driving off in the car. Information similar to that obtained by the patrolman will be requested to check for discrepancies. Significant differences from the original report will arouse the detective's suspicion. He will also want to know the reason for any delay in making the original report.

Most victims contact the police as soon as they become aware that their car is missing, but a delay of several hours or days in making the report is not unusual. Is the complainant in financial difficulties, does he have a prior criminal record? Has he made recent reports of burglaries or other thefts? He may have sold the car or hidden it with the intention of claiming money from the insurance company. The detective must verify these facts about the complainant.

For example, he may say the delay was due to the fact that when he discovered his car was missing near his office, he asked his wife to pick him up. On reaching his home in a neighboring suburb, he called the police, but they refused to go to his home to take the report because his home was outside of the city limits. After the weekend on his return to work he made the report. In this instance, his wife should be questioned as to when she picked him up at his office, and the complainant might be asked to name witnesses who could verify where and when he parked the car.

In the absence of any indications of a false report and clues to the identity of the thief, the investigation will conclude until such time as new leads arise or the car is recovered. The license number will have been recorded on the "hot sheet" of local thefts to be handed out daily to all patrolmen, and this number will remain on the "hot sheet" for several days. The VIN has previously been listed on NCIC across the country.

The auto theft detective may receive information from employees of service stations, garages and wrecking yards on car stripping, salvage switch operations or other illegal activities. Criminal informants may provide vital information, especially if they are members of a vehicle theft gang. A member who has recently married or become a father may become more fearful of a prison sentence and take steps to protect himself from this risk by providing a limited amount of carefully selected information to a detective.

In those states where dealers are required to keep daily records of all transactions, detectives may check these records, which include engine numbers and VINs. Failure to keep these records provides the basis for a search warrant, but this is not necessary if the owner signs a consent-to-search form. The search is a time-consuming, dirty, difficult task, as there may be from 50 to 3,000 vehicles scattered about in the lot, sometimes piled one on top of another, as well as doors with or without VIN plates stacked in long rows.

If the VIN plate is missing, a check should be made for the confidential number on the frame. Statutes usually permit officers to seize any vehicles with altered, changed or obliterated engine or vehicle identification numbers.

Surveillance of active auto thieves and fences will depend upon the availability of detectives. Background investigations on where they live and work and the names of their associates may provide promising leads. Utility records may show payment for electricity and natural gas at locations other than their homes. Ownership of a mini-storage warehouse may indicate the location of stolen auto parts.

Victims sometimes make independent investigations unhampered by those court restrictions which curb police investigations, as in the following example:

> Burglars forced open the gate at the rear of a paint shop, allowed a guard dog out of the lot, and removed four magnesium wheels, together with four radial steel tires, four Corvette transmissions and four Corvette hoods. The owner of the paint shop noticed from shoe prints in the earth that one of the burglars had very large feet. He recalled that an employee of a sports car agency, who had been in his shop the week before the burglary, had very large feet, and he obtained the home address of this young man from his employer.
>
> He went to the man's home, which was in a residential area of expensive homes surrounding a small park. No one was at home and in the backyard behind a tall wooden fence he found two of the Corvette hoods stolen from his paint shop. Numerous car parts were in the yard scattered around a small garden shed. He also noticed that on two sides of the two-car garage, attached to the home, were fans and filters consistent with the use of the garage for a car painting operation. The fans are needed to carry paint fumes from the enclosed area of the garage.
>
> A detective would not have had the authority to enter this man's enclosed backyard without the owner's permission, and he would not have had sufficient evidence to obtain a search warrant without the information obtained by the victim on his own initiative. A search warrant was obtained, and a stolen Corvette was found in the garage. It was mounted on blocks and had been

repainted in the garage. Parts of another stolen Corvette and two stolen motorcycles were also recovered.

In theft of farm and construction equipment, the victim should be asked if any part of the equipment is in need of replacement. Area dealers in this equipment should be notified, as the stolen equipment may be brought in for repair.

Identification of Stolen Vehicles

Officers on patrol should watch for stolen vehicles and also for clues that suggest the possibility a car has been stolen. A driver who seems out of place in a vehicle or shows a nervous reaction on sight of a police car should be checked out. A juvenile in a new car driving around in a poor housing area will not pass unnoticed. At one time police were advised to watch for poorly dressed persons in expensive cars, but today one often sees scruffy-looking persons driving late model luxury cars.

There is the car thief who becomes extremely careful on seeing a police car, going well below the speed limit and not only using his turn signals but also signalling with his hand. At the first opportunity, he turns off on a side street in the hope of avoiding possible further scrutiny by the police car. On the other hand, he may be so intent on watching the police car in his rearview mirror that he runs through a red light or stop sign. If the driver is unfamiliar with the controls, he may make a sudden jerky start, grind the gears or inadvertently turn on the windshield wipers on a sunny day.

Pry marks on windows, doors or the trunk and broken or missing door glass may indicate the driver has stolen a vehicle. License plates held in place with wire, or obscured by dirt, and a contrast between the plates and the car (dirty car, clean license plates; clean car, dirty license plates) should arouse suspicion.

If the driver appears to be under the age of sixteen, he can be stopped because he is too young to have a driver's license. Any traffic or vehicular violations, such as illegal turns, turning or changing lanes without signalling, defective lights, out-of-date safety stickers or license tags, obstructed windshield (something hanging from the rearview mirror) and bald tires will permit the officer to stop the car. The driver who hurries back to the police car may not want the officer to look inside his car.

The officer now has an opportunity to check the driver's license. The physical description on the driver's license should be compared with the appearance of the driver. Thus, the license may show a 300 pound person, five feet, eight inches in height, whereas the driver is 140 pounds and five feet, ten inches in height. The officer will also check the car registration papers and the VIN which can all be checked on NCIC. A bent, wrinkled VIN plate or one held in place with pop rivets rather than rosette head rivets may be a VIN plate from another vehicle. The use of plastic embossed tape as a replacement VIN number indicates that the car has been stolen. The officer should note if there are any wires hanging below the dashboard, which may indicate the car has been hot-wired.

The officer should ask the driver where he bought the car. If he states he just bought it in Kansas and the dealer's decal lists a location in Nebraska, further inquiry is indicated. Does the vehicle have six or eight cylinders; what is the mileage; when and where was the last oil change; are all useful questions. If the driver states that the car belongs to a friend or relative, then the owner of the car as recorded on the registration papers can be telephoned by the radio dispatcher, or if he lives in the area the patrol car can go directly to his home.

Passengers should be questioned separately from the driver. If they give totally different or exactly the same stories about the car, its origins, movements that day and so on, be on guard. If their stories are fairly close, they are probably telling the truth, e.g. the driver says he borrowed the car from his brother at a party, and his passenger states that the driver borrowed the car from a friend at the party.

When the officer has reasonable cause to believe the car is stolen, further questioning should be delayed until the driver has been advised of his rights. If the car has been stolen and the owner is not immediately available to give permission for a search, the police should search the car for inventory purposes to protect both the owner in securing his property and the police officer from later claims that property was misappropriated from the car while it was in the possession of the police.

If, however, the officer has reasonable cause to suspect that there is something illegal inside the car, he should obtain a search warrant. When in doubt, it is better to obtain a search warrant. Searches by warrant are presumed valid unless shown otherwise. In a search without a warrant, the burden is on the district attorney to prove that the search was warranted, but if the search is with a warrant, the burden is on the defense attorney of going forward and showing otherwise.

Unoccupied stolen cars are sometimes left in isolated areas. Juveniles who steal cars for their own use and for partial stripping will often pick a vacant lot near their homes. Indeed in some housing projects there are favorite spots for leaving stolen cars.

Searching Stolen Vehicles

If the engine is warm, the thief may still be in the vicinity and could return later. The coil wire should be pulled out, or the vehicle should be otherwise disabled so that the thief cannot drive it away. Surveillance of the vehicle should be maintained for several hours. If no one shows, the area around the vehicle should be checked for footprints and discarded papers. Persons living or working in the area may have noticed who abandoned the vehicle.

Stolen cars should be checked for fingerprints, particularly mirrors; the roof over the driver's head where he may place his left hand while driving; the posts between the wing and main windows; the trunk and gas tank spout areas; non-textured steering wheels, all levers and handles. Joyriders often leave empty beer cans and pop bottles that should be checked for fingerprints. If the car has been stripped of the battery, look for fingerprints on the hood. If the tires and wheels have been removed, look for fingerprints on the fenders above the wheel wells and on the bumper where the jack is mounted. If the transmission has been removed, look for prints under the car.

A search should be made for the broadcast teletype, computer broadcast or packing slip which is a computer print-out listing the VIN and equipment on a car (body type, paint color, engine type, transmission and accessories). This computer print-out is used by workers on the assembly line at the manufacturing plant, and just before the car leaves the assembly line, the print-out is stuffed in the seat springs, under the floor carpet or in Chevrolet Corvettes next to the gasoline tank. If the VIN on the car has been altered, this broadcast teletype may provide the correct VIN.

Articles left behind by the thief can lead to his identification. Check under seats and floor mats for notes, receipts, credit card slips, parking tickets, travel maps and so on. Fast-food containers indicate outlets whose employees may recall the vehicle and its occupants. Burglary tools, blood stains and bullet holes suggest the thief's involvement in other crimes as well as auto theft.

If the VIN has been altered, changed or obliterated the confidential number should be obtained (see Chapter 8 for information on restoration of numbers). The location of this number is provided to authorized agencies by the National Automobile Theft Bureau. This bureau also publishes annually a passenger vehicle identification manual listing vehicle identification number locations with an explanation of the numbering system for each make of car. Thus, the VIN, 2U87L8L113653 is made up as follows:

2: Manufacturers symbol—Pontiac
U: Car line—Firebird Formula
87: Body type—Hard top coupe
L: Engine symbol—8-350 4V
8: Model year—1978
L: Assembly plant—Van Nuys, California
113653: Sequential production number

The bureau can assist the detective in tracing the ownership of stolen vehicles, as the bureau lists the VIN, owner's name and license number.

It is sometimes difficult to locate the identification numbers on tractors and farm equipment and helpful information is provided in the *Official Guide on Tractors and Farm Equipment* published by the National Farm and Power Equipment Dealers Association, 10877 Watson Road, St. Louis, Missouri 63123. A

Location and Identification Guide for Construction Equipment is published by AED Research and Services Corporation, 615 West 22nd Street, Oak Brook, Illinois 60521.

Automatic License Plate Scanning System

Computer-based surveillance of license plates has been proposed. O'Hara notes that in an automatic license plate scanning system (ALPS):

> Electronic cameras mounted at strategic points along the highway, such as toll booths, would scan all passing vehicles, record and recognize all numbers and letters on license plates. The data would be sent by leased phone lines to a computer containing a list of all wanted license plates. If a scanned plate checks with a number on the wanted list, this fact together with other relevant information on the crime involved would be sent back to the scanning station within two seconds. The local operator would then radio a patrol car parked downstream along the highway to intercept the vehicle bearing the wanted plates. To operate ten ALPS scanners in a large urban area for five years would cost about $11,000,000. Such a system would be expected to cut the cost of all damages from car theft by an impressive $100,000,000 per year. Within a few years we should expect to see a nationwide link-up of computers maintaining up-to-the-minute lists of stolen cars, tied at strategic points to license-plate scanners (2).

Motorcycle Theft Investigation

Motorcycles are seldom stolen for joyriding, and the motorcycle thief is usually someone experienced in riding and repairing motorcycles who wants the cycle for himself, for its parts or for resale. He does not betray himself, as many auto thieves do, by difficulty in handling unfamiliar controls, by a nervous reaction on seeing the police or by looking out of place on the machine.

Arrests are usually made on the basis of information that a person is riding a "hot" motorcycle, a report that a machine brought to a reputable dealer for repair has stirred an employee's suspicion or because a suspect is known to be a repeat offender. If a rider commits a traffic violation, he can be stopped for a check of his driver's license, registration papers and motorcycle VIN.

Members of motorcycle gangs such as the Disciples, the Deadmen and the Sons of Silence are not noted for their respect for the law. When stopped by the police, they may arm themselves with bicycle chains as an act of intimidation and mill around so that if a stolen cycle is discovered, the officers will not be able to identify the rider. It is important to make each rider remain on or immediately alongside his machine until it has been checked.

It is much more difficult to check a motorcycle than a car to see if it is stolen. The majority of police officers lack the necessary skill, and police departments should make every effort to provide special training only for those officers who express a special interest. Officers without such an interest and with minimal training are likely either to overlook evidence of theft or to impound motorcycles because of the mistaken assumption that an identification number has been altered.

Many factors contribute to the difficulty in recognizing stolen motorcycles. Police officers are familiar with makes and models of automobiles and can easily verify vehicle descriptions on registration papers, but they do not have the same knowledge of motorcycles and may not know, for example, the difference between a Harley Davidson Sportster and a Harley Davidson Electraglide.

An officer can quickly tell the difference between a Model A Ford engine and a 1979 Ford engine, but many officers would have difficulty in telling the difference between a 1939 Harley Davidson engine and a 1979 model as their appearance has not changed significantly during this time. Many engines dating back to the 1930s and 1940s are still in use, and many stolen late model cycle engines are often covered by old titles.

Prior to 1970, the VIN on a Harley Davidson is the engine number. Since 1970, the VIN is the frame number, although the original engine on the cycle bears the same number as the frame. Since 1970, each VIN number has an unusual appearance in order to make it more difficult to alter or restamp the numbers. Thus, the number 5 is stamped at an angle and the number 8 is one triangle on top of another. Some officers will seize a Harley Davidson motorcycle because of the odd appearance of the numbers. Some other manufacturers also use distinctive numbers.

Some motorcycle manufacturers hand stamp all or part of the VIN numbers and the figures are often out of line. If a mistake is made in the number, some companies will just stamp another number over the wrong number. If the Harley Davidson Company makes a mistake, they will put a line through the entire number and stamp the correct number above or below, then add their trade symbol to show that the number is genuine.

A Kawasaki VIN includes letters, e.g. KAF as well as five numbers, but the title may list only the numbers. If the motorcycle is stolen and the VIN is taken from the title, then only these numbers will be placed on NCIC. If a police officer stops a person riding this stolen motorcycle and checks the motorcycle on NCIC, listing the full VIN including the letters, he will not receive a report that this motorcycle is listed as stolen. He should also list on NCIC the VIN numbers without the letters.

The VIN is often stamped on the frame on a raised round surface that will become flat or oval from grinding the frame to obliterate the number. An unusually thin boss may be visible to the naked eye. Experienced thieves will sandblast the surface to give it a textured appearance and hide file marks. The surface may be raised to its original level by using a liquid metal compound and this alteration is difficult to detect unless an acid solution is applied (see Chapter 8).

Air cooled motorcycle engines are made of an aluminum alloy, and it is much easier to obliterate the engine number than on a cast-iron car engine. File marks near the number or nicks on protruding parts of the engine suggest that the number has been altered. Heli-arc welding to obliterate the numbers may be very difficult to detect by eyesight alone, however, it may be possible to feel a difference in surface texture, and there may be hole marks from gas trapped in the metal.

If the engine has been painted, the purpose is usually to hide alterations of the engine number, and the paint over the number should be removed. Conversion of a 3 to an 8 and a 1 to a 4 or a 7 should be recognized relatively easily.

INVESTIGATION OF THEFT BY EMPLOYEES

Surveillance of employees is one method of detecting dishonest workers. Peep holes above cash registers in department stores make it possible to check store clerks who enter inexpensive items on the cash register and package these items with expensive merchandise, then hand the package to an accomplice. Undercover security officers who play the role of a shopper or new employee also check for these and other types of theft by employees, such as putting merchandise in trash cans and leaving it near a trash bin for later removal.

Discreet inquiries may reveal those employees who are living beyond their means, drinking excessively, gambling or in debt. All these investigations are usually performed by private detective agencies. Police detectives, during investigation of thefts, can often recognize inadequate security practices and advise with management on preventive measures to reduce theft by employees.

INVESTIGATION OF THEFT

The investigation of the theft of valuable items from jewelry stores requires not only inquiry regarding the appearance of the suspect, but also inquiry regarding persons in the store before or during the theft, as an accomplice may have aided in the theft by distracting the clerk's attention at a crucial moment. As in other crimes, it is important to record full details of the thief's method of operation. The jewel thief may, for example, always ask to see an emerald and never deviate from this approach.

INVESTIGATION OF SHOPLIFTING

Most shoplifters are arrested as the result of detection by private security guards and other employees. Police investigation of reports of shoplifting, including tracing of getaway cars, identification through physical description and method of operation, as well as review of mug shots by victims also contributes to arrests. Undercover private security officers watch for shoppers: who seem to be more interested in looking at store personnel than at the merchandise; who look in mirrors not to check their personal appearance, but to observe the movements of store clerks; who wear bulky clothing or carry packages that can be used to conceal stolen merchandise; who make unusual movements to conceal items; who take many items to changing rooms or who have a guilty, nervous appearance. One should not overlook the bold shoplifter who puts on an article of clothing and walks out of the store.

INVESTIGATION OF FENCES

Antifencing units in larger police departments, through the use of informants, wiretapping and surveillance of burglars, obtain the names and addresses of suspected fences of stolen property. Walsh (*Strategies for Combatting the Criminal Receiver of Stolen Goods*) has described the following antifencing strategies (3):

THE TRADITIONAL SURVEILLANCE/WARRANT STRATEGY. It consists of performing a surveillance or stakeout at the location of a fencing operation. It need not be continuous surveillance, but may occur when peak business with thieves is known to be conducted. The purposes of the stakeout are to document the thieves entering and leaving the premises and to develop specific information on which a warrant to search can be obtained. It is the thieves frequenting the premises that serve as the key element in developing information on which to base a warrant. Once a particular theft can be attributed to one or several of these individuals, the stolen property can be searched for on the fence's premises. Often this means that cases made through the stakeout method will be based on one or two items of property, unless other items in plain view can also be seized and identified as having been stolen. . . . In a slight variation of the stakeout strategy, an informant may be used to enter the premises before a warrant is sought to confirm the presence or absence of certain property items.

THE BUY-BUST STRATEGY. The term "buy-bust" is used to connote the idea that a fence buys a piece of property and is then busted. Some jurisdictions call this the "sell-bust," with the emphasis on law enforcement selling to the fence and then busting him. These two terms are interchangeable. . . . The buy-bust strategy proceeds to acquire and mark a piece of "bait property." Then either an informant or an undercover officer will be sent into the premises, concealing a body transmitter and carrying the bait property. The officer or informant is briefed to make certain that the item is represented to the fence as stolen in nature. This is critical and must be skillfully accomplished. The aim is to complete a transaction with the fence for the "stolen" item at which point the undercover operator leaves. Soon thereafter, backup officers who have monitored the conversation enter the premises to arrest the fence. On that basis they may receive consent to search for other stolen items, as well as to make limited searches in conjunction with the arrest. In any event, they will have one case built around the bait property item.

THE UNDERCOVER BUY STRATEGY. This strategy is similar to the buy-bust method described above except that it is a more sophisticated approach. It involves incriminating purchases from the fence rather than sales to him. The undercover buy strategy requires that undercover agents actively work to become customers of the fence, i.e., to buy stolen property from him that he has earlier received from thieves. This antifencing method relies heavily on skilled undercover officers and on trusted informants who can successfully introduce undercover officers into a fencing operation.

THE UNDERCOVER BUY-SELL STRATEGY. This is the most active of localized antifencing strategies. It is best utilized by a covert antifencing effort that has a relatively long time period in which to work, six to eight months, for example. This is because the undercover buy-sell will complete several transactions of different kinds with the fence in order to build its cases. Units working with this strategy will actively create scenarios within which to interact with the fence. To do so, they will need access to both property and investigative funds to use in buying and selling transactions (3).

STOREFRONT OPERATIONS

In storefront operations, undercover officers pose as fences with the object of arresting burglars and thieves who sell them stolen property. A vacant house, store or repair shop is rented, and surveillance equipment is set up so that videotape pictures can be taken from a concealed location of the criminals selling their loot. After a period of several months operation, the criminals are arrested at the storefront or elsewhere on arrest warrants.

The storefront should not be in a well-to-do area alongside a large office building, but should be in a rather seedy, suburban neighborhood, preferably in a small shopping area with businesses such as a donut store, filling station or auto-body shop that have many customers constantly coming and going. Parking should be available and a garage or bay area provides privacy for delivery of merchandise. Burglars do not like to carry stolen goods half a block from their parked car. A van can be parked nearby so that officers hidden inside can note license plate numbers.

The cover business should be one that permits temporary closing of the store without attracting attention. For example, a landscaping or surveying business or a transfer and storage agency. If a potential customer walks in and wants a residential lot to be surveyed, he can be told that the firm only does industrial surveying and vice versa. It is easy for the undercover officer to say that he just does the laboring work and the boss is out.

Alterations will be made to provide concealment for video-taping and sound-recording equipment. It may be necessary to add cork insulation to a wall to obtain better sound recordings. A colorful poster will encourage the thief to stand in a good position for the camera. A clock and calendar in the background provide a time and date record of the transaction on the video-tape.

One or two reliable informants spread the word that goods can be sold at the storefront and business soon picks up as one person tells another. The undercover officers should not offer too much money for stolen merchandise as this arouses the burglar's suspicion. The officer should offer the standard local price for new television sets and about 5 percent of the value of other goods.

Items purchased should not be allowed to accumulate for fear of attracting a return visit by a burglar. If a lot of money is needed to pay for merchandise, the officer should explain that he will have to get the money from his boss. This procedure reduces the risk of a customer setting up an armed robbery of the storefront. A weapon taped under a desk provides additional security for the officer. A backup team remains out of sight to provide protection.

The thieves may express concern that they are dealing with a sting operation. "This sounds and looks like a federal storefront," and the undercover officer will have to give a joking response. Most storefronts avoid any activities involving narcotics or gambling, but may obtain information on these activities. When the money available for purchasing stolen merchandise begins to run out; when few new thieves are coming in; and when the identities of most of the customers have been established; decision may be made on the closing date. On that day the burglars and thieves are arrested when they bring their stolen goods to the storefront. Others are arrested at their homes by other officers.

Storefront operations have been successful in recovering large amounts of stolen merchandise and in leading to the arrests of many burglars and thieves. Critics complain that the storefront operations encourage crime by paying burglars and thieves for stolen goods, that they do not put fences out of business and that victims are upset over the long delay between police recovery of their property and its return. The owner of an expensive stolen four-wheel-drive vehicle was bitter because the insurance company payment did not cover his loss, and at the time he made the settlement the police already had custody of his vehicle, but had not notified him as they wished to obtain more stolen cars from the auto-thief, who might become suspicious if he saw the owner in his vehicle.

REFERENCES

1. Fox, R. H. and Cunningham, C. L.: *Crime Scene Search and Physical Evidence Handbook*. Washington, U.S. Government Printing Office, 1974.
2. O'Hara, C. E.: *Fundamentals of Criminal Investigation*, 4th ed. Springfield, Thomas, 1976.
3. Walsh, M. E.: *Strategies for Combatting the Criminal Receiver of Stolen Goods*. Washington, U.S. Government Printing Office, 1976.

CHAPTER 8

SCIENTIFIC EVIDENCE:
THE CRIME LABORATORY

John M. Macdonald and Robert E. Nicoletti[*]

A little monograph on the ashes of
one hundred and forty different varieties
of pipe, cigar, and cigarette tobacco.
—Sir Arthur Conan Doyle
The Adventures of Sherlock Holmes,
The Boscombe Valley Mystery

IN CRIMES AGAINST the person, such as armed robbery and rape, there is a direct confrontation between the criminal and his victim, but in crimes against property, such as burglary and theft, there may be no direct encounter between the criminal and his victim, indeed there may be no eyewitnesses to the crime. When the accused claims innocence and there are no eyewitnesses to his crime, his conviction in court must be based upon indirect or circumstantial evidence.

Indirect evidence can be more effective in proving guilt or innocence than direct evidence. Expert testimony that the defendant's fingerprints were found on the windowsill of the victim's home, and that the defendant's signature was on the pawn ticket for the victim's television set may be more convincing to a jury than the victim's identification of the defendant's photograph based upon a fleeting glance of the burglar late at night in a dark hallway.

Indirect evidence can include the ownership of a burglary

---

[*] Lieutenant Nicoletti, Director, Bureau of Laboratories, Denver Police Department, received training in the scientific investigation of crime at the FBI Academy and at the University of Louisville. Sixteen of his twenty years service in the Denver Police Department have been in the Bureau of Laboratories.

tool and the inabiilty of the accused to account for his actions at the time of the crime. Other indirect evidence by experts from the crime laboratory provides a link between the criminal and his crime.

This chapter is not directed to the expert laboratory technician, but is written for the officer who responds to the scene of a burglary. This officer has to know what physical evidence to look for, where to find it and when to send for the laboratory technician. Ideally, this expert should respond to all crime scenes, but the reality is that few police departments have sufficient personnel for this purpose. The expert should be called to all major crimes and to any burglary involving forced entry.

The officer at the scene often has to decide what evidence should be preserved for laboratory examination. He needs to know both the capabilities and limitations of a modern police laboratory, and he should be familiar with the techniques for collection, marking and preservation of evidence. This chapter will attempt to present this information with an emphasis on practice, rather than on theory.

INDIVIDUAL CHARACTERISTICS

The criminalist is sometimes able to state with confidence that evidence has unique characteristics that clearly establish the identity of a person or an object. Fingerprints, for example, may point to one person and one person only. It is sometimes possible to link two objects together, for example, pieces of glass and wood when the broken or cut edges can be matched. Tools and tool marks, shoes and shoe prints, firearms and bullets can be linked together when there are sufficient distinctive characteristics present on both objects. Unique markings, which have identifying characteristics, may come from peculiarities at the time of manufacture or from use. But a manufacturing defect, for example, in the tread pattern of a tennis shoe may be present in many hundreds of pairs of those shoes.

CLASS CHARACTERISTICS

In the absence of special identifying characteristics, evidence may have to be classified by the criminalist as having class characteristics only. For example, glass fragments too small to permit matching of broken edges; pieces of wood without matching edges; tool marks, bullets, and shoe prints *when* the markings are insufficient for identification; paint such as from a safe or car; soil; hairs; fibers and blood have class characteristics only.

No matter how thoroughly this material is examined, it can only be placed in a class. A definite identification can never be made, as there is always a possibility of more than one source for the material recovered by the police officer. This material may still be useful as evidence, especially when there is a preponderance of matching class characteristics as, for example, paint with many layers all matching; soil with foreign matter such as paint chips, unusual seeds and perhaps even safe insulation; or building dust from the suspect's clothing, matching brick, mortar, plaster, paint, insulation and glass dust from the scene of the burglary.

Several separate pieces of evidence each with class characteristics may also be useful in court, as for example, similarities between the defendant's shoes and soil impressions at the scene of the burglary, as well as between both safe paint and safe insulation on his clothes and specimens from the scene. A transfer of several items, such as hairs and fibers from a burglar rapist, onto his victim together with a similar transfer from the victim to the suspect are unlikely to be due to chance.

This type of physical evidence may also be used to aid in the elimination of suspects. For example, the criminalist may be able to show that soil found on the suspect's shoes matches soil from the area where the suspect stated he was at during the time of the burglary.

APPROACHING THE CRIME SCENE

There is a need for caution in approaching the crime scene, as it is so easy to destroy evidence by driving or stepping on tire marks, footprints, bullets or other evidence that may be near the scene of the burglary. The officers may be responding to a call of a burglary in progress, and in their haste to capture the burglar they may walk over his tracks in the mud or snow, only to find that he has already left the scene and that the crime is murder.

PROTECTING THE CRIME SCENE

The precautions taken to protect the crime scene will depend upon the nature of the crime. A burglary involving the theft of an item valued at less than ten dollars does not justify the calling in of other officers to protect the crime scene. At a major crime scene, areas will have to be protected not only from the public, news reporters, television cameramen and political figures, but also from interested police officers not responsible for protecting or investigating the crime scene.

COLLECTION OF EVIDENCE

Physical evidence will be collected according to the legal requirements, that the officer should be able to identify it, describe its exact location at the scene of the crime and show the chain of custody. Care should be taken to store the physical evidence properly so that there will be no avoidable changes in this evidence between its collection and presentation in court.

"Examples of the type of changes that must be avoided are the use of unclean containers that would introduce chemical or bacterial contamination to a sample; the use of containers that allow spillage, evaporation or seepage of a sample, or alteration of an item by accidentally scratching, bending or even touching it, or cross-exchange, such as placing the suspect tool to be examined for paint in intimate contact with the painted wood from the scene" (2).

At a major crime scene the laboratory technician, whenever possible, will examine physical evidence before it has been moved. In a routine burglary the patrolman, while waiting for the laboratory technician, will place all moveable items of physical evidence in one convenient location, taking care not to obliterate fingerprints. This enables the laboratory technician to complete his work rapidly so that he can cover as many crime scenes as possible during his period on duty and also reduce the time spent by officers waiting for his appearance at other crime scenes.

In handling items that might have latent fingerprints, the officer should hold the item in areas where the burglar is unlikely to have placed his hand or fingers. Thus, a glass should be picked up by placing fingers inside of it, a bottle should be held by the top and bottom, a gun by the checkered grip or by a string through the trigger guard and broken glass should be held by the edges.

PHOTOGRAPHY

It has been said that a picture is worth a thousand words, certainly the photographs of a burglary scene often greatly simplify the work of the prosecutor and police witnesses at a jury trial. This is particularly true when there is widespread malicious destruction of property. A police officer can testify that motor oil and foodstuffs, including eggs, syrup, cereal, milk, pickles, ketchup and mustard, were thrown all over the kitchen, basement stairs and basement. He can also report that holes had been knocked in the wall; bedroom and bathroom mirrors had been broken; milk had been poured over one of the beds; and plants had been pulled out of their pots and torn apart. Only color pictures of the home, however, can show adequately the full extent of the damages.

Even when the burglar has been captured at the scene and his guilt does not appear to be in doubt, photographs may still be of value. At the trial when the defense attorney claims that his drunken client sought refuge on a bitterly cold winter night by wandering into an unlocked home, this defense will fall apart when the jury sees pictures of a chest of drawers with all the drawers pulled out, pictures of the loot piled alongside the rear door and pictures of the front door showing clear evidence of forced entry.

Photographs will be taken not only of the exterior and interior of the building, but also of items such as filing cabinets, strongboxes and safes that have been forced open. Fingerprints (when visible with or without development), distinctive foot and tire prints and all tool marks will be photographed. Crime laboratory technicians seldom have time to cast impressions of foot, tire and other prints, furthermore, good photography is sometimes better than castings.

Photographs of any scene should be taken from different

angles, as it may be claimed that a single picture gives a distorted or false impression of the crime scene. As photographs do not show the distances between objects, a crime scene sketch should be made listing important distances. This sketch need not be drawn to scale.

FINGERPRINTING

A fingerprint is an impression of the ridges on the skin surfaces of the fingers. Impressions can also be obtained from the palms of the hands, toes and soles of the feet. There are three types of fingerprints.

LATENT FINGERPRINTS. These result from the impression left by perspiration from the sweat pores on the ridges of the fingers. Body grease from hairy surfaces also contributes to the formation of latent fingerprints. These prints may not be visible on paper, but on other surfaces their presence can often be detected in the oblique beam of a flashlight.

Fingerprint powders are used to develop latent fingerprints on hard nonabsorbent surfaces, and these prints can be photographed with a special fixed-focus box-type fingerprint camera with its own light source. The prints can then be lifted by applying transparent tape, which is transferred to a clear plastic lift or a white or black card. Special techniques are used to develop latent fingerprints on paper and absorbent surfaces.

VISIBLE FINGERPRINTS. Fingerprints left from contact with paint, blood, grease, dirt or dust and ink do not need to be developed and should be photographed. The underlying surface can then be covered with transparent tape and preserved as evidence, but this is not always possible, as the surface may be part of a piece of furniture or other item of value.

PLASTIC FINGERPRINTS. Fingerprints left in butter, soap, warm chocolate or wax and fresh paint should also be photographed, and if necessary further procedures can be used to preserve the substance containing the fingerprint. Occasionally, a burglar will break through the same window two days in succession, and on his second visit he may leave his fingerprints in the fresh putty holding the new glass in place.

THE SEARCH FOR FINGERPRINTS

The crime laboratory expert will make a special search for fingerprints at the site of forced entry, including window frames and sills, window glass and glass doors. Broken glass outside the house is especially important, as glass forced into the house has probably been struck by some object, whereas glass outside may have been pulled out by the burglar. His fingerprints on one side and the edge of a piece of glass and his thumb print on the other side, could only have been placed there by someone removing the glass. It could not have been on the glass because he was a visitor or a workman in the home, as he may claim later in court.

The walls near light switches, the top shelves of closets that the burglar reaches for to check for items and the underside of toilet seats are possible locations of the burglar's fingerprints. Oblique light from a flashlight will show where a thin layer of dust has been moved by the burglar. Filing cabinets, coin banks, metal containers and jewelry boxes usually have smooth hard surfaces which are ideal for fingerprinting. He will also check liquor bottles and glasses as even the busiest burglar is tempted by a Chivas Regal®.

Any items that have been moved by the burglar should be fingerprinted. Even if no occupants are available to point out those articles that have been shifted from their usual position, the detective can often tell when items have been moved by the burglar. He will move pictures to see if money is hidden behind them, and even if he does not take firearms, he will often examine them. He may also open glass cabinets to remove small expensive plates, carved objects and antiques that catch his eye, but which he does not steal because he has no market for them. Juvenile burglars are particularly likely to handle unusual items.

Even if an eyewitness reports that the suspect was wearing gloves, this should not deter the search for fingerprints, as the burglar may have removed his gloves to open envelopes or eat food at the scene. There may also be a hole in his gloves. If he has covered his fingers with lacquer hair spray to conceal his fingerprints, the lacquer may gradually wear off during the burglary. When a burglary appears to be an "inside job" (no forced entry, burglar takes only large sum of money or coin collection from a secret hiding place) extensive fingerprinting may be pointless, as the suspect probably has legitimate access to the home, and if it is an accomplice, he goes straight to the hiding place and then leaves.

In the burglary of an office there may be papers scattered all over the room, and it is not practical to print them all. However, if a small strongbox has been opened in a house burglary and a relatively few papers from within are found nearby, then they should be examined. Very porous bond paper may have to be taken to the crime laboratory for chemical treatment to raise latent fingerprints.

If the burglar left his car at the scene, a search warrant should be obtained to permit a search and fingerprinting. If the burglar's car was not left in the driveway it may be difficult to identify, but officers will check on NCIC the license plates of cars in the vicinity that arouse their suspicion. For example, a car parked at an unusual angle or left with the motor running; cars with out of county license numbers or with license plates that have been bent or obscured with dirt to make identification more difficult for possible eyewitnesses; or an old car in a well-to-do neighborhood. NCIC search may show improper use of plates, a stolen vehicle or ownership by a known burglar.

Whenever a burglar is identified through fingerprints and there are further unidentified fingerprints, a list of the known associates of the suspect including names of persons listed on the suspect's police contact cards should be obtained to permit comparison of fingerprints with those found at the scene.

Batteries are a good source of fingerprints. The burglar who takes care to use gloves in his crimes may not have used them when he put batteries in his flashlight that he left at the scene. The victim, who neglected to record the serial number of his portable radio, put fresh batteries in the radio just before it was stolen in a burglary. The presence of these fingerprints on a radio, found in the possession of a suspect, contributed to his conviction on trial.

Burglary victims may think that recovery of a fingerprint

will lead to identification of the burglar. Such fingerprints are of value only when the detective has one or more suspects in mind and asks the crime laboratory technician to make a comparison. The arrest of a burglar with a distinctive method of operation will lead to a comparison of his fingerprints with those recovered in similar burglaries.

> It must be understood that if the identity of suspects is not known it is not possible to go to the main fingerprint file and search through it to establish the identity of latent prints. Fingerprint cards are filed according to a classification formula that is derived from a study of all ten of the fingers on a card. When only one or a few latent prints are found, it is impossible to make up a classification formula that will enable technicians to go to the main fingerprint file and search the appropriate section unless all or nearly all of the cards can be checked individually—an obviously impossible task, considering that fingerprint cards number in the millions in even medium-sized identification bureaus. It is therefore necessary either to have a suspect physically present so that his fingerprints can be recorded for comparison or to know the name of a suspect so that his fingerprint classification, and ultimately his fingerprint card, can be discovered in the main file (3).

It is not possible to go to the master fingerprint file when only one or a few latent fingerprints are found, however, many police departments keep a single or 10-1 fingerprint system in which each fingerprint is classified separately. Thus, if a single latent fingerprint is recovered, it is possible to classify it and to search for it through the single fingerprint system.

This procedure is very time-consuming, and the system is usually restricted to a limited number of major felons. In Denver, for example, persons convicted of burglary, robbery, rape and homicide are classified, and if they are not arrested again within five years, their cards are removed from the system. The cards are filed in age groups 19 and under, 20 to 25 and over 25 years of age. This classification further simplifies the search when the age group of the suspect is either known or suggested by the offender's method of operation.

Progress is being made by the FBI toward computer scanning for single latent prints, and it has been suggested that some day in the future it may become possible to determine a criminal's identity by placing his hand on an electronic scanner unit mounted in a patrol car (1).

TOOLS AND TOOL MARKS

Forced entry into a home or other building may leave the signs of toolmarks, whether from a screwdriver, pry bar, vise grips, pipe wrench or water pump plier. Drills are used on safes, and boltcutters are used on perimeter metal fences and padlocks. The door frame or any other object damaged by a tool should be photographed including close-up pictures of the toolmarks.

Any metal or wood damaged by toolmarks should be preserved as evidence. To enable positive identification of the tool used in the burglary, a comparison microscope may be used.

A tool may not be recovered until months or even years later when the suspect is arrested for another burglary or comes under suspicion through information provided by an accomplice or informant.

It is a simple matter to remove a doorknob or the striker plate from a door frame. Damaged sections can easily be cut out of an aluminum window frame, but a cutting torch will be needed to remove a section of a safe door. Victims, understandably, will object to any removal of material containing tool marks if such removal causes costly damage, but the damage from the burglary may be so extensive that the lock or aluminum door frame will have to be replaced anyway.

Almost every tool has unique characteristics either from manufacture or from continued use. Nicks and scratches appear, which contribute to the distinctive tool marks visible under the comparison microscope, on both the tool and the damaged object. The following two cases illustrate the value of this procedure:

> A burglar rapist was arrested at the scene of a rape in possession of a narrow screwdriver. Test markings from this screwdriver were compared with markings on the striker plate from the lock of the door which had been forced open by the burglar. Sufficient identifiable markings were found to identify positively

the screwdriver as the tool used to pry the door striker plate not only in this burglary rape, but also in four other burglary rapes. In each case the damage to the striker plate was slight, but fortunately all the striker plates in the previous offenses had been preserved as evidence.

A very successful safe burglar, who never left any fingerprints at the scenes of his numerous safe crackings, on one occasion took a small safe to his home where he used an electric drill to open it. The safe was later dumped in a vacant lot. He entered pleas of guilty when confronted with a laboratory expert's report that a ¾ inch drill, recovered on a search of his home, matched not only the toolmarks on the safe, but also toolmarks on the metal shavings from the safe recovered from a trash bin in his home.

The comparison microscope has largely replaced the casting of toolmarks, a cumbersome procedure now used by only a few experts when material containing the toolmarks cannot be removed for examination.

Photographs should always be taken at the scene to identify the location of the toolmarks. Close-up photographs at the scene may be used for class comparison purposes only. These photographs can show, for example, that an indentation in a wooden door caused by the levering action of a screwdriver, matches the shape and size of a screwdriver found in the possession of a suspect.

Trace material on a tool from a window frame, for example, can be compared physically, chemically or spectographically with material from the damaged area of the window frame. If the tool breaks during the forced entry it may be possible to match the broken piece left at the scene with the damaged tool recovered later from the burglar.

BROKEN METALS

Broken tools used by burglars to gain entry are not the only broken metals of value used as evidence. Fox and Cunningham note the following:

Items that are stolen are frequently broken from their mounts. In such cases, the mounts are important in proving that the object was the one stolen. There are many other possibilities for broken metals or objects to appear in evidence. For

example, an antenna broken from a "walkie talkie" used by a
suspect during the commission of a crime was important evidence
in a Kansas City burglary case which led to a conviction (2).

SHOE AND TIRE PRINTS

Photographs may be taken of shoe or tire prints left at the
scene by the burglar or his vehicle. These photographs of
impressions left in mud, snow, grease or paint will show the
shape, size, pattern and any peculiarities such as cuts, gouges
and areas of unusual wear.

Casts can be made of shoe, foot and tire prints, but the
procedure takes at least one and one-half hours. Busy crime
laboratory technicians, even if they are not responding to calls
from one homicide, two rape and several burglary scenes, are
not readily inclined toward this procedure, especially when
useful, but less time-consuming results can be obtained through
photography. If an arrest is not made within a month or so,
the surface of the assailant's shoe or tire may have changed
during this time from constant use.

BLOOD AND SEMINAL STAINS

While examination of blood and seminal stains found at the
scene of a burglary cannot provide positive identification of a
suspect, the tests may allow positive exclusion of a suspect as
the person responsible for the stains. On the other hand, if
the specimens match the blood tests on the suspect, the crime
laboratory expert can testify regarding the statistical probability
of such a finding. If a person is a secretor (approximately 65
to 80% of the population are secretors), then his blood type
can be determined from examination of other body fluid stains
such as sweat, saliva, semen and urine stains. Seminal stains
are left at the scene by burglars who masturbate, usually on
women's underclothing.

If a burglar cuts himself as he breaks through a window he
will usually leave a bloodstain on the glass fragments. If a
suspect questioned near the scene of the burglary has a fresh

laceration on his forearm and his blood type is different from that found on the bloodstained broken glass, clearly the suspect did not cut his arm breaking in the window. Blood enzyme studies should also be performed.

Officers responding to a silent burglar alarm arrested a man near the scene. The burglar had opened an overhead door in the building by punching a hole in the door, then reaching through the hole to unlock the door. On the door lock just inside the opening there were bloodstains and this lock was removed so that the bloodstains could be tested. The chemist reported that the blood was human blood, type A and that it contained the enzymes EAP-B, EsD 1-1, PGM 1-1. As the suspect had a fresh cut on his hand the night he was arrested, the detectives obtained a court order to draw blood from him. Tests showed that it was type A and had the above enzymes.

Laboratory tests can show if the stain is actually blood, whether it is human or animal blood, and if it is human blood, the blood group and the enzyme type. Tests on seminal stains, including microscopic examination, distinguish human from animal semen, not that animals are likely to remove a bra from a dresser drawer and then masturbate on it. The test will also show the blood type in secretors.

Many police departments provide kits which contain instructions for the collection of both moist and dry blood samples together with the necessary saline, swabs and containers. The officer should be careful not to touch specimens with his own hands, as he may be a secretor and could contaminate the specimen.

Materials stained with blood or semen should be allowed to dry in a draft-free area, and no attempt should be made to hasten the drying by exposure to heat or sunlight. If the blood-stained material is not completely dry before being placed in a paper bag for removal to the laboratory, the blood may undergo changes which interfere with the tests.

When bloodstained items cannot be sent to the laboratory, the dried blood should be scraped from the surface with a clean knife or razor blade, and the scrapings should be placed in a container which can be sealed to prevent loss. Scrapings from the nonstained area around the stain should also be collected and placed in a separate container. These scrapings are also tested to see if the material affects test results.

Another method of collecting dried blood is to place a drop of saline onto the bloodstain and after fifteen seconds, soak up the saline on a piece of cloth by moving it around over the stain. Saline may be placed on the cloth first though, which may then soak into the stain. The cloth should be handled with tweezers and not with the fingers and allowed to dry before being sent to the laboratory.

Liquid blood should be collected with a clean medicine dropper and added to an equal quantity of isotonic saline solution (0.9 percent sodium chloride) in a small glass bottle or vial.

HAIR AND FIBERS

Burglars run the risk of unexpected encounters with a homeowner or his dog in which there may be a transfer of hairs. It may be helpful to recover hair from the clothing of both suspect and victim and to take hair samples from the parties involved, although the suspect may not always be immediately available, and a watchdog may not appreciate the necessity for removal of hairs from various parts of his body. In the burglary of a fur store, the offender may come in contact with several types of animal fur. In a burglary rape it will be necessary to obtain both head and pubic hair samples from both victim and suspect.

The laboratory expert can distinguish between human and animal hair. He can tell the race and body area of human hair, whether it has fallen out or been pulled out, and he may be able to provide information on the use of hair dye and the presence of trace evidence such as hair cream. He can also tell the species (cat, dog, etc.) of animal hair. This is class evidence as it is not possible to make a positive identification from hair.

Hairs obtained by the use of a clean comb or clean tweezers should be placed in clean paper inside a container, taking care not to kink or crush the hairs. There should be about twenty hairs in each sample.

Fibers may be torn from burglar's clothing when he crawls through a window, struggles with an occupant of the building or escapes over a chain link fence. His clothing may also contain fibers from a victim's clothing, draperies or furniture. Fibers should be removed from a surface with tweezers or with an evidence vacuum sweeper equipped with a filter and can be identified as synthetic (nylon, Dacron®), vegetable (cotton, linen), animal (wool, silk) or mineral (glass, asbestos). If a suspect is arrested, comparison can be made between fibers from the suspect's clothing and fibers found at the burglary scene or on the victim's clothing. This is class evidence, as it is not possible to make a positive identification from fibers.

PAINT AND GLASS

Paint on a door or window frame may be transferred to a pry bar or other instrument that is used to gain forced entry into a building. Samples of paint can be chipped off an area adjacent to the tool marks and submitted for microscopic, spectrographic or other chemical analysis. A suspect in a burglary involving the removal of a safe to an isolated area, where it was forcibly opened, was known to have the use of a pickup truck. Foreign paint removed from the truck matched four-layered paint particles from the safe.

Glass fragments from a broken window at the site of a burglary can be matched with glass fragments found in the clothing of a suspect. This matching can be on the basis of shape or physical properties such as density, light dispersion and refractive index.

> While on patrol in the early morning hours, a Virginia police-man approached the broken glass door of a clothing store and saw a person standing inside. The burglary suspect saw the officer, broke the glass in a side door, and fled through the opening.
>
> A short distance from the crime scene, the officer spotted and apprehended the suspect. Because he had lost sight of the suspect for a few seconds, the officer submitted the man's clothing and

glass samples from both broken doors to the FBI Laboratory.

Subsequently, a Laboratory expert testified in local court that the glass specimens from each door had different properties, and that glass fragments found on the suspect's clothing matched glass specimens from the two doors. The suspect was convicted and received a 1-year sentence (*FBI Law Enforcement Bulletin,* April 1971).

SOIL, WOOD AND BRICK

Soil on the suspect's shoes or clothing can be compared with soil from the scene of the burglary. Glass fragments, splinters of wood, brick, dust, cinders, unusual seeds or safe insulation may be found in both samples. Wood debris recovered from a burglary suspect's clothing should be compared with splintered wood found at the point of the break-in.

In order to break a window to gain entry, the burglar may use a brick, which he has taken from his own home or backyard. This brick may help convince a jury of his guilt, because the laboratory expert matches it with other bricks from his home. Bricks, prior to modern mass production, were often made in relatively small hand-mixed batches with considerable variation in their composition, which can be analyzed.

DUST

Manufacturing plants have distinctive contaminants in the air, thus, the dust in a bakery is very much different from that in a clothing factory. Following a burglary, a specimen of the dust disturbed at the point of entry should be preserved as evidence. If a suspect is arrested, this dust can be compared with that recovered from his clothing. Following the burglary of a custom grinding business, an officer recorded the license number of an unoccupied car parked nearby. The owner of the car was questioned by the police before he had a chance to change his clothes. Dust from his trousers was compared with dust from a thick layer near the window through which the burglar gained entry. Both samples contained trace amounts of eleven different elements including various metals and alloys.

RESTORATION OF SERIAL NUMBERS

Whenever a serial number has been altered or obliterated and restamped, every effort should be made to restore the original number. Serial numbers are placed on the frame, engine or both on motor vehicles, on firearms, watches, cameras, binoculars, household appliances, typewriters, professional and sports equipment. Sometimes an owner will have his name stamped on valuable items. "An appliance repair store was asked to repair a commercial-type vacuum cleaner. The repairman noticed that the serial number had been obliterated and he informed the police. The original number was restored and it was found that the machine had been stolen in a burglary. Further investigation resulted in the arrest of the man who brought the machine in for repair."

Prior to restoration of obliterated vehicle identification numbers (VINs), it is useful to make a cast of the new number that has been stamped on the frame to preserve toolmark evidence. The Toolmark Unit of the FBI Laboratory uses a unique plastic replica, distributed under the trade name, Lucitone®, in the casting of all altered vehicle identification numbers. Lucitone, an acrylic resin-base material, is convenient and highly durable and sets rapidly to produce an almost unbreakable cast suitable for long-term retention (*FBI Law Enforcement Bulletin,* August 1978).

FIREARMS

Although statistics are not readily available, many experienced police officers believe that burglars are more likely now to carry and use firearms than formerly. The criminal who sets out on a burglary may commit the more serious crimes of armed robbery, kidnapping and murder. If he shoots at a householder or security guard who appears unexpectedly, the police officer at the crime scene should look for the bullets, and if an automatic pistol was used he should also look for the shell casings. Their location should be photographed and recorded on a sketch of the scene that lists the distances between a piece of evidence and fixed points of reference. The combination of photographs and a sketch map should aid in reconstruction of the crime. Shell casings are usually ejected behind and to the right of the shooter.

After noting the positions of the hammer and safety catch, the officer will unload any firearms. In order to avoid obliteration of fingerprints, the weapon should be handled by the side of the trigger guard, the checkered portion of the grips or by rough surfaces. Note should be made if the bullet under the firing pin has been fired, and a record should be made of the position of fired and unfired bullets in a revolver.

The officer will place his initials on the base of bullets, on the inner surface of shell casings and on any firearms recovered. It is not sufficient to record the weapon's serial number, the officer should also place his initials on the firearm, as the defense attorney may later claim that manufacturers have been known to use the same serial number on two different weapons.

If the suspect has been arrested, his hands should be tested for gunpowder residue. A nitric acid swab test should be followed by a trace metal detection test (TMDT). If more than six hours have elapsed since a weapon was fired, or if .22 caliber ammunition other than federal brand was used, the chances are slight that significant residue will be present.

FIRES AND EXPLOSIONS

The burglar who attempts to conceal his crime by setting fire or explosives to a building may be detected through careful scientific study of the crime scene. Experts may be able to identify the type of accelerant used to set the fire or the type of explosive. Carpet or other items that may contain an accelerant, such as gasoline, should not be allowed to dry, but should be placed in a tightly sealed can or mason jar. Fragments of a bomb, including watches and tape, may provide useful clues. Thus, the laboratory study may show that the watch used as a timing device is one of a batch of watches stolen in a burglary by the same suspect, or that the tape used to bind the sticks of dynamite together was similar to tape found in the possession of the suspect.

SAFE INSULATION

Fire resistant safes usually contain insulating material, which may come in contact with tools, clothing and shoes of a burglar who forces his way through the safe wall. Safe-insulation has been found in the nail holes of shoe heels several weeks after a safe burglary. This material may be a decisive factor in proving guilt.

The variations among insulations make it valuable as evidence. Many older safes made prior to 1930 contained an insulation composed of natural cement. This product is made by calcining certain argillaceous limestones and has been used without sand or gravel, only as safe insulation. Many modern safes use an insulation composed of diatomaceous earth, portland cement and vermiculite mica. This combination of materials has only been used as insulation for safes. The experienced laboratory examiner can, therefore, state positively that the above materials on the clothing or tools of a burglar came from a safe. This alone is valuable testimony in cases of safebreaking or possession of burglar's tools. Further, many brands of safes contain distinctive insulation, samples of which are maintained in a file in the FBI Laboratory. It is, therefore, often possible to compare insulation from a suspect's belongings with insulations in the file and name the make of safe from which it came.

Some safes, however, use gypsum containing woodchips as insulation. This material cannot be positively identified as safe insulation, but side-by-side comparisons of particles from tools or clothing with the insulation from a burglarized safe can lead to valuable court testimony affirming or denying a suspect's complicity in a crime.

The FBI Laboratory can usually determine that even a very small particle of material came from a safe, the brand of safe from which the particle came and whether or not questioned particles are the same as or dissimilar to insulation from a burglarized safe.

The mere presence of safe insulation material on the clothing or shoes of a suspect can, with other circumstances, be a strong indication of guilt. Generally, persons would rarely come in contact with this type of material in the course of normal activities unless, of course, they are employed in the manufacture or the repair of safes.

Hammers, chisels, punches, drills and pries utilized in safebreaking will often be found to have quantities of insulation material adhering to them. This is good evidence of the purposes for which they have been used and may be the basis for the proof of intent necessary in cases involving possession of burglar's tools (*FBI Law Enforcement Bulletin,* November 1974).

TEETH MARKS

The burglar who bites an apple or a victim at the scene of a burglary may be identified through his bite marks. Forensic odontologists claim that with thirty-two teeth in a full set, the odds against two people having identical teeth are two and one-half billion to one. As one expert stated, "You can lie in your teeth, but your teeth can't lie."

A burglar while ransacking an office building removed an apple from a secretary's office drawer and took a single bite in it. Before leaving, he set fire to the building causing $56,000 worth of damage. The apple, which was not burned, was rushed by the police to a dental surgeon who placed it in preserving fluid. Five days later police picked up a suspect whose home was only a few streets away from the office building, and his criminal record included an incident where fire had been used. The suspect agreed to have impressions taken of his teeth, and an expert found that the bite in the apple provided forty-six points of similarity with the suspect's teeth. Although there was no other evidence pointing to the suspect's guilt, he was convicted of arson and sentenced to three years in jail. His conviction was upheld by the British Court of Criminal Appeal.

THE CRUCIAL LINK

A set of fingerprints recovered at the scene of a burglary points to one person and one person only. Other physical evidence that does not provide such a specific link between the crime and the suspect may nevertheless be crucial to successful prosecution of the burglar. During the burglary of an expensive home in Denver, Colorado, the burglars encountered the homeowners, but the victims could not identify the intruders who were wearing ski masks. No fingerprints were recovered because the burglars used gloves. Criminal investigation suggested that professional burglars from Chicago committed the crime. Physical evidence recovered at the scene included adhesive tape used to bind the victims, as well as paint and body metal from the burglar's car, which hit a chain across the driveway during the getaway. Gloves, ski masks and two rolls of adhesive tape were recovered from a car that was being driven by the suspects at the time of their arrest in Illinois.

Crime laboratory experts were able to match ends of the tape, used to bind the victims, with torn ends of the two rolls of tape found in the suspects' car. Fibers and other debris on the adhesive surface of the tape used on the victims, matched material found on the suspect's gloves. The paint and body metal on the chain across the driveway matched the paint and body metal on the getaway car.

The importance of such physical evidence needs no emphasis, but at a burglary scene it is not always easy to determine what material should be preserved as evidence. It is better to err on the side of collecting too many items, as the laboratory is not burdened with having to test these items unless further investigation indicates the need to do so. Three burned paper matches in the ashtray of a stolen car may not attract the investigator's attention, but they may provide a crucial link between the crime and the criminal as in the following case:

> Early one morning a police department in a midwestern state received a report of a stolen car. The stolen vehicle was spotted by an officer in a patrol car who gave chase but lost it in heavy traffic.
> Later that day, the stolen car was found abandoned in a corn-field near the city limits. In the car's ashtray were three burned paper matches. Investigation led to the arrest of a suspect, and a partially used book of matches was found on his person.
> The burned matched from the stolen vehicle's ashtray and the partially used book of matches were sent to the FBI Laboratory for examination. Examination revealed that two of the three burned paper matches were torn from the partially used book of paper matches.
> An expert from the Laboratory testified to his findings in state court. The suspect was found guilty by a jury and sentenced to serve three years in prison (*FBI Law Enforcement Bulletin,* June 1970).

The chain of custody should be kept as short as possible.

The officer who discovers the burglar's wallet, at the scene of a burglary, should not hand it to a group of other officers for inspection and then leave it to someone else to mark it and check it into the police custodian's office for preservation as evidence. A skillful defense attorney will quickly show that this officer cannot recall exactly where and by whom it was found at the crime scene.

Items should be marked clearly with the officer's initials, and he should select the same location for marking from one item to another. For example, he should mark, whenever possible, a shirt in a particular location so that when he is asked to identify a shirt on the witness stand he goes straight to the right place. Juries are not impressed by anxious officers who fumble around on the witness stand looking from one place to another for their initials.

His mark should be clearly visible one year later when the suspect is brought to trial. An officer's initials on the black surface of a suspect's wallet were not visible when the case came to trial; fortunately, the crime laboratory was given time to raise the initials, which they were able to do only after considerable effort and expense. The officer should have placed his initials on a gum label on the wallet and then seal it in a plastic bag.

It is better to mark a piece of evidence properly and destroy some part of it in the process than to mark it improperly and run the risk that it will not be accepted as evidence in court. An officer who marked the base of a bullet with two dots was asked by a defense attorney to select the bullet he had marked from a group of bullets all with two dots on the base. He was unable to do so.

Trace material from one item of evidence should not be allowed to contaminate other items. Two suspects were arrested near the scene of a burglary, and their clothing was seized as evidence. Each man's trousers contained dry wall dust from the site of the forced entry. Unfortunately, the two pairs of trousers were placed in the same plastic bag, and at trial each suspect claimed that his trousers were clean and that the dust must have come from contact with the other man's trousers.

Defense attorneys were successful in excluding both pairs of trousers from presentation as evidence to the jury.

FUTURE ADVANCES

Rapid progress is being made in many areas of laboratory investigation including blood typing. In this chapter, we have not listed all the sophisticated techniques, which include neutron activation, emission and mass spectography, chromatography and x-ray diffraction. The choice of test to be used should be left to the crime laboratory expert who has a responsibility to keep police officers informed of any new developments which broaden the scope of scientific investigations.

REFERENCES

1. Federal Bureau of Investigation: *The Science of Fingerprints.* Washington, U.S. Government Printing Office, 1978.
2. Fox, R. H. and Cunningham, C. L.: *Crime Scene Search and Physical Evidence Handbook.* Washington, U.S. Government Printing Office, 1974.
3. Inbau, F. E., Moenssens, A. E. and Vitullo, L. R.: *Scientific Police Investigation.* Philadelphia, Chilton Book Company, 1972.

CHAPTER 9

CRIMINAL INTERROGATION

*Questioning is not a mode of conversation
among gentlemen.*
—Samuel Johnson, Boswell, *Life*, 1776

IT IS OFTEN SAID that criminal interrogation is an art which
cannot be described, but can only be learned through years of
experience. This viewpoint might appear to gain support from
those highly skilled interrogators who cannot explain their
remarkable ability to obtain confessions from previously uncooperative criminals. The psychologist may talk of the criminal's
urge to confess, but this urge has to be uncovered, and its
presence does not detract from the accomplishment of an interrogator who succeeds when others have failed to obtain any
admission of guilt.

Those police officers with a natural talent for interrogation
have qualities of temperament, perceptiveness and sensitivity
that enable them to succeed without any need for textbook
instruction. There are, however, many younger patrolmen and
detectives who lack experience in interviewing and who seek
practical guidance. All too often they are told only that skill
comes with experience. In this chapter an attempt will be made
to provide practical advice, much of which is well-known but
frequently disregarded in practice.

There are a variety of approaches and each officer has to
learn for himself those approaches that seem best suited to his
personality and most effective in helping him to secure information from criminal suspects. If the officer feels uncomfortable
using a technique, he is not likely to use it with success as
the suspect will quickly sense his discomfort and lack of
confidence. Some officers can play the role of the stern, harsh,
unfriendly interrogator and can shift without difficulty into

the opposite role, suddenly becoming understanding, friendly and compassionate. Other officers are unable to make such a change comfortably and should avoid using this approach.

One cannot anticipate every possible situation that may arise and provide advice upon it, but there are some very simple rules that everyone should know even though they are not always observed. There is an exception to every rule, but one should have a good reason for going against the stream. On the other hand, slavish obedience to rules is not the mark of the gifted interviewer. Some detectives seem to have a lucky star, they break all the rules in the book, yet achieve remarkable results. Perhaps it is because suspects sense the genuineness of these detectives, no matter what they might say, for these gifted interviewers sometimes make very candid critical comments to suspects.

The writer, on appointment by the court, examines defendants charged with serious crimes usually following pleas of "not guilty" and "not guilty by reason of insanity." There is not the usual doctor-patient relationship, and the defendant is advised that this is not a privileged relationship and that anything he says may be reported to the court. However, information obtained for the first time will not be used as evidence on the innocence or guilt issue unless the defendant or his attorney so desire. If the defendant decides to fake insanity and conceal information regarding the alleged crime, the forensic psychiatrist will face similar problems to those encountered by detectives questioning uncooperative suspects.

PREPARATION

Whenever possible, the interrogator should prepare himself for the interview by reviewing all available information on the suspect and his alleged crime or crimes. If the man has a prior criminal record, the patrolman or other detectives who have dealt with him in the past may know his family, his personality, his strengths and his weaknesses. Self-confidence is essential, and this comes from knowledge and experience. Both the beginner and the expert obtain knowledge of the suspect from a careful preparation. "The mother of a man charged with rape and murder told me that her son had no prior sexual problems. She denied that her son had ever attempted to rape her and when I read her son's account of the incident to her, she said, 'You jogged my memory.'"

It is sometimes helpful to jog people's memories as in the following example: "A skyjacker who parachuted from a United Air Lines jet plane with a large sum of money claimed amnesia and said that if he did commit this crime, he must have been out of his mind as he had a fear of heights and his only previous air flights had been to and from Vietnam. After I showed him a copy of his army discharge papers, which listed him as a qualified helicopter air gunner, his memory improved considerably."

There is the risk that if you know all the information available on the suspect that you will tend to focus on what is known and the suspect quickly becomes aware of what you know. You think you know everything, but you don't and you begin to make up your mind. Without being aware of it you exclude from consideration new information that does not fit in with what is already known or suspected.

The "blind" interview is even a greater challenge to one's interviewing skill. If you know few of the facts, you tend to probe harder and in many different areas that might not occur to you if you already knew some of the answers. At the end of your interview, you can compare your information with that obtained by others. This provides a good check on your interviewing skill, either failure to obtain important facts previously provided to others or success in eliciting vital new material.

If a burglar is arrested at the scene of a crime, the sooner he is interviewed the better and the detective should not wait until he has accumulated all possible information about the offender before talking to him. Immediately after his arrest at the scene the burglar is probably not in the best of spirits. If he thinks, "I've had it, they've got me cold," he is more likely to talk to the police than at any other time. If no detective is available, the patrolman who arrests him should take advantage of his willingness to talk.

By the next morning, twelve cell mate jailhouse lawyers have advised him not to talk to the detective. A self-assured confident defense attorney, eager to sell himself as an unusually gifted courtroom veteran, has restored the suspect's morale with promises of a speedy release on bond and later acquittal at trial. The lawyer has pointed out that victims and witnesses often make false identifications, and that awkward pieces of evidence can be excluded from presentation to the jury.

His parents or wife have visited him in jail and have expressed their confidence in him and their firm belief that he did not commit the crime. He has had time to dream up an explanation for his possession of six new microwave ovens, and all in all he feels much better than he did at the time of his arrest. The opportunity to obtain a confession may have been lost. Strike while the iron is hot.

THE INTERVIEWING ROOM

Interrogation requires concentration on the part of both the interrogator and the suspect. The latter welcomes any distraction that will take his mind off the painful subject under discussion. The suspect prefers a room with large windows or glass partitions that enable him to watch bypassers or secretaries and other police department employees at work. The detective is so intent on his task and so familiar with his surroundings that he does not appreciate the interest the suspect has in his framed diplomas, textbooks and pictures.

Following John Gilbert Graham's arrest for a plane bombing in which forty-four persons were killed, it was considered that his state of mind at the time of his confession might become an issue at his trial because he had undergone many hours of interrogation. I attempted to assess his state of mind during the questioning by checking his powers of observation and his memory for the period. He described the interviewing room including pictures on the wall of World War II Nazi saboteurs and of the history of fingerprinting.

An interrogator confirmed only the presence of the pictures of the saboteurs. On checking the room I found that Graham's recall of the room was better than the interrogator's, as there was a picture on the history of fingerprinting. The interrogator's mind was probably focused entirely upon Graham and the plane bombing, whereas Graham was probably doing all he could to think of anything at all rather than of hotshot batteries, timers and sticks of dynamite.

Some terrorist groups instruct their members on resistance to police questioning. For example, they are taught to concentrate their mind on some object in the interrogation room. One terrorist at his trial claimed that the police had forced him to remember a six-digit number. The police were puzzled by this accusation, and on checking they discovered that a file on the interrogating officer's desk had this number, which the suspect seized upon as a method of distracting his attention from his interviews.

Confession is often difficult, and one should not add to the criminal's burden by asking him to reveal himself in the presence of several persons. Ideally, there should only be one or two interrogators in the interviewing room with the suspect.

Privacy can be obtained in almost any situation. If one talks to a suspect on the street, his mind may be intent on creating a tough guy image for the benefit of bystanders. In the police car his words cannot be heard by spectators, he is no longer tempted to play to the gallery, and he can now concentrate on explaining his possession of the contents of a Wells Fargo truck.

The need for privacy should require no emphasis, and it is surprising how often this rule is neglected. Perhaps the questioner feels that the suspect has no intention of talking anyway, or that a confession is not needed as there is sufficient evidence to secure a conviction.

But one never knows if a suspect will talk, committed other crimes or if other evidence will indeed be sufficient for a successful prosecution. So one should always attempt to obtain a confession no matter how difficult this may appear and no matter how trivial the offense may be. There are exceptions to the rule for the need for privacy. Thus, it may be more important for a questioner to seize the right moment to obtain a confession, rather than run the risk of losing it by delaying questioning until privacy can be assured, as in the following example:

> A young man charged with shooting a police officer admitted to committing only those burglaries for which he had been convicted in court. I pointed out that most burglars commit 50 to 100 or more burglaries for every one they are charged with in court, and that he had to feed his heroin habit, however he persisted in his denial of other burglaries. After I had completed my psychiatric evaluation I was taking him back to his cell when a policewoman passed us in the corridor.
>
> This was the first time I had seen a policewoman in this small city, and I drew his attention to the young woman. He suddenly became very friendly, his eyes lit up and he commented that I must have been a tiger when I was young. It was obvious that mistakenly he had assumed that my interest in the policewoman was of a sexual nature. I seized the moment of friendliness to question him about his burglaries. It was awkward standing writing notes in the busy narrow corridor of the corrections center, but the opportunity for obtaining this information might well have been lost if I had taken him back to the interviewing room.

The use of a recording device is an invasion of privacy and may discourage a criminal from revealing himself. Although some experts recommend the use of a concealed microphone and a hidden recording device, this procedure does seem rather unsporting and may at some future date be outlawed by the Supreme Court. Even if the suspect raises no objection to a tape recorder, he may nevertheless be more on guard and less talkative.

The interrogator himself may be inhibited by the use of a tape recorder. He becomes self-conscious, stilted and formal in his statements because of his awareness that everything he says will be reviewed by others.

> A burglary detective, noted for his skill in questioning, permitted a detective from a suburban police department to attend the interrogation of a young burglar. The visiting detective produced a pocket tape recorder, said that he had writer's cramp and obtained the suspect's permission to use his recorder. He then dictated a long statement listing the names and titles of everyone present, the time, location and other information in a most officious and rather pompous manner, thereby defeating the whole purpose of the interview as the suspect became very guarded in his answers.

Interrogators who use tape recorders sometimes seem to be more intent on demonstrating to some future jury how courteous and considerate they are to the suspect than upon obtaining a confession. In their eagerness to demonstrate their fairness they make a point of repeating for perhaps the sixth time the *Miranda* warning, "You have the right to remain silent; anything you say can be used as evidence against you in court, you have the right to talk to a lawyer before questioning and have him present during questioning, if you cannot afford a lawyer, one will be appointed for you before questioning," and so on.

But there may be no tape for the jury to listen to because the suspect, although he has already signed the advisement form, "knowing my rights and understanding them, I now wish voluntarily to talk to you" suddenly has second thoughts about talking. After hearing his rights repeated over and over again by the arresting officer, as well as by the detectives, he finally catches on to the idea that perhaps, after all, he should ask for a lawyer before talking to the police.

The investigator who takes notes during the interrogation may discourage a suspect from talking. The detective with a good memory will prefer not to write anything down until after he has a full confession. At this time he will write down the important admissions or he will repeat parts of the interview, writing out questions and answers. Alternatively, a police department stenographer will be brought into the interviewing room to make a record of the suspect's statements. A tape recorder is often useful at this stage.

Victims and witnesses, who are not as helpful as one might wish, should be interviewed in the police building. The familiar surroundings of their own home or office and the support of family members or fellow employees make it easier for them to avoid revealing information that they do not wish to share with the detective. Victims and witnesses should, of course, be accorded the same privacy as suspects, but this is not always easy to obtain in an office or home.

MEETING THE SUSPECT

In the introductory phase of the questioning, the detective attempts to establish a friendly relationship and to win the confidence and trust of the suspect. The investigator is not likely to accomplish this purpose by adopting a false, overly friendly attitude and by showing excessive concern for the suspect's welfare, "Would you like a cigarette? Can I get you a cup of coffee? Would you rather have a can of pop?" This criminal is on one side of the fence, the police officer is on the other side, and the offender greets such an approach with the same suspicion that a car buyer has for the blandishments of a used-car salesman.

The hustle and bustle of the modern world business is often conducted in uncivilized haste. In former times, such behavior was considered ill-bred, and a gentleman would always pass the time of day and inquire about another's health or well-being before mentioning vulgar commercial affairs. The investigator would do well to engage in civilized pleasantries with the burglar before questioning him about his felonious activities. "What are you doing these days?"—"Oh, I'm working for a burglar alarm company." "What's your brother doing?"—"Ten to fifteen." You can see how useful such questions can be. They make the suspect feel you are interested in him and not just in his felonies, and the answers may tell you something important about the suspect.

Answers to such questions are useful in court when the defense attorney suggests that the detective put words in the suspect's mouth. The detective's knowledge of the names, ages and occupations of the suspect's brothers and sisters, as well as other personal information surely can come only from the suspect.

Every man has something he is proud of, whether it is his skill at baseball, his intellect, his sense of honor, loyalty to companions, muscular development or physical appearance. Attention should be directed toward his source of pride. An uncooperative soldier, suspected of strangling his girl friend, responded quickly when his biceps were felt and favorably appraised. A poorly educated but intelligent murderer confessed after his interest in books and wide range of knowledge were remarked upon.

It is helpful for the interrogator to find something that he shares with the suspect, whether it is an interest in football, service in the Marine Corps or even awareness of some slang expression. An uncooperative black suspect was asked by an officer who had worked in the south, "Were you ever caught toting sugar?" (i.e., illegal alcohol). After this question the suspect became quite friendly.

In an emergency situation there is no time for the leisurely establishment of friendly relations, but the officer should take care not to antagonize anyone. A patrolman questioning a couple parked in a car near the scene of a burglary should simply ask the couple if they noticed anyone leaving the building. An immediate demand for a driver's license or other identification arouses anxiety and resentment, especially if the man is married and the woman is another man's wife. So the officer does not get vital information on the burglar's car.

CONTROL OF THE INTERVIEW

At all times the investigator should be in control of the interview, but this does not mean that he should be domineering and authoritarian, although upon occasion he may be, not because it is his nature, rather because he feels it will be the most effective approach. At another time he may adopt a passive role, but still remain in control of the interview.

Self-control is important. A murderer's account of a triple slaying upset me, and my face betrayed my distress. The murderer rebuked me saying, "You shouldn't let yourself be emotionally involved. You should be cool, detached and clinical. A good psychiatrist should cultivate that ability." The questioner should try to conceal any negative emotional responses.

If you become angry and insulting, the suspect will conclude that you are frustrated because you do not have enough evidence to press charges against him, and this strengthens his resistance to interrogation. Upon occasion it may be rewarding to show or express negative feelings toward the suspect.

The suspect may challenge your control of the interview. A middle-aged woman charged with burglary and forgery was a very controlling, assertive person who had mixed with senators, governors, chiefs of police and other prominent officials. At one time with some success she impersonated a colonel in U.S. Army Intelligence. She challenged all my efforts to direct the questioning. She was overweight and needed exercise, so at the end of each interview I would ask her to walk upstairs rather than use the elevator. She did not like this, and one day while walking through a crowded lobby she shouted in a loud voice, "Dr. Macdonald I am menstruating, and if you make me walk upstairs there will be blood on every step." After that we always used the elevator.

Some women use tears to control men, and the interrogator must be on guard not only with the tearful suspect but also with the tearful victim.

> A young woman, held up while working alone in a small store at night, was so distraught that it was difficult to obtain from her a description of the bandit. She was sobbing hysterically and seemed quite unable to give a coherent account of the robbery. The detective tried to comfort her and asked someone to call her mother. Actually, she was a runaway living with two young speed freaks who had told her to accumulate money in the cash register rather than to put more than was needed for change in the drop safe. Once she had $200 in the cash register she removed it and called the police to report that she had been robbed at gunpoint.

VIGILANCE

The skillful interrogator, no matter how relaxed and casual he may appear, is alert and watchful at all times, sensitive to changes in mood and behavior and quick to note the slightest discrepancy in the suspect's statements. He cannot afford negligence or lack of attention; like the hunter of wild game, he must be totally absorbed in his pursuit.

He does not relax his vigilance when questioning anyone

regarding a crime—suspect, victim or witness—because the victim may become the suspect, and the witness may conceal his knowledge of the crime or provide false information. One drawback of the term, criminal interrogation, is that it suggests that suspects should be questioned differently from victims and witnesses. The initial approach may be different, but the need for careful scrutiny remains constant.

An investigator's sympathy for a victim injured in a burglary-robbery or a burglary-rape may lead to his overlooking small, but significant changes in the victim's original account of the crime and to his turning a deaf ear to improbable tales that suggest a false report—a red and white plaid jacket becomes blue and white.

Persons who have been stabbed or shot accidentally in family arguments, in suicide attempts or in the commission of a crime may give another explanation for their injuries. Thus, a false report is made of a burglar breaking in a home and attacking the householder. A woman who has to explain her pregnancy to her husband reports a burglary-rape and may even injure herself to give credence to her claim. The able questioner will pick up some discordant factor which points to perjury.

The observant interviewer recalls that a silver ring with a unique bear claw design on a female suspect's finger was reported stolen in a burglary and notes needle tracks on the suspect's arm. The presence of the tattoo, *Death before dishonor,* rather than suggesting high moral standards is more likely to indicate its opposite, and the man will probably offer to become a snitch. The presence of insulation from a safe, clinging to the suspect's trousers, should not pass unnoticed.

NONVERBAL COMMUNICATION

A man's bodily movements can be very revealing. If he jacks a shell in his shotgun he is telling you something, and his action speaks louder than words. More subtle nonverbal communications include twisting a lock of hair; slightly hesitant speech for the first time; a change in the tone of voice or rate of speech; a flush, rising from the base of the neck; or a sudden downward look, which suggests the whole truth is not being told.

"A man suspected of murder said that he lived on good terms with his recently deceased neighbor, but at the same time he clenched his fist." "An employee of a hamburger stand while being questioned about the armed robbery that had just occurred kept looking down. It was a false report, and he was looking at the cupboard where he had hidden the money." "A man in a wheelchair, who had just reported the theft of $600, wheeled himself over to where his wife was standing and smiled at her. Persons who have just suffered the loss of $600 do not smile." A sudden interest in something in the interviewing room may point to deception as in the following example:

> A middle-aged chronic alcoholic man, who pleaded not guilty by reason of insanity to a charge of murder, was friendly and cooperative on psychiatric examination. He spoke freely and when questioned directly on any subject he replied without hesitation. It was noted that he appeared somewhat ill at ease when describing his school record. The subject was therefore raised again at a later interview and once more he appeared somewhat discomforted. His answers were not as spontaneous as previously. He turned half away from the physician and appeared to be interested in the contents of a glass medicine cabinet. In view of his change in demeanor, it was assumed that he was withholding some information.
>
> He denied this, but became more obviously distressed, and then suddenly with considerable abreaction he revealed that at the age of twelve he had seen his father shot and killed by a revenue officer. He rushed inside, picked up his father's loaded shotgun, went outside and killed the revenue officer. His placement in a reform school had interfered with his schooling. On his release from prison he had traveled to another state, married and settled down.
>
> This man had been successful in keeping this information a secret from his wife for their thirty years of married life. The earlier murder conviction was not on his police records, but was confirmed by correspondence with the reform school (3).

THE QUESTIONING

Let the Suspect Tell His Story Without Interruption

When a suspect is questioned about a burglary or theft, he should be allowed to tell his story without interruption. If he mentions that he drove to the area of the crime in his girl friend's car, do not interrupt him with questions on the make, model, color and year of the car. Such questions can always be asked later and interrupt the flow of conversation. It also tends to place him on guard and reduces the interview to a series of direct questions and answers. Liebling expresses this viewpoint well (2):

I had a distaste for asking direct questions; a practice I considered ill-bred. This handicapped me not as much as you might think. Direct questions tighten a man up, and even if he answers, he will not tell you anything you have not asked him. What you want is to get him to tell his story. After he has you can ask clarifying questions such as, "How did you come to have the axe in your hand?"

If the suspect makes a statement that you know to be untrue, do not immediately confront him. If he wishes to tell tall tales, allow him to do so. If he wants to dig a ditch for himself, let him do so. Let him bury himself in a host of contradictions, inconsistencies, improbable explanations and false statements. These will make him vulnerable to sudden massive confrontation and will also weaken his position in court. When he has finished explaining his behavior at the time of the crime, direct questioning on many issues becomes necessary.

Vague General Questions Should Be Followed by Narrower Questions

A surprising number of criminals will give helpful answers providing they are asked the right questions. The broad question, "What did you do after leaving San Francisco?"—"I took a United Airlines flight to Denver," should be followed by the very narrow question, "Was it a nonstop flight?"—"No I spent three days in Las Vegas." The suspect's activities during these three days may be very revealing, but they might have escaped notice in the absence of the important second question.

The narrow question alone may provide an escape for the suspect. "Did you steal the $540?"—"No," he replies in good conscience, and he does not add that it was $545. The suspect cannot so easily evade the broader question, "Did you steal the money?" He may deny the theft, but feel less at ease in doing so and betray his discomfort by looking away.

Make Sure That the Crime Itself Is Properly Covered

On the crime itself and other vital issues, be sure to check: WHAT, WHEN, WHERE, WHO, WHY and HOW.

Questions Should Be Clear-Cut and Not Ambiguous

Even such an experienced investigator as Inspector Clousseau made this elementary mistake. You will recall that he asked the manager of the hotel, "Does your dog bite?" "No," replied the manager, but when the inspector patted the dog, he was promptly bitten on the hand. He complained to the manager, "I asked you if your dog bites" and the manager replied, "That's not my dog."

Make Sure That Your Questions Have Been Answered

Often a suspect will start to answer a question and then shift to some other topic, likely to arouse the detective's interest. I have read many transcripts of interrogations in which key questions were not answered, and the detective was clearly not aware that the suspect had successfully distracted his attention from some vital issue.

Catching the Suspect by Surprise

The suspect may be disconcerted by the unexpected attitude and manner of the interrogator. There is an old adage, "Treat a duchess like a whore, and a whore like a duchess." Unexpected kindness will often catch an offender off guard. A woman charged with murder did not answer any questions, but after she was given some picture postcards to send to her children she cried and began talking about her crime. She said later that she had expected an angry response to her initial failure to answer.

The occasional question that has no relation to the crime puzzles the suspect, and his answer may, if only by chance, contribute to a better understanding of his personality. Routinely

I ask persons, "What kind of car do you drive?", and the answers are sometimes of psychological interest. A young woman who had burned her parents to death came to see me some years later. She was driving a red Pontiac Firebird.

A detective should not hesitate to ask questions based on his hunches. If his intuitive guess proves correct, the suspect will often be caught by surprise and will assume either that the detective is an insightful person or that he has important sources of information. I once asked a suspect if he had ever been a police officer, and he replied that he had been a police cadet for several months. Later I wondered why I had asked that question, and then I remembered that he had told me that he "worked out" regularly lifting weights, an activity favored by many police officers.

Winning the Suspect's Respect

It is important to gain the respect of the suspect because this places the interrogator in an advantageous position. One experienced detective put it this way:

> I don't try and bullshit people. I don't use any tricks. I don't lie to them. I tell them the truth. They don't like to hear it. "I know you shoot heroin, I know it, you know it, God knows it." They respect somebody who comes forward with it. They don't like you but if they respect you, they'll talk to you.
>
> If the guy says, "I ain't shooting nothing, I just gave blood," and if the detective says, "That's probably true, you did," the guy says to himself, "I can snow him." If you say, "I know you've been shooting, they don't take blood out of the wrist," he thinks this guy's sharp. You've got to win their respect. You've got to be honest. You've got to treat them like humans, don't look down on them.

Making It Easier for the Suspect to Confess

The detective, by avoiding use of words such as burglary, rape and murder, makes it easier for the suspect to talk about his offenses. When the victim has provoked a crime, reference to this may facilitate admission of the offense.

Many offenders are very reluctant to inform on their partners of crime, and one method of easing this burden is to tell the man, "I'm going to go out of the room. When I come back, if I find a name on this piece of paper, no one can ever say you told me." Another approach is to say "Was Frank the other guy?" On receiving a negative answer the detective says "If I put his picture in the mug-shot book, nobody will ever know"— "You won't tell anybody, well you might put Frank's picture there."

Confronting the Suspect

The detective may decide to confront the suspect with a host of issues that point to his guilt early during the initial interview. This may overwhelm the first offender who is drawn down by the shock of his arrest and by feelings of guilt. The more experienced or more resilient offender will not succumb so readily, and it is better to delay confrontation. When confronted, he will often be very adept in quickly thinking up excuses.

If, however, he is suddenly faced with many issues in quick succession, he becomes mentally fatigued and may give answers which point to his guilt. For example, one offender, toward the end of a questioning session, on being told that a witness had identified him replied, "It was too dark in that place and the broad was too scared." Even career criminals sometimes will throw in the towel when suddenly subjected to massive confrontation.

Varying the Approach

A technique that has long been used by detectives is for one officer, usually an older detective, to adopt a brusque, unsympathetic manner, while his younger colleague, who plays a less active role in the questioning, is friendly and under-standing in his manner. When the stern detective leaves the interviewing room, the younger detective using a low key approach is often successful in obtaining a confession. The "hot-cold" approach can be used by a single interrogator, who is cold and remote at one interviewing session, then warm and kind at the next session.

Involving the Parents

The father (or mother) of a juvenile suspect will be present during the questioning, and often he is naturally inclined to believe in his son's innocence, to be protective and to be suspicious of police harrassment. If, however, the detective's questions and the juvenile's answers begin to raise doubt in a parent's mind, there is gradually a change in attitude so that when the juvenile refuses, for example, to take a lie detector test, the parent will intervene and ask his son why he refuses to take the test. Juveniles are quick to sense loss of parental support, and after a private conversation with his father, the juvenile may confess his burglaries.

Persistence of Effort

There is a general rule that you should continue questioning for another fifteen minutes after you have decided to stop. One should not become discouraged easily, as interrogation is sometimes no more than an endurance contest.

> A man arrested in Denver in possession of a stolen car was suspected of murdering the owner, because the trunk of the car was bloodstained and the owner had been missing from his home in California for some weeks. For about five hours the author interviewed him while he was under the influence of a barbiturate drug before he described the murder and the location of the burial site near a radio tower in New Mexico. Information obtained from such prolonged questioning without interruption would probably not be admissible in court.

A stimulus to continue the interview is provided by constant repetition of such answers as "Not that I recall"; "Do I have to go over this again?"; "I don't really know"; "I don't remember"; "To tell you the truth"; "Truthfully"; "Frankly"; "Honestly"; "I swear to God"; "They can send me to jail for life, but I didn't do it"; "Believe me"; "I was drunk"; "I passed out"; "I blacked out"; "Do you think I'm a liar?"; "I didn't do it but I'll pay it back."

CONCLUSION

Above all the interrogator should listen carefully and thoughtfully, he should always remember that his object is to obtain rather than to reveal information, and he should not talk down to nor belittle the suspect. Information obtained through the use of threats or promises cannot be used in evidence.

The guidelines or rules for criminal interrogation described in this chapter remind the writer of the taxi driver in Dublin who pulled up at a traffic light, look around and then drove on. When his passenger complained that he had gone through a red light, the driver replied, "Tis a matter of philosophy, sir. Traffic lights are there to help us, not to hinder us." Well police questioning is like driving a taxi in Dublin. You need to know the rules, but you don't have to obey them if there's a better way of getting to your destination.

REFERENCES

1. Inbau, F. E. and Reid, J. E.: *Criminal Interrogation and Confessions.* Baltimore, Williams and Wilkins, 1962.
2. Liebling, A. J.: *New Yorker,* 35:108, April, 1959.
3. Macdonald, J. M.: *Psychiatry and the Criminal,* 3rd ed. Springfield, Thomas, 1976.

CHAPTER 10

PREVENTION AND PUNISHMENT

*I would give all my fame for a
pot of ale and safety.*
—Shakespeare, *Henry V*

L AW ENFORCEMENT AGENCIES, security companies and businesses are constantly planning new methods for reducing financial loss from burglary and theft, while at the same time the criminals are busy devising countermeasures and plotting new tactics. The struggle continues and the only thing certain is the expense. If the burglar is determined to break-in he will succeed, as it is very difficult to make any home or building completely safe from burglars.

Much can be done to reduce the risk of burglary and theft by simple measures, such as taking steps to avoid attracting the attention of burglars by removing the key from the ignition of the car, by using door locks and shutting windows, by watching out for the safety of others and by providing community support for an effective criminal justice system. In general the objectives are—

1. to make it harder for the burglar to break in through improved physical security.
2. to increase the risk of detection and arrest at the scene of the burglary through community reporting of suspicious activity, burglar alarm systems and more effective police patrol.
3. to reduce theft by employees through greater use of standard internal security measures.
4. to improve identification of stolen property through stamping of serial numbers by manufacturers and personal stamping of social security numbers.
5. to make disposal of stolen property more difficult through

antifencing strategies and through better regulation of pawnshops and secondhand stores.

6. to improve criminal investigation and crime laboratory studies of physical evidence.
7. to provide speedy trials and to provide safer bail bonding systems.
8. to rehabilitate younger offenders and to confine career criminals in jails.

The social scientist will demand changes in those social conditions which contribute to crime. Preventive measures will be reviewed for the various forms of burglary and theft.

HOME SECURITY

The householder should not advertise his absence from home by leaving a note on the door, and if he is going to be away overnight or for an extended period he should arrange for a neighbor to collect his mail and newspapers each day. The society columns of the local newspaper almost every day give the names of persons who are about to leave on a thirty-day European tour or who are participating in some fund-raising charity show that will be held on a given date. The society burglar will have no difficulty in obtaining the home address from a telephone or city directory.

Police answering a silent alarm from a home, arrested a twenty-eight-year-old man who said that he had been in Denver only two days. He was found hiding in a shower stall adjoining the master bedroom, and he had on him $283, credit cards and jewelry belonging to the victim. A .38 caliber revolver and a flashlight were found near the shower stall. The suspect was carrying a newspaper clipping listing more than fifteen couples who were to attend a Colorado Women's College benefit theatre party. The owners of the home were the first couple on the list.

Doors should always be locked, yet all too often homeowners will leave without checking their exterior doors. People seldom realize how quickly a burglar can rifle through a house. Even if the householder does not leave a key under the door mat, in a flower pot or at some other obvious location, the burglar can be in and out within a very few minutes. This is less time than it takes a housewife to drive to the nearest convenience store to pick up a few grocery items. Householders will often leave their garage door open while making such a trip because they will be back in a few minutes.

At night, a lighted porch and dark house attract the burglar. Lights should be left on in more than one room, and automatic timers can be used to turn these lights on and off at predetermined times. The timer can also be used to turn a radio on and off.

It is unwise to plant large shrubs near the front door, as these prevent neighbors from checking on the activity of any stranger who walks up to the door. Large fences provide privacy for both the householder and the burglar. A low fence and a large watchdog do much to discourage the burglar. The house street number should be clearly visible from the street, so that if the police are called they can respond without delay.

Dead bolt locks should be set in solid wood rather than hollow doors, and the door frame should be of sound construction so that the burglar cannot simply kick the door open. If there is a glass window in the door, a double cylinder dead bolt lock should be installed if the window is within forty inches of the lock. Otherwise, a burglar can break the window in the door, reach in and turn the thumb screw on a single cylinder lock.

Not everyone would want a double cylinder lock that has to be opened with a key on both sides of the door. In the event of a fire it may delay a hasty exit while one looks for the key. One pays a price for increased security. The large watchdog may bite your visitor's children, and the window bars may convert your house into a deathtrap in the event of a fire.

> "We can't get out, we can't get out" cried a family trapped in a fire behind steel bars meant to keep burglars out. Instead the bars kept out firemen. The bars were finally dislodged with crowbars and chains, but one of six children and an adult in the house died of smoke inhalation and burns. The six survivors, three unconscious, were huddled at the back door. The key to the security grate was unreachable near the front door where the fire was hottest.

Sliding glass patio doors or windows with aluminum frames can often be forced open without difficulty. Special locks are available, and screws should be placed at ten to fifteen inch intervals in the channel above the top of the glass frame. These screws should be adjusted so that they just allow the door or window to pass beneath and prevent the burglar from lifting the frame out of the lower channel. Metal rods or wooden dowels have been used in the track of the lower channel to brace the door closed, but burglars can remove them with a short piece of wire.

Windows that slide up and down can be prevented from moving more than a few inches by nailing a strip of wood in the channels at the side of the frame. The slats of glass in louver windows can be removed easily from their metal holders unless glue is used to hold them in place.

If the decision is made to install a burglar alarm, the Better Business Bureau should be consulted, as some fly-by-night security companies do not provide satisfactory service. Householders who arm themselves with firearms run the risk of having the gun used against them by the burglar. There is also the risk of shooting a family member in mistake for an intruder.

> A thirty-six-year-old man was shot in the abdomen and seriously wounded early in the morning at his home when his wife mistook him for a burglar. The couple were awakened by barking dogs, and the husband went to the garage to investigate. His wife got up also, armed herself with a revolver and went to the hallway leading to the garage. She said she saw someone coming toward her and asked, "Who is it?" When she received no reply, she fired two shots wounding her husband.

Any suspicious activity in the neighborhood should be reported to the police. A youth sitting on a lawn or waiting in a car with the motor running may be the lookout for an accomplice who is breaking into a neighbor's house. "Neighborhood Watch" programs have strengthened community action to prevent burglary and have contributed to the arrest of burglars at the scene of their crimes. The person who comes to the door to ask if Mr. Jones lives there may well be a burglar looking for a home where no one answers the doorbell. The door-to-door salesman selling vegetables at ridiculously high prices is clearly not in the vegetable-selling business.

Householders should not invite strangers into their homes.

If a person claims that his car has broken down, make the telephone call for him, but do not invite him in. The person who claims he is doing a marketing survey may in fact be doing a survey to see if your home would be a good target for burglary. The woman who permits the use of her home in a "Home and Garden Show" may have over 300 visitors, one of whom may be a criminal doing his homework. Persons who employ babysitters without checking their credentials may find that the babysitter invites over boyfriends who are burglars.

A list should be kept of the serial numbers of radios, TV sets, electrical applicances, cameras, binoculars and firearms. Valuable jewelry should be photographed. Many police departments make electrical pencils available without cost so that householders can record their social security numbers on items without serial numbers.

COMMERCIAL SECURITY

Physical security for large commercial and industrial premises begins with a seven foot tall, perimeter chain link fence, with as few gates as possible. A separate fenced area for employee parking makes it more difficult for employees to take stolen merchandise to their cars, as there is no opportunity for an employee to drive his car to the building where he works or near the receiving and loading docks. Sewers, culverts and utility tunnels running through or under the perimeter fence should be protected by bars or locked doors.

Protective lighting should illuminate the area between the perimeter fence and the buildings, and this area should be kept as uncluttered as possible to permit easy detection of intruders. According to Bunn, three out of four commercial burglaries are committed against buildings that have either no lights or inadequate lights. He recommends that alleys, the rear of the businesses, and all entry points should be well-lighted. Night lights should be placed over the safe; inside night lights should be to the rear, so that an intruder's silhouette can be seen from the street; and night lights should be wired so that an alarm is set to go off if the lights go out.

Windows, unless needed for emergency exit, should be protected by bars or metal screens if they are less than eighteen feet from the ground. Access to the roof should be denied the burglar by storing ladders, placing utility poles some distance from the building and constructing fire escapes for easy exit, but for difficult entry. Skylights and ventilators on the roof should be protected.

Solid wood doors should have adequate dead bolt locks. Studies have shown that doors, windows and even safes are often left unlocked by employees leaving at night. An employee should be assigned to check the building at closing time to see whether anyone is hiding inside, to lock all doors and windows, to turn on the alarm system and to check the safe.

The appropriate type of burglary-resistant safe will depend upon the maximum amount of money and valuables likely to be kept inside, but the minimum amount necessary for the conduct of business should be kept on hand. Dishonest employees will neglect to pay money into the bank or hand it over to an armored car service because a burglary or armed robbery has been planned with an accomplice, and they want to steal as much money as possible. Very strict rules are essential regarding prompt transfer of money to the bank when in excess of a certain amount. Even heavy safes should be anchored to the floor or set in concrete, as burglars have been known to remove safes weighing up to one ton. First floor safes should be near a window in a lighted room so that the safecracker will have to work in public view.

Alarms

Audible alarms mounted high on the outside walls of buildings are intended to scare the burglar into leaving before he has completed his burglary. Neighbors and bypassers are expected to call the police, but usually no one has told them, and they may assume that the alarm also registers at police headquarters. Neighbors often object to the loud ringing sound or other noise that can be heard for several hundred feet, which may continue for several hours until the owner arrives to turn it off. The mere presence of the alarm or of a window sticker advertising its presence is sufficient to deter some burglars.

Silent alarms are preferable because the police may be able to respond in time to catch the burglar, who is not aware that he has triggered a signal to a burglar alarm company or to police headquarters. When the silent alarm is activated, the signal has to be processed by the burglar alarm company. Is it a valid alarm? What is the location? The information has to be telephoned to the police dispatcher who has to select the nearest available police car and relay the information.

According to a study reported in *Crimes Against Small Business* (U.S. Government) the average time required to get alarm information to the police car is 1.3 minutes, and the average police travel time is 3.81 minutes giving a total response time of 5.11 minutes. Police cars are not always immediately available, and it may be ten to twenty minutes before the police arrive at the scene of a silent alarm. There is always the risk that the burglar has a radio scanner with him tuned into police radio wavelengths.

A more serious problem is the frequency of false alarms. A vibration alarm may be set off by heavy truck traffic, an ultrasonic motion detector may be activated by a furnace turning on and a sonic alarm by incidental noises other than those caused by an intruder. Wind storms rattling windows and doors, lightning storms and power failures affecting electrical communications or an employee entering the building forgetting to turn off the system also contribute to false alarms.

Whenever there is a high percentage of false alarms the police tend to become less efficient in responding to these calls, and there is also a substantial waste of service time. Another problem is the failure of alarm company equipment or staff so that either the alarm fails to function or the call is not reported to the police.

Burglary detectives who checked to see why a noise detector alarm had not been activated during a $15,000 burglary were told that the equipment was working perfectly. Later they received a letter from the alarm company employee who explained:

> Immediately after I was informed that a burglary had taken place I went into our monitoring room to check the receiver module. What I found was that the sensitivity knob was set at

the lowest position. The sound system is activated by noise, and the level of noise to activate the system is determined by the position of the sensitivity knob. When the knob is turned all the way down, you can practically walk up to the microphones and beat on them with a hammer without the sound being heard in the monitoring station. The reason I failed to mention this to you is that it would have cost me my job. Obviously if this information was known to the client, the alarm company would be open to a suit for negligence.

Modern sophisticated alarm devices using radar systems, capacitance relays or photoelectric cells with infrared rays can cost $1,000 or more for installation alone and are usually only in banks, jewelry stores and warehouses containing expensive items. Simpler devices using magnetic switches and plunger switches are inexpensive and suitable for filling stations, taverns, convenience stores and restaurants. In a large school the system can be confined to key locations such as the room with a safe, the office, and the musical instrument storage room.

A few burglars use ingenious methods to overcome alarm systems or obtain information on unprotected points from an employee or ex-employee, but some burglars are caught through prompt response of police to a call from a burglar alarm company.

Burglar Traps

Tavern keepers and owners of small stores, enraged by repeated burglaries, will sometimes lie in wait with a gun to shoot anyone who breaks in. Occasionally, a burglar trap will be set using a loaded gun. Over a period of several years, three men were killed in a trap at a grocery store in Everman, a suburb of Fort Worth, Texas.

A twenty-one-year-old ex-convict died from a bullet fired from a pistol the grocer had rigged to discharge when the back door was opened. A nineteen-year-old youth was also killed at the same store by a shotgun blast while he was trying to burglarize the store. The owner of the store was wounded by his own burglar trap and eventually was killed by it when he was struck in the chest by a shotgun blast. A butcher who witnessed the accident said he thought the owner had disconnected the trap, rigged to fire when the rear screen door was opened. The sixty-three-year-old owner was carrying out a box of trash at the time.

Internal Security

One of the most important, yet frequently neglected, measures for preventing theft by employees is thorough screening of all applicants for employment. In gasoline stations there is often no attempt to check the employment application form, not even scrutiny of the driver's license to check the date of birth or to record the license number. Shortly after he is hired though, the new employee closes the gas station late at night and leaves with several hundred dollars that he should have deposited in the drop safe. His home address is nonexistent and his previous places of employment are all out-of-state and likely to prove fictitious.

Many businesses are reluctant to provide information in writing on the dishonesty or suspected dishonesty of former employees, and even if the personnel manager or owner does not provide such information over the telephone, his manner of responding to questions may betray his reservations about the person under discussion. The check may reveal that the applicant has provided false information regarding his length of employment, salary or reason for leaving.

The greater the opportunity for employee theft the greater the need for a thorough background check. A listing of each job since leaving school, including dates of beginning and ending, will quickly reveal an unstable work record. This by itself raises questions of uncertainty and may also show prolonged periods of unemployment that could be due to confinement in a penal institution. Although, a prior criminal record should not lead to automatic rejection of the applicant.

Other important preventive measures are payment of adequate wages to employees and fair labor practices. Whenever employees have a justified feeling of resentment, the risk of internal theft increases. An overbearing foreman or supervisor can cause a drop in morale, and management should be ever alert to any changes which lead to widespread feelings of grievance. Even when adequate wages are paid and working conditions are good, there will always be employees who will take advantage of any opportunity to fill their pockets. Measures should be taken, therefore, to decrease temptation and the opportunity for theft.

Specific measures to prevent employee theft include control of movement within a commercial operation. Reference has already been made to an enclosed area for employee parking so that employees' cars cannot be parked, even briefly, near receiving and loading docks or alongside buildings. This procedure makes it more difficult for transfer of merchandise from the plant to a car. All employees should leave by the same exit if this is possible. Incoming and outgoing goods should be checked carefully, otherwise, a dishonest employee can acknowledge receipt of more items than actually have been received. He may have an accomplice who is employed by another firm and shares the profits with him.

Alternatively, a dishonest employee can certify, for example, that three microwave ovens were placed on a delivery truck when in fact five ovens were placed on the truck. Double checking, gate exit checks and surprise checks by security personnel reduce the risk of these types of theft. Movements of stock within the plant should be documented by vouchers and receipts. Careful inventory records should be maintained so that stock shortages can be traced to the original point of loss.

Employees should not be allowed to make sales to themselves, and special arrangements should be made for employees who wish to make purchases. This should be through a supervisor, or all purchases should be checked in a package room. Employees in the mailroom may mail stolen items to themselves or to their friends and relatives, and there is a need for supervision and periodic checking. Merchandise may be hidden in an outdoor trash container and picked up later either by the employee or by an accomplice of a trash disposal company. Trash should either be compacted or checked at intervals and containers should not be placed on loading or receiving docks.

Key control is essential. All keys should be numbered, and records should be kept to show who has each type of key. In large companies, keys should not leave the complex, and persons authorized to have keys should leave them at the security office at the close of work. Failure to do so should result in the person being asked to return his key immediately, regardless of the hour of day when its absence is discovered. (A 2 AM telephone call to return a key need only happen once, as the word soon gets around the factory.)

If an outer door key is lost or stolen, it may be much cheaper to pay for a change of keys and lock-core than to pay for a new electric typewriter or other items that may be stolen. Submaster and master keys should be given to as few employees as possible. Particular care should be taken over the control of keys for use by janitorial companies, which often have a high employee turn-over rate. "Investigation of theft from some offices in a large building showed that the building maintenance company had five to six persons working in the building every night. Most of these men are hired from labor pool organizations and are paid by the day. The keys were kept in an unlocked cupboard on a display board with labels for each set of offices."

Electronically controlled locks have the advantage that the code numbers for opening the locks can be changed quickly whenever necessary without additional expense. Large hotels are beginning to use electronic locks operated by disposable plastic cards similar to credit cards. When a guest registers, the desk clerk inserts two or more blank cards into a device that punches a code for them. One card is given to the guest, and the other is placed in the appropriate slot in the master console. When the guest inserts his card in a slot outside his room, the card is electronically compared with the corresponding card in the master console and if the two match, the door will unlock with an audible click.

Employees who drink to excess, gamble, are in debt or are reluctant to take a vacation will come under the suspicion of security personnel investigating internal theft. In small businesses, as well as in larger companies, cash receipts should be kept in a secure location and be deposited in a bank each day. Often large sums of money are counted then placed in bank bags and left lying on top of a desk in an unlocked room while the cashier is talking to another employee in the next room before leaving for the bank.

PREVENTING SHOPLIFTING

The sales staff who can do much to prevent shoplifting should be given training on the behavior and methods of shoplifters (see Chapter 2) and should be told what to do when they see a shoplifter at work. A code word or phrase can be used to warn, directly or by telephone, other clerks or the store detective regarding the presence of a suspected shoplifter. Sales clerks should serve customers as quickly as possible and should not leave their area unattended. Lunch hours and coffee breaks should be arranged so that no area is left with too few employees at any one time.

The fewer the entrances the better. The store should be well lighted without high displays that obstruct easy surveillance of large areas. Very expensive items should be in locked display cases or otherwise secured. Cheap items can be kept near exit doors, and the more expensive items should be further from these doors, preferably in an area that is well staffed.

Convex mirrors are of limited value because the distorted images make it difficult to see at a glance what is going on. Flat, conventional mirrors are a more useful aid to the checking of blind areas or important locations. Offices eight to ten feet above floor level with large windows overlooking the main first floor shopping area provide good observation posts and have good deterrent value. Closed circuit television also helps to keep people honest. It is difficult to assess the value of signs warning that shoplifters will be prosecuted.

In order to prevent shoplifters from obtaining money by returning merchandise for refunds, there should be a very strict policy requiring receipts before payment and also when larger sums are involved, a record should be kept that lists the driver's license or other identification of the person requesting the refund.

Electronic article surveillance machines at exits set off bells, buzzers, or flashing lights whenever a customer walks out of a store without paying for an item. When the clerk accepts payment, he removes with a special device, a plastic tag from the item purchased. This tag contains an electronic chip which can be detected by the machines at the exits. The manufacturers claim that the system will pay for itself in less than two years in a store that has a sales volume of $500,000 or more a year.

PREVENTING VEHICLE THEFT

Educational programs conducted by police departments, automobile clubs, insurance companies and other groups have focused upon the need for drivers when leaving their vehicles to close all windows; lock all doors; keep packages or valuables out of sight; leave *only* the ignition key with parking lot attendants; keep spare keys and vehicle registration papers in wallet or purse rather than in the car. The spare key should not be attached to the car frame. It also is important to park in a well-lighted area with the front wheels turned sharply to the right or left, thereby making it more difficult for the professional thief to tow it away.

Some car owners install *tapered door lock buttons* that make it almost impossible for the thief to pull them up with a coat hanger; an *alarm system* that makes a loud noise when the thief tampers with the car; a *concealed toggle switch* either between the ignition switch and the safety switch or between the ignition switch and the coil; a *concealed fuel switch* which shuts off the flow of gasoline; and a *lock bar*, which locks the steering wheel to the break pedal.

A few drivers will even remove a coil wire on leaving their vehicle and secure the hood with a case-hardened cut-proof steel chain.

Unfortunately, the skilled professional car thief quickly develops a solution for any new antitheft devices or procedures. Thus, if a car is left parked with the front wheels turned sharply, the professional car thief will tow the car by raising the front end after first removing a cotter pin under the car which enables him to shift the transmission from the locked to the neutral position. Tapered lock buttons may defeat a coat hanger, but not a "slim jim." An alarm system can be circumvented by towing the car.

The toggle switch between the ignition switch and the coil can be bypassed, or the thief can find this switch and also the fuel switch. Lock bars can be cut, and the case-hardened chains holding the hood down can be sprayed with Freon, freezing the chain. Once the chain has been frozen it can be broken without difficulty. Even if the thief does not have a replacement coil wire with him, he can substitute one of the wires from a spark plug. The car may not run as well, but he can drive it away.

Thus, the conventional antitheft procedures will not defeat the professional car thief, but they may send the amateur car thief in search of an easier vehicle for theft.

Various legislative measures have been recommended as a means of reducing the problem of auto theft. It has been suggested that federal legislation requiring placement of the vehicle identification number on all major parts of new vehicles would make it easier to both trace stolen auto parts and also to detect persons involved in auto theft for car stripping and sale of stolen auto parts. Another suggestion has been that more states should pass laws requiring all motor vehicle dealers, used parts dealers and persons involved in vehicle salvage or destruction, to keep a daily record of all transactions involving secondhand or used auto parts and equipment. This record is to be open for inspection at all times by law enforcement officers. The law would also permit officers to seize vehicles with altered, changed or obliterated vehicle identification numbers.

THE VICTIM IN COURT

"Much law but little justice"
Thomas Fuller, *Gnomologia.*

Justice is due not only to the accused, but also to the victim of a crime. Yet all too often the victim suffers twice over, first at the hands of the criminal and then at the hands of the courts. It is not unusual for a skillful defense attorney to obtain on a variety of pretexts one continuance after another. The victim, who has already suffered financial loss at the hands of the burglar, has to take time off from work to appear in court not once, not twice, but several times.

If the defendant fails to appear for a hearing the case is continued once more, but if the victim fails to appear, the

charges may be dismissed. It matters not that he has previously
been faithful in attending and that no inquiry has been made
by the court as to whether the next court date suits his convenience. It is not surprising that managers of some businesses
are unwilling to press charges of burglary; they have learned
from experience that sending skilled employees to wait for
hours in courtrooms only to be told to reappear at some future
date adds to their financial loss.

Victims of burglary are often out for blood and expect the
courts to take a stern attitude toward the criminal. Radzinowicz
quotes a letter written to a newspaper by a victim whose sense
of justice was outraged by a burglar's jaunty exit from court
after being placed on probation.

> Those of us who try to do right need to see something un-
> pleasant happen to those who do wrong. It is not a matter of
> revenge or deterrence or reform. It is a matter of satisfying the
> inner longing for justice. I was once burgled. The police efficiently
> caught the burglar. He pleaded guilty and asked for twenty other
> burglaries to be taken into account. I sat stunned at Quarter
> Sessions while the Chairman addressed him in kindly and en-
> couraging words and put him on probation. Nobody spoke to me—
> I was only the victim. The man who had stolen my peace of mind
> left the court on his wife's arm and smilingly raised his hat to
> mine. My respect for the English courts has never recovered from
> that morning's experience (6).

It has been suggested that offenders convicted of burglary
and theft should be ordered to compensate victims for the
losses they have suffered. Such payments give the burglar a
better appreciation of the effects of his skulduggery on persons
whose homes he has visited. A burglar in Kennewick, Washington was ordered to pay the burglary and theft insurance (over
$200 a year) of a restaurant from which he had removed the
safe. The judge said that it was time burglars realized that
their acts drive up business costs.

There is, however, little point in ordering the offender to pay
restitution, unless he is in a position to do so. Any money in
his possession at the time of arrest is likely to be in the hands
of his defense attorney at the time of his conviction. Some
burglars, if placed on probation, would have to pay their

narcotics dealer first and would need a regiment of policemen to prevent them from continuing their criminal careers while at liberty.

PUNISHMENT

"Laws and institutions are constantly
tending to gravitate. Like clocks,
they must be occasionally cleansed,
and wound up, and set to true time"
Henry Ward Beecher, *Life Thoughts.*

Hanging, maiming and branding of burglars and thieves have not entirely disappeared. There are still a few countries where light-fingered persons can lose their hands or their heads if they continue to steal. Under Islamic law the punishment for theft consists of cutting off the right hand and in the case of a second theft, the left foot. If there are still further thefts, and also if the other hand or other foot are not fully usable, the thief is merely imprisoned until he shows repentance (7). In 1979, on the occasion of the Prophet Mohammed's 1,409th birthday, Pakistan, a Moslem nation of 75,000,000 people, legalized the Islamic penal code.

The President of Pakistan, anticipating criticism in the West of the new Islamic penal measures, said that the philosophy is not to chop off a hand or stone a man dead, it is to create a fear, a deterrent so severe that offenses are not committed. He added that in Saudi Arabia, where the Islamic code is enforced, the threat of hand or foot amputation has reduced thefts and made it safe to leave jewelry shops open and unattended.

The United States has a somewhat different approach to the punishment of theft. Although penalties vary from one jurisdiction to another, there is general agreement on the need for protection of the rights of juvenile offenders and widespread recognition of their need for special consideration. They are at a vulnerable stage of life development and care should be taken not to confine them in some institution where they might be exposed to the influence of violent, recidivistic older offenders.

Overburdened juvenile court judges, handicapped by an insufficient number of trained experienced consultants in social work, vocational guidance, psychiatry and other specialties and hampered by a lack of suitable alternatives to custody, often do no more than utter pious expectations of better future behavior before placing a burglar on probation. On the offender's record card at the police juvenile bureau the initials L and R, standing for lectured and released, are placed in the disposition column alongside his latest burglary. There are already many L and Rs on his record card.

The judge may have ordered conditions of probation, but in this fantasy land no one gives serious consideration to these restrictions. The judge is never directly confronted by a follow-up study of his labors, how could he be when there is not even a check on juvenile offenders to see whether they are following the requirements of their probation orders? Those parents who are concerned have long since learned that expression of this concern falls on deaf ears.

Juvenile offenders may well be at a critical stage of their psychological development, but they are neither stupid, nor incapable of recognizing indecisiveness and lack of authority. "Me and Harry was pulling weeds up for my mom and it was hot so I went in my house for a glass of Kool-Aid®. When I came out Harry said, me and Robert are going to hit up this house and I said where. He said down at the corner and I said no, that's too close to my house. Harry said, man I'll get you some speakers for your stereo and if we get caught nothing will happen to you but you will have to give back the speakers."

The juvenile offender needs to know that if he commits a crime something unpleasant will happen to him, and that with each succeeding offense the penalty will become greater. The adult offender also needs to know this, but in the courts, justice is neither swift nor certain. Regardless of his record of prior offenses, the burglar will probably be quickly released on bond.

Release on Bond

In 1977, a New York social agency that screens defendants and gives advice to judges recommended that David Berkowitz, the confessed "Son of Sam" multiple killer, be released on his own recognizance. By referring to him as AKA "Son of Sam," the agency, which is financed by the federal government and the city of New York, showed it was aware that Berkowitz had been accused of six lover's lane murders and seven attempted murders. But the agency pointed out that he was a first offender and had a permanent residence as well as a steady job with the post office, criteria routinely applied in determining whether a defendant is likely to skip bail. Mayor Abraham Beame commented, "Obviously no judge would accept such a recommendation in the 'Son of Sam' case, but it does make us wonder whether judges on other occasions, confronted with busy court calendars, are accepting recommendations that could permit dangerous criminals to walk the streets on little or no bail. This monumental irony underlines my contention that we must crack down on loopholes in the criminal justice system."

A significant number of persons released on bond do not return to court when required to do so. Almost 10 percent of felony cases before the New York Supreme Court in 1970 went unprosecuted because the defendants did not appear for arraignment. Burglars while on bond may commit more crimes, sometimes to raise enough money to pay for a prominent defense attorney.

> A sixty-year-old man confronted a burglar in the living room of his home and was told, "You saw me and I'm going to have to kill you." Despite repeated stab wounds the victim was able to escape and ran to a neighbor's home. The thirty-two-year-old burglar who was arrested by the police had a history of thirty-eight prior arrests and had been convicted twice for burglary and twice for receiving stolen goods.
>
> At the time of this arrest he was free on bond while awaiting trial on five other charges: three burglaries, one armed robbery and carrying a concealed weapon. All except one of these crimes occurred during the twenty-month period while he was free on bond. Following his arrest on the charge of armed robbery he was released on a $10,000 bond. Less than a week after his release he was arrested for burglary, but was released on a personal recognizance bond. The following month he was charged with possession of narcotics and carrying a concealed weapon. Once again he was released on bond.
>
> The judge who granted his repeated requests for release on bond said he was sensitive to the possibility of accused felons committing crimes while on bond, but he said the primary purpose of bond is to assure a defendant's appearance in court.

Prison Sentences

A study in Washington, D.C. of 1,665 adults arrested in 1974 and later convicted of felonies showed that about one-third of the burglars and nearly one-third of those offenders who displayed or used a dangerous weapon were given probation or a suspended sentence. Krohm has estimated that an adult burglar runs less than one chance in 400 of being sent to prison for any single offense. It might well be that crime does pay.

The burglar does face additional hazards. He may be shot by one of his victims or he may lose his life accidentally.

A burglar who tried to get in a London house down the chimney fell more than thirty feet down the flue and died a slow death jammed in pitch darkness against the soot-choked brick work. His body, partly mummified by humidity and smoke from the fireplace, was found six years later by workmen repairing the chimney. He was identified as a thief by dental work done during a term in prison. The probable year of his death was fixed by the date of coins in his pockets.

A householder on returning home noticed a broken window, heard noises inside the house and saw a youth jump through the double glass window in the living room. He chased the burglar who collapsed after running two blocks. He died a short time later from a large laceration on his left side from jumping through the window. He had previously been arrested for burglary and auto theft. Jewelry from the home was found in his pockets.

A thirty-year-old intruder in a Bronx apartment house apparently panicked when a girl in the apartment started screaming. Instead of jumping through a window leading to a fire escape, he jumped through a closed window and fell four floors to his death on the courtyard beneath.

The victim of a burglary or friends of the victim on discovering the identity of the thief may take private revenge as in the following example:

In 1975, the body of Joseph Arce, a known burglar and heroin addict, was found lodged between rocks in the surf below the 250 foot high cliff along the Palos Verdes Peninsula near Los Angeles. His car was found parked at his apartment house, and it was considered unlikely that he would have walked to the Peninsula. A police informer suggested that the police ask a woman burglary victim how she got her television set back.

Further investigation revealed that this woman had reported a burglary, but had not reported recovery of the stolen television set.

Her former husband and his friends had accused an acquaintance, Joseph Arce, of the burglary and Arce confessed, naming an accomplice and a fence who purchased the television set. The accomplice and the fence admitted their involvement, but no action was taken against them because neither had known the burglary victim. Joseph Arce was driven to the Palos Verdes Peninsula and thrown over the cliff. His burglary victim pleaded guilty to a charge of false imprisonment and was placed on two years' probation. Her former husband and two other men pleaded guilty to a charge of voluntary manslaughter and were sentenced to one to fifteen years in the state penitentiary.

Revolutionary groups operating outside the law and without prisons of their own may also resort to violence against criminals. The Irish Republican Army of Northern Ireland has attempted to keep the police out of some residential areas and have, themselves, punished burglars and thieves. The offender may be required to participate in some community project, but if he continues his wayward behavior he risks kneecapping, a painful and disabling punishment resulting from a bullet fired at close range through the knee joint.

In the United States, those burglars who are sentenced to prison usually receive much shorter sentences than armed robbers and rapists. Very long sentences are rare and tend to be reserved for older offenders with a long record of previous convictions.

> In 1970 in Dallas a thirty-two-year-old man was sentenced to life in prison after a jury found him guilty of stealing fifty cents. He was convicted of breaking and entering a car and taking fifty-one cents from an ashtray, but he dropped a penny in the car. The life sentence came under the Texas habitual criminal law when the jury found that he had served another prison sentence for burglary.
>
> In Oklahoma City in 1971 a forty-one-year-old man was sentenced to ninety years in the penitentiary for stealing less than five dollars from six parking meters. The jury recommended the term, and the judge sentenced him to six consecutive fifteen-year terms.

Indeterminate sentence laws were hailed as a means of avoiding the disparity in sentences handed down by different judges. The principal argument in favor of indeterminate sentence laws is that it is not desirable to decide at the outset how long a person should remain in confinement, but that it is advantageous to watch the development of his personality, his adaptability to training and his desire and will to become rehabilitated, and to reach a decision as to when his release date should come on the basis of the progress of events (3).

In practice, these laws resulted in many prisoners being confined for much longer periods than if they had been sentenced under conventional statutes. Other prisoners under indeterminate sentence were released very quickly indeed, often independent of any clear change in their outlook and behavior. Prisoners became the pawns of liberal and conservative parole boards or prison wardens, and their fate was determined by the philosophical views of their custodians rather than by any change within themselves. Those prisoners who were locked up too long seldom had effective means of publicizing their hardship. There was occasional public outcry over a quick discharge from prison.

> In 1969 the police chief of Bellevue, Iowa was found lying face down in a pool of blood at the scene of a forced entry into an auto-dealer's garage. Apparently he surprised his murderers in the commission of the break-in and was bludgeoned to death with a shovel. William P. Sweeney known to have a history of assault and battery charges was arrested and charged with first-degree murder along with another man and an eighteen-year-old girl. Sweeney was convicted and sentenced to seventy-five years in prison.
>
> Two years and eight months after entering prison he was freed on parole. An Iowa corrections official commenting on the case said, "He has received the maximum amount of treatment, his attitude and progress were excellent, and it was the staff opinion that now was the best time to release him if we expect complete rehabilitation. . . . Our only excuse for keeping him incarcerated any longer would have been just to punish him. And to keep him only to punish him is not in keeping with the attitude of correcting."

In recent years, the trend has been toward abolition of indeterminate sentence laws, partly because of the wide disparity in judicial sentencing and the abuse of discretion by parole boards and partly because of lack of confidence in correctional rehabilitation programs. Many legislators have been influenced by the report of Robert Martinson and his colleagues on 231 rehabilitation programs in the United States and abroad that showed with few exceptions the rehabilitative efforts that have been reported so far have had no appreciable effect on recidivism (5).

A number of states have passed legislation which provides for determinate sentences for felonies. Curiously, both liberal and conservative legislators are united in seeking fixed prison terms, although there has been some disagreement on the length of the fixed sentences. Usually, judges still retain some discretion, but not to the same extent as formerly.

> Under the California Uniform Determinate Sentencing Act of 1976, all felonies, except those punishable by a life term or the death sentence, carry a possible prison term of one of three lengths; e.g., two, three or four years; five, six or seven years. A sentence to prison must specify which of the three possible terms is being imposed. The middle term must be imposed unless the court has found circumstances in aggravation or mitigation after a hearing on a motion made by the prosecution or defense. In addition to the upper, middle or lower term for the offense, called the "base term," the new law prescribes certain additional terms of imprisonment, called "enhancements," if specified facts were charged in the indictment or information and are found to be true. The facts giving rise to enhancements include: service of a prior prison term; having been armed with a deadly weapon; using a firearm; taking or damaging property of great value; and committing great bodily injury. Imposition of the additional prison terms for enhancements is mandatory, unless the court finds mitigating circumstances and strikes the additional punishment. The law governs dispositions imposing a prison sentence; it makes no change in the trial court's discretionary authority to grant probation or to make another disposition of the case, such as imposing a fine or a jail term when authorized by the substantive portion of the California Penal Code (2).

Prisons are unpleasant, dangerous places with a high incidence of homosexual rape, assault and murder. They are schools for crime and many prisoners leave with less, rather than with greater, respect for life and property. Why then should we

send burglars, thieves and other felons to prison? Radzinowicz
and King give the following answer:

> People are not sent to prison primarily for their own good
> or even in the hope that they will be cured of crime. Confine-
> ment is used as a measure of retribution, a symbol of condemnation,
> a vindication of the law. It is used as a warning and deterrent to
> others. It is used, above all, to protect other people, for a longer
> or shorter period, from an offender's depredations.

REFERENCES

1. Bunn, V. A.: Business management for crime prevention. In *Crime
   Against Small Business.* A Report of the Small Business Administration. Washington, D.C., U.S. Government Printing Office,
   1969.
2. California Uniform Determinate Sentencing Act: Abstract. *Criminal
   Justice Abstracts,* 9:269, 1977.
3. Holtzoff, H.: In Branham, V. C., and Kutash, S. B.: *Encyclopedia of
   Criminology.* New York, Philosophical Library, 1949.
4. Krohm, G.: The pecuniary incentives of property crime. In Rottenberg,
   S. (Ed.): *The Economics of Crime and Punishment.* Washington,
   D.C., American Enterprise Institute for Public Policy Research,
   1973.
5. Martinson, R.: What Works?: Questions and answers about prison
   reform. *The Public Interest,* 35:22, 1974.
6. Radzinowicz, Leon, and King, Joan: *The Growth of Crime.* New York,
   Basic Books, 1977.
7. Schacht, Joseph: *An Introduction to Islamic Law.* Oxford, Clarendon
   Press, 1964.

INDEX